MAKING POSTERS

BLOOMSBURY VISUAL ARTS
Bloomsbury Publishing Plc
50 Bedford Square, London, WC1B 3DP, UK
1385 Broadway, New York, NY 10018, USA

BLOOMSBURY, BLOOMSBURY VISUAL ARTS and the Diana
logo are trademarks of Bloomsbury Publishing Plc

First published in Great Britain 2020

Copyright © Remrox LLC and Natalia Delgado, 2020

Scott Laserow and Natalia Delgado have asserted their rights under the Copyright,
Designs and Patents Act, 1988, to be identified as Authors of this work.

For legal purposes the Acknowledgments on p. 239
constitute an extension of this copyright page.

Cover design: Scott Laserow & Natalia Delgado

All rights reserved. No part of this publication may be reproduced or transmitted in any form or
by any means, electronic or mechanical, including photocopying, recording, or any information
storage or retrieval system, without prior permission in writing from the publishers.

Bloomsbury Publishing Plc does not have any control over, or responsibility for,
any third-party websites referred to or in this book. All internet addresses given
in this book were correct at the time of going to press. The author and publisher
regret any inconvenience caused if addresses have changed or sites have
ceased to exist, but can accept no responsibility for any such changes.

A catalogue record for this book is available from the British Library.

A catalog record for this book is available from the Library of Congress.

ISBN: PB: 978-1-3500-9015-6
ePDF: 978-1-3500-9017-0
eBook: 978-1-3500-9016-3

Original book design by Scott Laserow & Natalia Delgado
Typeset by Lachina Creative, Inc.
Printed and bound in India

To find out more about our authors and books visit
www.bloomsbury.com and sign up for our newsletters.

MAKING POSTERS
From Concept to Design

Scott Laserow and Natalia Delgado

BLOOMSBURY VISUAL ARTS
LONDON · NEW YORK · OXFORD · NEW DELHI · SYDNEY

TABLE OF CONTENTS

6 *Foreword*
8 *Introduction*

1 THE BEGINNING

13 The Beginning
15 Historic Timeline

2 CONCEPTUALIZING

23 Conceptualizing
24 Know Your Project
26 Train Your Eye
27 Know Your Facts
27 Know Your Message
29 Know Your Audience
30 Define Your Resources
31 Ideation Techniques for Conceptualizing
35 Case Study: Splendent Sun by Dermot Mac Cormack
38 Exercises
39 Gallery

3 EXECUTION

51 Execution
52 Image Making
54 Line
57 Type as Image
58 Figure/Ground
59 Color
60 Composition and Hierarchy
61 Using a Grid
62 Symmetry and Asymmetry
64 Rule of Odds
64 Focal Point
66 White Space
67 Creating a Poster Series
68 Context
68 Aesthetics
70 Methods and Materials
74 Making Mistakes
76 Evaluate Your Design
77 Case Study: Dead Leaf by Christopher Scott
80 Exercises
81 Gallery

4

4 GRABBING ATTENTION

- 101 Grabbing Attention
- 103 The Power of Contrast
- 103 Using Color to Demand Attention
- 105 Adjust the Thermostat: Contrasting Temperature
- 105 Opposites Attract: Using Complementary Colors
- 107 The Power of Three: Triadic Color Palettes
- 108 Burst of Color: Using Four Colors or More
- 111 Scale
- 112 Rhythm and Pattern
- 113 Movement
- 114 Eye Gaze and Pointing
- 114 Disruption
- 117 Case Study: Converse/Marimekko by Andrew Lewis
- 120 Gallery

5 ART OF PERSUASION

- 137 Art of Persuasion
- 139 Rhetorical Figure
- 139 Metaphor
- 140 Metonymy
- 140 Synecdoche
- 142 Other Figures
- 148 Building an Emotional Connection
- 149 Fear and Shock
- 151 Humor
- 152 Arousal
- 154 Case Study: Somos de Maíz by Natalia Delgado
- 156 Gallery

6 STORYTELLING

- 167 Storytelling
- 168 Creating Your Visuals
- 171 Structuring Your Story
- 171 Nostalgia and Reminiscence
- 173 Telling Your Story with Type
- 175 Multiple Narratives
- 175 Narratives across a Poster Series
- 177 Case Study: Storytelling by Joe Scorsone and Alice Drueding
- 179 Gallery

7 BEYOND THE PRINTED SURFACE

- 193 Beyond the Printed Surface
- 194 Interactive Posters
- 194 Smell
- 195 Touch
- 196 Taste
- 199 Sound
- 200 Moving Posters
- 200 Animated Posters
- 202 Music and Sound
- 206 Augmented Reality Posters
- 209 The Future of the Poster
- 211 Exercises
- 213 Case Study: Blood Oil by Scott Laserow
- 215 Gallery

- 228 *Glossary*
- 232 *Bibliography*
- 233 *Index*
- 239 *Acknowledgments*

FOREWORD

The Public Life of Posters By Elizabeth Resnick

"Posters endure as one of the most permanent and solid forms of visual communication, and they exert a palpable physical presence, shaping spaces while reflecting and altering human behavior."[1]

This book is about making posters. The goal is to provide the reader with a structured experience to create, analyze, and evaluate posters through a multitude of exploratory research and brainstorming methodology, keeping the focus firmly on conceptualization (the forming of ideas).

Why a book on making posters in this digital age? Simply put, posters are message systems—informing, educating, or inspiring—whether they are viewed in public spaces, in galleries or museums, or while browsing the internet. "From the confrontational and political, to the promotional, persuasive and educational, the poster in all its forms has persisted as a vehicle for the public dissemination of ideas, information and opinion."[2] They are windows onto our world in the service of our collective community conscience.

Posters also function as effective memory triggers. You see an image and are instantly transported back to a specific time and place in your past. Sights, sounds, smells, places, people, and objects can all act as strong memory triggers. I'd like to offer two personal experiences in this vein, both of which have shaped my work as a designer, educator, curator, collector, and author.

In the early 1960s, when I was a pre-teen living in Queens (a borough of New York City), my family took the subway into Manhattan for outings, entertainment, or dining out. Most New York City subway stations are subterranean environments. You descend several flights of stairs into a darkened underground cavern-like space, glaringly lit with fluorescent lights. This environment would feel gray and lifeless if not for the large, colorful posters that line the tiled walls in every station. A cacophony of bold images and words shouting out cultural events and advertising commercial products and services, all crying out "look at me" as each poster competes for attention.

During this time, most of the posters displayed in the subway espoused lifestyle choices, showing sophisticated pretty women and attractive young men enjoying cigarettes or alcoholic beverages with the aim of influencing ordinary people to buy their product. Other posters touted the latest time saving conveniences or remedies for the morning after like Alka Seltzer's "plop, plop, fizz, fizz, oh what a relief it is!"

As a young person traveling into the city, I loved being cocooned in this sea of visual distraction, yet only one poster campaign still resonates: "*You Don't Have to Be Jewish to Love Levy's Real Jewish Rye.*" Each large poster depicted a photographic portrait of a distinctly non-Jewish person eating a sandwich made of rye bread. It is very doubtful that the Black, Asian, Italian, and Native American models pictured in these ads were Jewish. It was also very rare to see any person of color or non-white ethnicity featured in advertising of any kind.

The campaign, which began in 1961, was developed by American ad agency Doyle Dane Bernbach (DDB) for a small family-owned bakery in Brooklyn. Although the campaign transformed Levy's into New York's top seller of rye bread, it actually did more than simply promote rye bread. This campaign was widely acknowledged as one of the first sensitive and successful uses of cultural and racial identity in public advertising.

The 1960s was also when paper posters transitioned from public spaces to private spaces in the service of lifestyle decoration. The first poster I ever thumbtacked to my dorm room wall was Milton Glaser's *Dylan* poster. As the story goes, John Berg, then art director at Columbia Records, asked Glaser to create a poster that could be folded and packaged into Dylan's "Greatest Hits" LP in 1967. Glaser depicted Dylan with kaleidoscopic hair, a visual nod to the rock posters being produced in San Francisco at the same time. Glaser has always maintained he took his inspiration for the Dylan profile from a 1957 self-portrait by Marcel Duchamp. Glaser used a similar composition but maintained that Dylan's curly mane, with its swirling streams of color, was his own invention. Personally, I've always thought that Glaser was channeling Peter Max— an enormously popular American artist known for using bright colors associated with psychedelic art, pop art, and counterculture. Or, perhaps, it was simply the cultural and visual climate of this era. Nevertheless, this powerful and colorful visual statement came to define a generation.

Making Posters from Concept to Design is a book—for learners with a basic understanding of art and design principles—that will exemplify effective methods for creating posters that can engage, inform, reflect, and shape our material world. It will undoubtedly resonate for years.

Dylan | **Artist:** Milton Glaser | © Milton Glaser | **USA** | 61 x 91.4 cm

INTRODUCTION

How This Book Works

Making Posters—From Concept to Design has a companion website (www.making-posters.com) that works alongside the book. The website offers additional content, including resource website links, videos, animated and digital interactive posters, a list of participating artists, and an interactive poster history timeline.

Book Key

MPR Denotes additional content found at www.making-posters.com/resources.

[A] Denotes Augmented Reality posters. To view these posters, download the free Artivive® application to your handheld device.

QR Codes will link to animations and videos.

Always check www.making-posters.com for the latest app updates.

Making Posters—From Concept to Design is written as an educational tool for undergraduate graphic design and advertising students. While this book offers useful and interesting content for all levels, those in second, third, and fourth year will benefit the most. The book can be a teacher's companion for those who are teaching a poster course or any graphic design course as well as a supporting bibliography for those teaching introductory or advanced graphic design courses. The book is also helpful for professional designers who want to learn more about this specific area and for non-designers who want to explore this topic. Although *Making Posters* is an educational resource, the posters represented are so diverse that anyone with an interest in posters will relish this book.

Making Posters—From Concept to Design demonstrates effective methods of creating posters that engage and inform by reviewing the fundamental design principles that designers continue to apply to deliver compelling work. It presents the origins of the poster through a timeline that traces its role and remarkable transformation throughout history, helping readers to understand its relationship with art and advertising and its use as a social communication device.

With a focus on conceptualization, this book provides a structure to create, analyze, and evaluate posters and leads readers through various methods of research and brainstorming techniques. It analyzes the art of image making and takes a critical look at the persuasive power of the poster, its use as a storytelling device, and how a narrative can dictate the way a message is received.

Going beyond the printed surface, *Making Posters* reviews how emerging technologies continue to offer designers new tools, allowing the process of making a poster to expand and evolve while still maintaining its core purpose—to communicate quickly and convey its message.

About the Authors

Scott Laserow

Scott Laserow is a full professor of Graphic and Interactive Design at Temple University, Tyler School of Art, in Philadelphia, PA, USA, where he has taught for over twenty-eight years. His curriculum includes traditional graphic design; branding, identities, page layout, packaging, posters, and emerging technologies; animation; augmented reality; digital publication; tablet applications; and website design and development.

For over thirty years, Scott has brought his unique approach to graphic design in the form of print, web, interactive design, and animation. Between Scott's client work and poster design, he has won over seventy-five prestigious national and international awards, been featured in over sixty publications, and been included in over sixty exhibitions in sixteen countries, all peer-reviewed. Since 2004, Scott has focused increasingly on posters as a design challenge and an instrument of social change. Since he started creating posters, he has been involved in many social, environmental, and political causes. Scott's posters have appeared in numerous international publications and exhibitions; many have received international awards and are in permanent collections worldwide. Scott has also refereed and judged various international poster competitions.

A Pivotal Moment

In the summer of 1974, at the age of eleven, I discovered the poster! This was about the same time the Watergate scandal was winding up and Richard Nixon was stepping down as president. A neighbor sold posters, bubble gum machines, and other strange and wonderful things out of her home. You might have thought an eleven-year-old would have been interested in the novelties, but I was more excited by and drawn to the vibrant and surreal posters. One of those posters still hangs on a wall in my studio today. It is a 1973 Third Eye Inc. dayglow, blacklight poster titled *Watergate* by the incomparable Ralph Reese and Larry Hama. I still set it aglow every now and again. Of course, I had no idea what Watergate was, I just thought it was a cool poster that would look wicked on my bedroom wall. Mind you, this poster was tame in comparison to my 1970s bedroom. Imagine walls painted the color of bananas just before they ripen and turn bright yellow, and a matching yellow and gold shag carpet. My comforter was a velour leopard print complete with a giant oversized coordinating footprint pillow. There were blacklight posters covering practically every inch of wall space, a strobe light, and two or three blacklights illuminating all the intense colors. Although some of the poster themes may have been a bit over my head at the time, it was the electric comics that captivated me with colors and images floating in an endless space. I remember often getting lost in their visuals for hours.

As I grew older, my tastes changed, and the groovy banana yellow room was repainted. Yet I found that the colors and images of posters still ignited my curiosity. First it was band

Kyoto Travel Poster | 43.2 x 27.9 cm. © the author

posters, then album covers. My love for music and visual narrative led me to discover many musical artists by purchasing their albums simply because I liked the cover. Like my Watergate poster, many of my favorite album covers adorn my walls today. I am still enamored with their images that bring back memories of great music and questionable fashion.

In 1985, I began to study graphic design at Tyler School of Art, Temple University. My first poster was created in a typography class and was a sort of travel poster for Kyoto, Japan. While it may not have been the strongest poster, it taught me about concept, typography, composition, and white space. Little did I know at the time that I would end up here, not only designing posters but writing a book about posters and poster design.

Natalia Delgado Avila, Ph.D.
A design strategist and educator with more than fifteen years of experience in her field, Natalia has a bachelor's degree in Graphic Communication Design, a master's degree in Science and Arts for Design from the Universidad Autónoma Metropolitana, and a Ph.D. in Art Education from the University of Victoria.

Natalia has shared her original design process and vision in conferences and workshops around the world. She's been the recipient of numerous awards and has juried some of the top international poster competitions. Her work has been exhibited in more than 100 locations and published in multiple magazines, websites, and books.

She worked as a consultant and facilitator for the international non-profit organization *Poster for Tomorrow* and helped to develop the curriculum and program design for the United Nations Funded *Draw Me Democracy!* Project. She is a co-founder of Poster Poster, a virtual community that celebrates the power and influence of posters in our culture. Natalia's interest in contemporary social issues has been a critical element in her work, which emphasizes the importance of considering design in its historical, social, and cultural contexts. She currently resides and teaches in Montreal, Canada.

Poster Passion

Even before I knew what graphic design was, I had a fascination with posters. It was a time before Facebook and social networks, when the internet was taking its first baby steps, and we had to switch between being online and using a landline phone to make a call. Access to large printed images was limited and expensive, but my friend and I managed to sweet-talk the manager of the local movie theater into letting us have the posters that were taken down from the displays after the movie stopped showing. I still remember taping *The Last of the Mohicans* to my bedroom wall. Of course, at the time, I was more interested in Daniel Day-Lewis's handsome face than the color or layout of the design!

There were many memorable moments during my studies that confirmed my career choice. I remember attending the Mexican Poster Biennial exhibition in Mexico City and falling in love with the images covering the walls. I even bought the catalog, which was a significant expense for my modest student budget. In 1999, I went to Cuba, where I came upon a poster exhibition about El Che Guevara. This was my first encounter with a thematic exhibition, and I was mesmerized by the variety of conceptual and technical alternatives that could be used to address the same topic.

After I graduated, I designed posters for some events but found it challenging to find exciting work because the poster culture was poor in Baja California, and most of the posters were printed in tabloid size. I was hungry to create, and I couldn't find anything that I felt challenged me and helped me grow as a designer. So I took the matter into my own hands and decided to enter Good 50x70, an international poster competition focused on social communication that was launched that year. Of the briefs proposed that year, my attention was especially drawn to the issue of prostitution. This subject is delicate and difficult to handle, and to this day, this image is one of the most potent and controversial ones in my portfolio. I focused my concept on pimps, the hidden characters in the world of sex trafficking, and used the metaphor of the woman as property that gets commercialized. I poured my heart and soul into making it, and I was ecstatic when it got selected. It was a career-defining moment, and my life changed completely after that.

Posters have, in different ways, taken me all over the world and led to some of the most exceptional experiences and friendships in my life. Sometimes your passion screams at you, sometimes it whispers.

For Sale by Owner | 50 x 70 cm. © the author

1

*"Poster is essence.
The extraction of a topic.
The distillation of a thought.
No more, no less."*

Miguel Angel Rangel

CHAPTER ONE THE BEGINNING

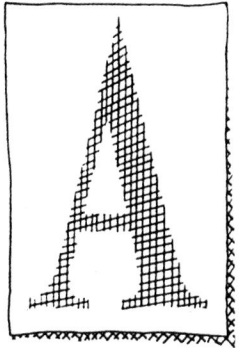

A poster or bill is a pictorial form of communication that often appears in public places to post notice. They are generally found on vertical surfaces and may include both graphic and typographic elements or may be solely graphic or typographic. Posters are a visually striking and informative tool used in advertising and promotion to grab an audience's attention and generate interest in a particular topic. They are also frequently used by social, political, and environmental groups to communicate a message or point of view.

Posters are a flexible medium and can range in size from A4 to the size of a billboard or can appear on digital screens as electronic images. Posters reflect pop culture, a literal sign of the times. They are a portal to the past and a record of how typography, image, and color were used to publicly disseminate information. The poster has always embraced change and will continue to do so. The electronic tools that poster artists are experimenting with today will become a virtual record of how twenty-first-century posters are designed and executed. As technology continues to impact how we receive information, the poster's form will undoubtedly change, but its vibrant role of informing society will remain.

THE BEGINNING

Image courtesy of István Orosz

| 1787–1799 | | 1855 | 1865 |

The French Revolution

Posters Take to the Streets

The Birth of the Lithographic Poster

Illustration of the French Revolutionary emblem with text: *Unite, Indivisibilite de la Republic Liberte, Egalite, Fraternite ou la Morte*. (Photo by Time Life Pictures/Mansell/The LIFE Picture Collection via Getty Images)

Die Erste Berliner Litfasssäule, 1855. Photo by Ullstein bild via Getty Images

Jules Chéret, *Folies-Bergere, La Loie Fuller Poster*, 1893. Photo by © Historical Picture Archive/CORBIS/Corbis via Getty Images

Alphonse Maria Mucha, *Petroleo Gal Para El Pelo—Perfumeria Echeandia* (Photo by Swim Ink 2, LLC/CORBIS/Corbis via Getty Images)

The French Revolution
The French Revolution is known as the first milestone in the history of posters. It was a period of social and political rebellion in France and its colonies that began in 1789 and had a profound influence on political and social trends throughout Europe. From this time forward, posters were increasingly used for advertising products and services, often following the AIDA formula: Attention, Interest, Desire, and Action.

Posters Take to the Streets
In 1855, Ernst Litfaß, a German printer and publicist, devised a free-standing cylindrical advertising pillar, named Litfaßsäule. During this time, there was also the emergence of sandwich board men, who were hired to carry wood panels with posters on their front and back to call the attention of people strolling down the street.

The Birth of the Lithographic Poster
Although lithography was invented in 1798, it was not until the 1860s that Jules Chéret created the three-stone lithographic process (usually blue, red, and yellow), which allowed artists to achieve just about any color they could imagine. This process offered an economical way to mass-produce large-scale visuals. Chéret is considered the world's first full-time poster artist. His pioneering adoption of a single central image became a model for other poster designers.

The First Golden Age: The Belle Époque & Art Nouveau
The Golden Age of posters, the Belle Epoque featured Parisian nightlife and romanticized the theaters and cabarets of the city. Natural forms and structures, flat colors, bold contrasts, curved lines, balanced asymmetry, and embellishment inspired by Byzantine icons, pre-Raphaelite romanticism, Japanese prints, and Celtic art are all a part of this style.

TIMELINE

| 1875 | 1885 | 1895 | 1905 | 1915 |

The First Golden Age
Glasgow School Collective in Britain
Jugendstil
Vienna Secession
Plakatstil

Charles Rennie Mackintosh, *Glasgow Institute of Fine Arts*, 1896

Glasgow School Collective in Britain

In Britain, the Glasgow School of Arts represented the Art Nouveau movement. A group of designers known as *The Four*—Charles Rennie Mackintosh, sisters Margaret and Frances Macdonald, and Herbert MacNair—created posters inspired by the Arts and Crafts movement and Celtic illuminated manuscripts.

Henry van de Velde, *Tropon*, 1899. Digital image, The Museum of Modern Art, New York/Scala, Florence

Jugendstil (Jugend-style)

In Germany, Art Nouveau took the name *Jugendstil*, stemming from *Die Jugend (The Youth)* magazine, which featured many Art Nouveau artists. Before 1900, the style mainly focused on floral and organic shapes and lines; its later stages became more abstract, influenced by the work of architect and designer Henry van de Velde. The style was a benchmark for German and Austrian modern design. It emphasized workshops where designers and manufacturers worked together.

Moser Koloman, *Poster for the 13th exhibition of the Viennese Secession*. Color Lithography. Printed by Albert Berger: Vienna, 1902. Photo by Imagno/Getty Images

Vienna Secession

The desire to rebel against academic tradition led to the formation of secessionist associations like the Vienna and Munich. Satirical magazines became popular during this time.

Robert J. Wildhack, *Poster for Opel automobiles*, 1911. Photo by Fine Art Images/Heritage Images/Getty Images

Plakatstil

Artists from Scotland's Glasgow School, Austria's Vienna Secession, and Germany's Deutscher Werkbund shunned rounded decorative forms in favor of rigid geometric arrangements based on functionalism. As a result of this, 1905 saw the birth of the German *Plakatstil* (*Poster Style*), led by Lucian Bernhard in Berlin and Ludwig Hohlwein in Munich. The style used flat colors and shapes as well as an abstract and modern visual language that allowed a more natural appreciation of the advertising message.

1905 1915

The Cappiello Style

Constructivism

World War I

16

Leonetto Cappiello. *Maurin Quina Absinthe*, Italy, 1905. Photo by Leonetto Cappiello/Buyenlarge/Getty Images

The Cappiello Style
Italian artist Leonetto Cappiello produced over 1,000 posters during his 40-year career. The father of modern advertising revolutionized poster design with a new graphical style that used a single simple image, often humorous or bizarre, placed against a dark background, making it pop and capture the viewer's attention. His eccentric poster design style would reign supreme through the Art Deco movement of the 1920s.

Filippo Tommaso Marinetti, *Futurism*, 1932. Photo by Fine Art Images/Heritage Images/Getty Images

Cubism, Dadaism, Futurism, and Surrealism
Four of the most influential art movements of the time were Cubism, Dadaism, Futurism, and Surrealism. Cubism was marked by a departure from representational art through the use of various simultaneous vantage points to portray its subjects. Dadaism challenged the definition of art itself and embraced chaos, absurdity, and irrationality. Futurism praised machines, speed, and innovation while experimenting with expressive typography. The Surrealist movement introduced the notion of intuitive art and automatism, exploring the world of the unconscious, merging dreams with reality, and combining a variety of media.

Poster for *German Domestic Arts Exhibition*, 1914. Photo by Found Image Press/Corbis

Deutscher Werkbund (German Association of Craftsmen)
Deutscher Werkbund was founded in 1907 by Hermann Muthesius and emerged from the need to strengthen the competitiveness of German companies in global markets through a partnership between design and mass production. The style employed simple forms, bold colors, and clear typography.

Vladimir Stenberg and Georgii Stenberg, *The Burden of Marriage*, 1925. Photo by Buyenlarge/Getty Images

Constructivism
The Russian Constructivist movement began in 1913 and rose to prominence after the Revolution of 1917. Inspired by the ideal of social change and a functional approach to artmaking, the posters featured a minimal color palette, dramatic diagonals, strong typography, and photomontage. The style began with a political aim but quickly spread to the world of advertising and publishing. The leading artists of the time were Vladimir Tatlin (the father of Constructivism), Alexander Rodchenko, El Lissitzky, Gustav Klutsis, and the Stenberg brothers.

1925　　　　　　　　　　　　　　　　　　　　　　　　　　　　　　　　　1935

Cubism, Dada, Futurism and Surrealism

Deutscher Werkbund

De Stijl

Bauhaus

Art Deco

War Poster *"Britons, your King wants you. Join your country's army! God save the King,"* 1914. Photo by Universal History Archive/Universal Images Group via Getty Images

Theo Van Doesburg, *Archer*, 1919. Hulton Fine Art Collection. Photo by Fine Art Images/Heritage Images/Getty Images

Joost Schmidt, *Bauhaus the 1923 Weimar Exhibition*, 1923. Photo by Apic/Getty Images

A.M. Cassandre, *Normandie*, 1935 (French Line Poster). Photo by Found Image Holdings/Corbis via Getty Images

World War I and the Bolshevik Revolution

During WWI, posters became political tools to campaign and broadcast propaganda. From raising money to recruiting and provoking outrage, the war created an unprecedented advertising campaign. The United States produced over 2,500 posters and printed 20 million copies in two years. The Bolsheviks acknowledged the incredible impact these poster designs had in America and began using the same tactics for their propaganda.

De Stijl

The artists' association *De Stijl* was founded in the Netherlands in 1917. Led by Piet Mondrian and Theo van Doesburg, the movement sought a return to order after the chaos brought by the war. The main characteristic of this style was simplicity, reflected in the total abstraction of form. Geometric shapes, lines, and primary colors were all artists needed to create their powerful images.

Bauhaus

In 1919, Walter Gropius founded the Bauhaus in Weimar, Germany. The school had a crucial role in the evolution of design education. It encouraged the embrace of modern technologies and promoted a pragmatic view of design through the principle of "form follows function." The school had three locations: Weimar, from 1919 to 1925; Dessau, from 1925 to 1932 under the direction of Hannes Meyer; and Berlin, directed by Ludwig Mies van der Rohe from 1932 to 1933 until the Nazi regime closed it down.

Art Deco

Art Deco, also called *Style Moderne*, originated in Paris in the 1920s. The style made distinctive use of sleek geometric forms and intense colors. Its central themes were power and speed, and the movement drew its inspiration from many sources, including jazz, modernist artistic movements, and the exotic arts of Persia, Egypt, and Africa. One of the most iconic designers of the Art Deco style was A.M. Cassandre, famous for his airbrush techniques.

1935　　　　　　　　　　1945　　　　　　　　　　1955

World War II

Taller de Gráfica

Mid-Century Modern

New York School

Golden Age of Polish Posters

British propaganda poster during the Battle of Britain. *Never Was So Much Owed by So Many to So Few*, 1940. Photo by David Pollack/CORBIS/Corbis via Getty Images

World War II
During the Second World War, the poster once again played a central role in rallying support for the troops, earning the nickname "weapons on the walls." Designers used photography and offset printing to produce posters on a massive scale. Some featured patriotic messages to boost morale; others highlighted the importance of solidarity in terms of scarcity, while others used fear to emphasize the importance of secrecy.

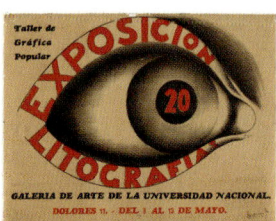

Francisco Dosamantes, Exposicion Litografias, *Taller de Grafica Popular*, Galeria de Arte de la Universidad Nacional, 1942. The Museum of Modern Art, New York/Scala, Florence

Taller de Gráfica
Founded in Mexico in 1937 by artists Leopoldo Méndez, Pablo O'Higgins, and Luis Arena, *Taller de Gráfica* is acknowledged by many as one of the most influential printmaking collectives of its time. The group was primarily interested in using art to promote revolutionary social causes.

David Klein, *Las Vegas*, 1960. Photo by Buyenlarge/Getty Images

Mid-Century Modern: '50s Style
The end of World War II brought the emergence of a new consumer society. Posters adapted to the times by changing their focus from propaganda to advertising, giving birth to the vivid, playful, and colorful boom of the early 1950s.

Saul Bass, *The Man with the Golden Arm*, 1955. Photo by Movie Poster Image Art/Getty Images

The New York School
The New York School was a group of artists closely associated with abstract expressionism and other avant-garde art movements. The movement started in the 1940s and quickly grew, making New York the cultural center of the world during the 1950s and 1960s. The artists were interested in the open and direct presentation of ideas and played with shape, contrast, and texture to accomplish this mission. In the field of graphic design, this resulted in the symbolic use of form and an interdependent relationship between text and images. During this time, many influential boutique advertising agencies were established, leading to the creation of iconic designs that are still in use today.

1965　　　　　　　　　　　1975　　　　　　　　　　　1985

Swiss Style

Pop Art

Cuban Revolution

A Polish poster for the Paramount Pictures movie 'Roman Holiday,' titled 'Rzymskie wakacje', 1953. Photo by Movie Poster Image Art/Getty Images

The Golden Age of Polish Posters
In 1950s Poland, the film industry was state-run. Without commercial constraints, artists had the freedom to express themselves, resulting in posters featuring vibrant colors and often a single surreal, intriguing, or provocative image that, in many cases, made little to no reference to the film it represented.

Erik Nitsche, *Atoms for Peace*, *General Dynamics*, 1955. Digital image, The Museum of Modern Art, New York/Scala, Florence

The Swiss Style
The Swiss Style, also known as the International Typographic Style or International Style, arose from modernist and constructivist ideas guided by its pursuit of simplicity. It featured highly structured and systematic designs made up of essential typographic elements and striking photography. The government actively promoted posters and the printing industry during this time, allowing the Swiss Style to become a landmark and expand outside the country to the rest of the world.

Roy Lichtenstein illustrations on the windows of a gambling and gaming casino in London, UK. Photo by In Pictures Ltd./Mike Kemp/Corbis via Getty Images

Pop Art and Expressionism
Led by Andy Warhol, Roy Lichtenstein, James Rosenquist, and Claes Oldenburg, Pop Art was a movement that emerged in the late 1950s and became internationally prominent during the 1960s and 1970s. It is recognized by a bold chromatic aesthetic and elements from popular culture to create iconic images and striking patterns.

Antonio Perez Ñiko, *Hasta la Victoria Siempre*, 1967. poster courtesy of artist © Antonio Pérez Ñiko.

Cuban Revolution and Movie Posters
Fueled by the success of the Cuban Revolution of 1959, the poster thrived in Cuba as a tool to showcase the new political, economic, and social changes of the nation. That same year, the Cuban Institute of Cinematographic Art and Industry (ICAIC) and the *Casa de las Américas* were founded, creating key cultural opportunities for poster design.

1965   1975

Chicano Poster Movement

Psychedelic Posters

Punk

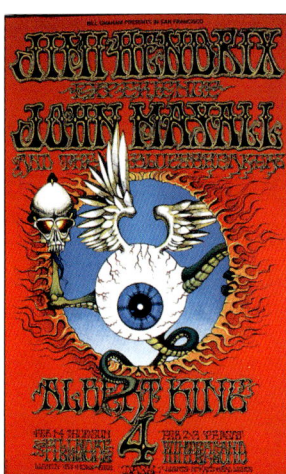

Xavier Viramontes, *Boycott Grapes, Support the United Farm Workers Union*, 1975. Smithsonian American Art Museum, Gift of Tomás Ybarra-Frausto. Photo by Cathy Murphy/Getty Images

Chicano Poster Movement

The Chicano Poster movement can be traced back to 1965, when Cesar Chavez created the United Farm Workers (UFW) union. What started as a labor movement quickly became a civil rights movement. Since posters were cheap and easy to mass-produce, they became a powerful medium to disseminate the message of the cause. The movement featured unique and distinctive iconography that drew from bicultural and bilingual elements and was influenced by the Mexican muralist movement and Cuban political posters. The posters were overtly political and portrayed the life and struggles of Mexicans in the United States. Popular iconography included the use of Aztec gods, Day of the Dead images, and the Virgin of Guadalupe.

Rick Griffin, *Jimi Hendrix* concert poster at the Filmore Auditorium 1968. Photo by GAB Archive/Redferns/Getty Images

Psychedelic Posters

Psychedelia flourished in the United States, particularly in San Francisco during the 1960s. It frequently featured intense contrasting colors from opposite ends of the color wheel that created a visible vibrational effect. The typography was fluid and at times difficult to read, making onlookers work to decipher the content. Another common psychedelic approach involved making repeated photocopies of photographs, then reducing them to simple black-and-white shapes.

Sex Pistols, God Save the Queen, 1977. Europunk exhibition at the Villa Medici, headquarters of the French Academy, in Rome. Photo credit ANDREAS SOLARO/AFP/Getty Images

Punk

The Punk aesthetic glorified chaos and anarchy, making use of lo-fi and DIY approaches, including collage and décollage. Designers attacked the page, mixing contrasting shapes, colors, and textures. As the popularity of punk rock grew at an unprecedented rate and experienced many reinterpretations in the late 1970s, so too did the Punk aesthetic, including the addition of hand-drawn illustrations. A principal Punk poster designer was Jamie Reid, who created the iconic artwork Sex Pistols, God Save the Queen.

Niklaus Troxler Design, *McCoy Tyner Sextet,* 1980. © Niklaus Troxler

Postmodernism

Postmodernism, as its name suggests, emerged as a response to what many perceived as the rigid and dogmatic rules of modernism. Postmodernism first appeared in the 1970s but did not become widespread in Europe and America until the 1980s and 1990s. It was characterized by a distrust of theories and ideologies, a revival of ornamentation, and the use of historical references, humor, and irony.

1985　　　　　　　　　　　　　　　　　1995　　　　　　　　　　PRESENT

Postmodernism

Memphis Style

New Wave/Swiss Punk

Deconstructivism

Ettore Sottsass. Detail from the photograph of the exhibition Design Radical at The Met Breuer on July 20, 2017, in New York City. Photography: John Angelillo | UPI / Alamy Stock Photo

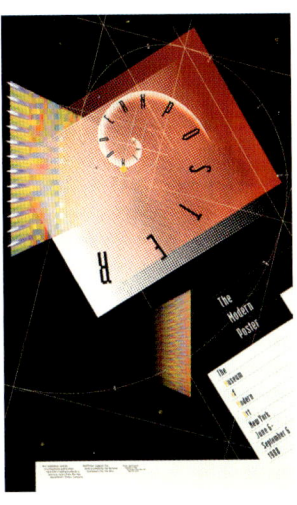

April Greiman, *The Modern Poster*, 1988. © April Greiman

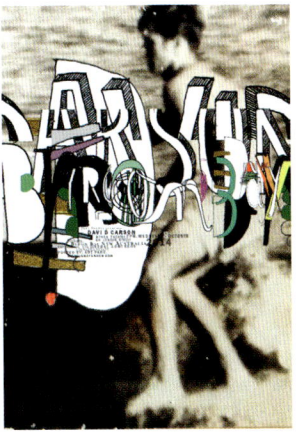

David Carson, *Byron Bay*, 2014. © David Carson

Memphis Style

The Memphis design movement began in 1981 in Milan, Italy, with the creation of the Memphis group founded by designer Ettore Sottsass. Influenced by Art Deco and Pop Art, the style valued humor, fame, and outrage, featuring geometric shapes in a colorful palette. The Memphis style experienced rejection at first but quickly gathered a cult following.

New Wave or Swiss Punk Typography

New Wave or Swiss Punk Typography can be traced back to Wolfgang Weingart in the early 1970s at the Basel School of Design. Many of his students, including April Greiman, Dan Friedman, and Willi Kunz, further developed the style. New Wave used analog and digital tools to create geometric shapes and isometric patterns that challenged previous notions of how type should appear on the page. The evolution in technological developments allowed designers to break the rules and experiment with type, color, and layout, creating chaotic compositions. New Wave defied strict grid-based arrangement conventions in favor of inconsistent letter spacing, varying type weights, and unexpected alignments.

Deconstructivism: The Grunge Art Movement and the New Typography

Grunge, a type of rock music known for its rough guitar and lethargic vocals, became popular around 1985 as part of the Seattle underground subculture. In the early 1990s, this artistic movement crossed over to the visual arts and design. Known for its experimental approach to typography and jumbled composition, Grunge gave rise to a new movement that sought to break the rules of traditional graphic design. Leading the way was David Carson, who served as art director of *Ray Gun* magazine for its first three years. His unique style quickly caught on and would forever change the way we look at graphic design and typography.

2 ideas DO NOT NEED to be *esoteric* to be ORIGINAL or exciting

— Paul Rand

CHAPTER TWO CONCEPTUALIZING

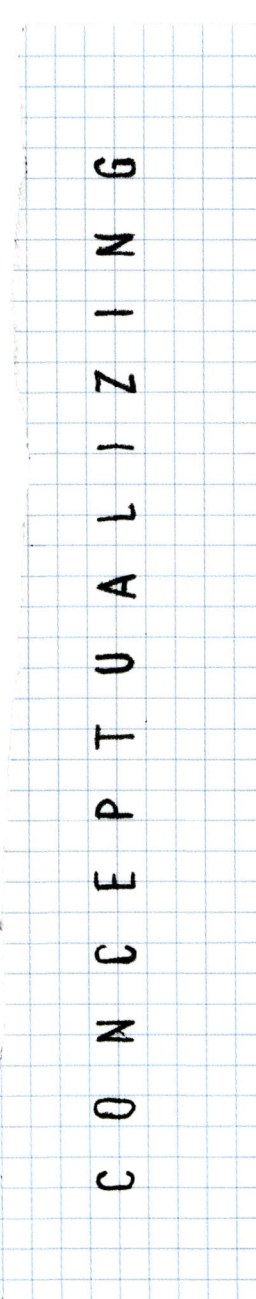

pon embarking on any poster project, designers and artists set out on a path to generate ideas, laying the groundwork for concept development. A concept is the main ingredient of any message and will ultimately influence the decisions you make during the image making stage of the design process. Your concept will keep you on track while the path twists and turns many times until resolution. The concept becomes the underlying narrative and the mechanism that provokes your audience; it should therefore inspire, influence, and even offer additional information outside of the main message. It is the designer's responsibility to combine resourcefulness and knowledge gained through discovery to develop effective concepts. During this time, you will explore many techniques for generating solutions to assigned problems. A successful result is achieved when all the elements of your poster support one another and speak in one voice. Whether it is a call to action to promote an event, seduce, entertain, or sell, a strong concept will allow you to unlock complex, seemingly unsolvable challenges.

(above and facing page) Illustration: Scott Laserow

To create your concept, you should be aware of three things:

1. The context where the communication is taking place.
2. Your persuasive intent (or that of your client).
3. The beliefs of the audience about the issue.

Know Your Project

Research is the backbone of any successful idea and requires time and dedication. This is the stage when the designer seeks to build a deeper understanding of the assignment. Therefore, the more time you spend educating yourself, the more likely you are to succeed. Strong research from reliable sources can provide the most recent and relevant information. Even if you believe that you already understand a subject or have previous experience with it, you will find that there is always more to learn and discover. Designers and artists should be open to the unexpected and have an insatiable curiosity, for what you uncover may serve as a deviation and offer a revitalizing change. Finding something new can be the most exciting part of this journey. Zora Neale Hurston, an influential author of African-American literature and anthropologist, said, "Research is formalized curiosity. It is poking and prying with a purpose."[3]

The following are important questions to ask yourself before you begin: Who? What? Where? When? Why? How?

- Who is the poster directed to? Who will it benefit or affect? Are there any target segments or stakeholders you need to reach?
- What is the topic? What is the purpose of the poster? Is it for a contest, exhibition, event, etc.?
- Where will the poster be displayed? Is it for a specific country or will it be shown internationally?
- When is this poster being produced? Is there an urgency about the topic?
- Why is this poster being made? Why is the topic important or relevant?
- How will it be reproduced? How will it be used?

While learning as much as you can about a subject, be sure to pay attention to specific visuals that you may use as a reference later. Regardless of how familiar or straightforward an object may appear to you, never rely solely on memory. Everyday objects have subtleties and nuances that, if overlooked, will result in weak visuals. Even the most celebrated artists throughout history used references. As you collect imagery, you will naturally start imitating the things you like and incorporate them into your designs. Do not plagiarize, but rather be stimulated by your inspirations and make them your own. Poster designers often pay homage to artistic movements or specific artists. This expression of respect and honor should be used only as inspiration and should not in any way resemble any particular poster or image unless that is your intention. For example, when you design with a retro or vintage aesthetic, you pay homage to a period or previous artistic movement.

You may also be motivated and inspired by the many visual styles created by design's rich history of image-makers. Although you may be familiar with and have used photographic collage, did you know that this style was pioneered in the early 1930s by Swiss photographer and poster designer Herbert Matter (Figure 2.1)? Another impactful design style makes use of figure ground. Famed Japanese poster designer Shigeo Fukuda demonstrates his mastery of this technique in his 1975 *Woman and Man's Legs* poster (Figure 2.2). If you prefer a minimalistic approach to image-making, consider master poster designer Saul Bass's 1959 *Anatomy of a Murder* poster (Figure 2.3). Perhaps the iconic style of Milton Glaser's 1966 *Dylan* poster (Figure 2.4) or Seymour Chwast's famous 1967 *Bad Breath* poster (Figure 2.5) is what excites you. Regardless of your taste, there are many artists whose work continues to influence us today.

CHAPTER TWO CONCEPTUALIZING

Figure 2.1 | *Pontresina Engadin* | **Artist:** Herbert Matter | Digital image, © The Museum of Modern Art, New York/Scala | **Florence** | 101.6 x 63.8 cm

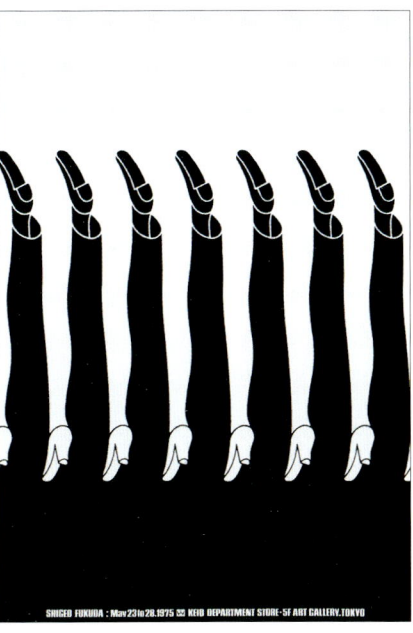

Figure 2.2 | *Woman and Man's Legs* | **Artist:** Shigeo Fukuda | © Shigeo Fukuda | Mary Evans/Scala | **Florence** | 73.7 x 104.1 cm

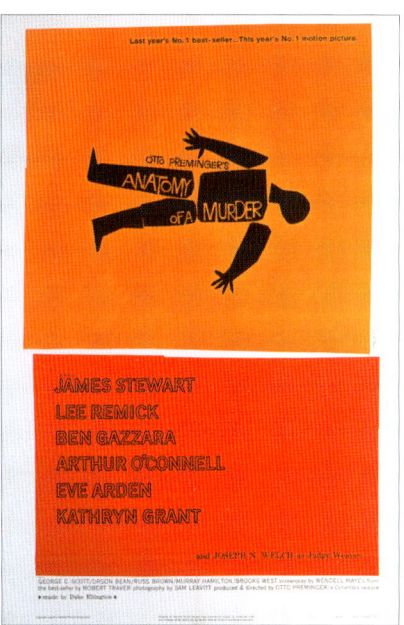

Figure 2.3 | *Anatomy of a Murder* | **Artist:** Saul Bass | LMPC / Contributor | **Contributor:** Movie Poster Image Art | **USA** | 68.6 x 104.1 cm

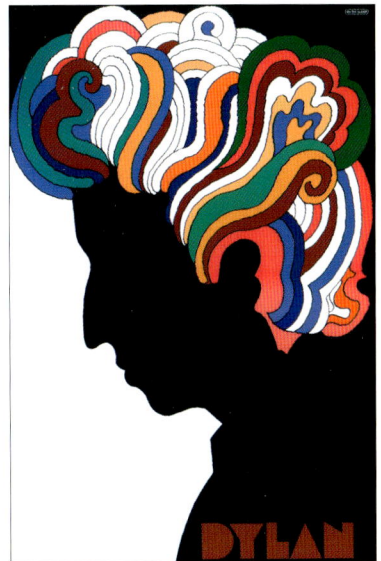

Figure 2.4 | *Dylan* | **Artist:** Milton Glaser | © Milton Glaser | **USA** | 61 x 91.4 cm

Figure 2.5 | *Bad Breath* | **Artist:** Seymour Chwast | © Seymour Chwast | **USA** | 61 x 94 cm

Figure 2.6 | *Bitter Campari* | **Design/Illustration:** Robert Rodriguez | © Rodriguez | **USA** | 57.8 x 88.3 cm

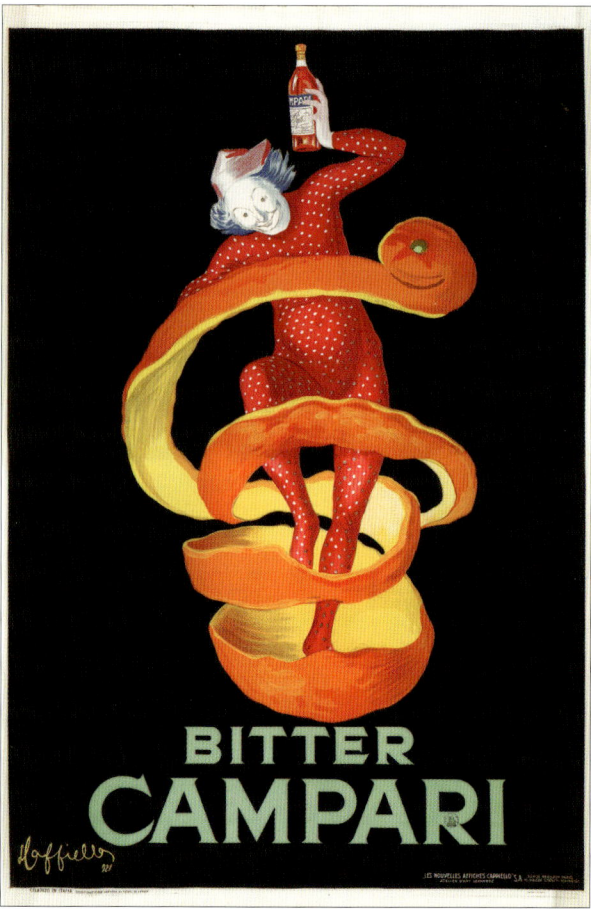

Figure 2.7 | *Bitter Campari Alcoholic Beverage* | **Photography**: © Swim Ink 2, LLC/ CORBIS/Corbis via Getty Images | **Artist**: Leonetto Cappiello | **Italy** | 66 x 106 cm

Illustrator and designer Robert Rodriguez pays homage to the classic turn-of-the-century Italian advertising poster aesthetic with his 2011 *Bitter Campari* poster (Figure 2.6). As compared to Leonetto Cappiello's 1921 *Bitter Campari Alcoholic Beverage* poster (Figure 2.7), Rodriguez's illustration uses current techniques to reinvent this classic style of poster design. Drama and intensity are created to command attention, as the viewer is naturally drawn to the use of color, shadow, and contrast. The pop of white in the clown's face and his pointed hat direct your eyes to the BITTER CAMPARI typography, which is expertly executed to give the illusion of something vintage. Notice how Rodriguez balances the juggled bottles to rise and fall in places that do not obstruct the typography.

Train Your Eye

Observation is a habit that can bring deeper meaning to your research. It is an ongoing skill that will grow stronger the more you practice. Experience all the design that surrounds you, like billboards, signage, artwork, window displays, packaging, or anything that may arouse your curiosity. Training your eye will hone your senses and allow you to create a visual repertoire that may provide ideas for future projects.

Ask yourself: What do I like and why do I like it? Look around and see what things attract you the most; study them and find what they have in common. Is it the color, the texture, the use of typography, or maybe a clever concept? You will see that patterns and trends start to emerge. This approach tends to lend itself to alternative views of a particular topic, as our focus is diverted by the environment.

Know Your Facts

The best path to robust research is through a thorough review and analysis of your topic from both web-based and print media. However, do not spend too much time on any single source, as you may fixate on one view rather than exposing yourself to numerous perspectives. Seek insight from many resources to gain new knowledge by surfing the internet, reading books outside of your general interests, flipping through magazines with unusual topics, and building a collection of ephemera that might include toys, games, vintage clothing, packaging, matchboxes, bottle caps, or anything that visually excites you. Often, valuable riches come from surprising places.

As you carry out your fact-finding mission, you will notice that generally two types of data emerge: qualitative and quantitative. There is extensive literature available about these two types of data, but simply put, quantitative refers to numerical or quantifiable information, while qualitative refers to exploring material without being inhibited by predetermined findings.[MPR]

Once you have conducted a broad search, revisit all that you have collected and start to narrow the focus to the information that is most relevant, then begin to analyze the refined pertinent data. This may include primary research collected firsthand, such as interviews, observations, or focus groups, as well as secondary research, which may consist of articles, statistics, images, design movements, design trends, typographic styles, color palettes, and other reference materials you may find online or in books and other printed materials. Both primary and secondary research are necessary for generating your concept. The time needed to collect and interpret all the data may become extensive and will depend upon the scope and complexity of your project. This is time well spent, as you will gain the knowledge necessary to develop your targeted message and discover visual reference materials to help you in the design process.

Gustavo Morainslie's poster *A Lot at Steak* (Figure 2.8) illustrates how calculable information can become the foundation for the visual while the visual itself derives from exploratory research. Calculable research establishes the fact that 25 percent of global land use is driven by beef production, while the exploratory research builds the compound visual of the T-bone steak and tree trunk. Other research may have included beef, cattle, livestock, deforestation, and wasteland. By combining these two research methods, Morainslie creates a meaningful poster that makes a strong statement.

Know Your Message

A clear and memorable message is a vital component of any design project. It must resonate with your target audience and provoke the appropriate response. A message can be defined as the content of your poster, which seeks to convey an underlying theme. The originator of the message is the sender, and the person on the other side of the communication is the receiver. Communication is effective only if the receiver understands the message, which is why it is often referred to as encoding and decoding. If the exchange is successful, the message will be understood and stimulate the receiver in a meaningful way. Therefore, to create a great poster, you must craft the message to be easily decoded by the viewer.

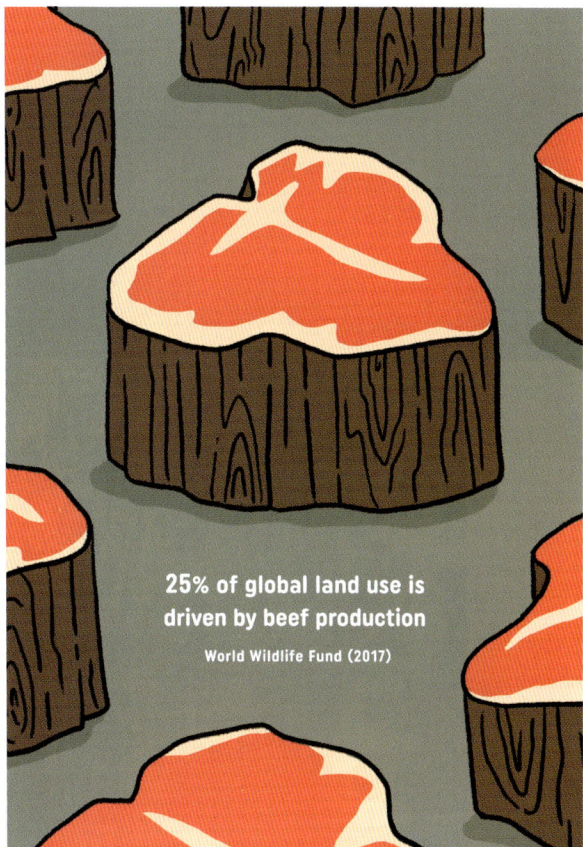

Figure 2.8 | *A Lot at Steak* | **Design**: Gustavo Morainslie | © Gus Morainslie | **Mexico** | 70 x 100 cm

Generally, for a poster to be effective, it is essential that the audience learn something new or perhaps somehow change their perceptions. A successful concept paints a mental picture for the audience and attempts to reach them on an emotional level. However, before considering your audience, you must be clear about the message you want to communicate. Having a stated purpose or objective will make for a more efficient and productive exercise. Often, we start designing without having a good understanding of the problem. It is essential to interpret and evaluate the information collected from your research to be sure your message does not become confusing, or your audience may not believe it or find it relevant. If you do not thoroughly understand the topic, it is highly unlikely that your message will be received as intended. Although you may go through many iterations of a concept during ideation, the underlying message must endure.

Your message will emerge from the results of your research. A common mistake is to confuse the topic of the poster with the message you want to communicate. Although the subject may be broad and general, the message must be as specific as possible. An excellent way to achieve this is to picture it as a conversation between you and a friend. Ask yourself: If you could tell this person just one thing, what would that be? To be clear about your message, it is a good idea to write it down. Ideally, your message should be as short and as concise as possible. As you brainstorm, you might find that multiple messages emerge. This is not unusual; however, be sure to keep them separate to avoid mixing them. In the end, you will have numerous options that will allow you to create different proposals for the same topic.

As you write your message, keep the following criteria in mind:

- Keep it short and straightforward.
- Use language that is easy to understand.
- Articulate the main point of your argument.
- Use real, meaningful, and relevant information.
- Appeal on a rational level.
- Appeal on an emotional level.
- Make it memorable.

Do not worry about the prose or style as you write your message. Get started with whatever comes to mind and then check it against the project criteria and refine. In the end,

Figure 2.9 | *Plastic Waste/Real Threat* | **Artist**: Maria Karasova | © Maria Karasova | **Slovakia** | 50 x 70 cm

you will choose only the two or three strongest messages to carry forward to the next stage. Keep all your results, as it is common to find hidden gems in what initially appeared to be weaker solutions.

The posters in Figures 2.9, 2.10, and 2.11 were created by three different designers for the competition Segunda Llamada, a poster contest with the topic of plastic pollution awareness. Despite having the same topic, you can observe how each poster focuses on a different message. The poster *Responsible Handling of Plastic Waste* (Figure 2.9), by Maria Karasova, focuses on the danger element, featuring plastics as a literal ticking time bomb. The poster *Greener, More Beautiful* (Figure 2.10), created by Zhang Yong, offers a green alternative to the problem, proposing baskets instead of plastic containers and highlighting the additional benefits of this option with the slogan *more green,*

Figure 2.10 | *Greener, More Beautiful* | **Artist:** Zhang Yong | © Eddie Zhang | **China** | 50 x 70 cm

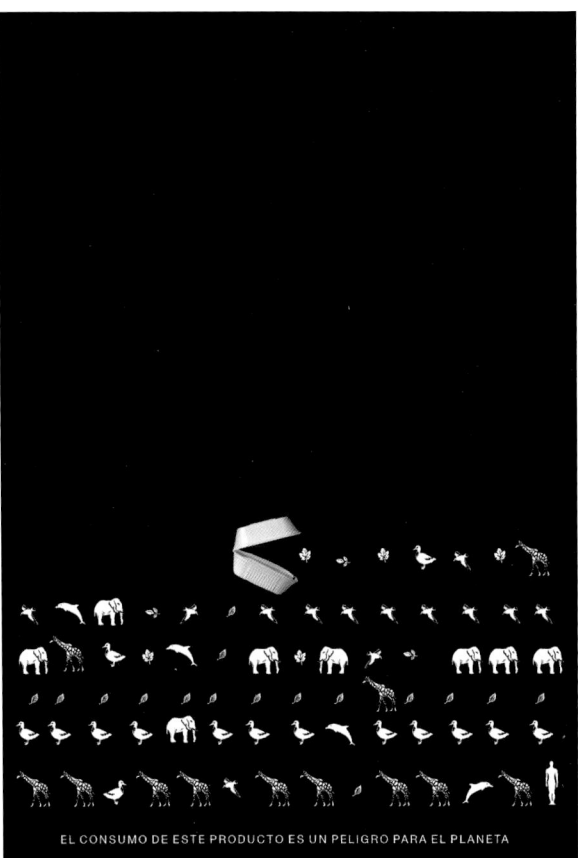

Figure 2.11 | *Consumption of This Product Is a Danger to the Planet* | **Artist:** Obed Meza Romero | © Obed Meza Romero | **Mexico** | 50 x 70 cm

more beautiful. The third poster, *Consumption of This Product Is a Danger to the Planet* (Figure 2.11) by Obed Meza Romero, emphasizes the impact of plastic pollution on wildlife by using the unicel container as a Pacman devouring different animal species that are headed for extinction.

Another common mistake is to confuse the message with the actual text that appears on the poster. While there might be some phrases or information to include in your design, it is crucial that you define your message(s) first. After all, many great posters do not incorporate text yet deliver a powerful message.

Know Your Audience

A poster does not need to appeal to everyone. To send a meaningful and effective message, you must know your audience—how they think, feel, and act. Many find it helpful to document this information by writing it down or creating a chart. This is a common practice for marketing and advertising agencies. They record comprehensive descriptions of their target audience to create a detailed and vivid profile of their customers. The same can be done for any poster project. In some cases, there might be more information available than in others, but it is always key to gather as much material as possible.

There are two main elements to consider while targeting an audience: demographics and psychographics. Demographics considers things like age, gender, marital status, geographic location, household income, etc. Psychographics looks at attributes, like hobbies, interests, values, and priorities. As you build your target audience profile, you will gain a greater understanding of their motivations, which will focus your message. Even though a topic may alienate a group of people, a powerful poster is hard to ignore. A compelling image will surely spark an emotional response even from a community outside of your targeted audience.

Figure 2.12 | *México Dulce y Querido (Mexico Sweet and Dear)* | **Design/Illustration**: Julieta Murga | © Julieta Murga | **Mexico** | 70 x 100 cm

The *México Dulce y Querido* poster series (Figure 2.12), by Julieta Murga, for the International Mexican Poster Biennial, promotes the colors, flavors, and sensation of traditional Mexican sweets. As a Mexican designer, Murga has a lifetime of experience enjoying candy and was easily able to identify the most popular and iconic sweets in her country. Going further with the theme, Murga framed the candy as a celebration of Mexican culture and made a link with traditional dances or *bailes típicos* for her poster series. The *concha* bread makes the skirt of the traditional dancing costume of Jalisco's *Baile Tapatío*, the *borrachitos* represent the iconic dance of *los viejitos* (the old men) from the state of Michoacán, and the *paleta/chupirul* is a celebration of the *Danza de los Quetzales* from the state of Puebla. The text *México Dulce y Querido (Mexico Sweet and Dear)* is a play on words, referring to both the sweetness of the candy and the candor of Mexican culture. The bright colors commonly used in their arts and crafts are also representative of this.

Define Your Resources

There are important considerations you must take into account before you begin the design process. Keep in mind everything that is involved from initial research through completion. Set realistic goals for each achievement and give yourself enough time to explore a topic thoroughly. Consider other daily responsibilities and other projects that may appropriate your attention. Having an accurate sense of time will allow for an organized plan with a successful outcome. This will also stop you from staying in the ideation stage for too long before you move on to the next step to meet your deadline. A common mistake is to be overambitious with your design, failing to accomplish your objective in time. It is essential to know your limits and capabilities so that you can manage your time accordingly. If you find yourself rushed, you may make many errors, so it is better to start with something that you feel confident you can finish on time. As you gain experience, you will become more aware

Ideation Techniques for Conceptualizing

Conceptualization requires the designer to engage both sides of the brain. When using the left side of the brain, we tend to look at problems analytically. Although a purely critical view may sometimes lead to intriguing conclusions, it can also cause creative blocks and a reluctance to take risks and experiment. Conversely, the right, or creative, side of the brain allows for an open and intuitive view of the problem, but it can produce too much information, which may make it difficult to narrow down to just a few points of view. This difference in analyzing information may present challenges for some poster designers when shaping a compelling and concise message. You might identify more with one of the scenarios or find that you oscillate from one side to the other; whatever the case may be, it is essential to develop ways to overcome these obstacles. The following ideation techniques will help you create more and better solutions.

of what you can accomplish within a restricted time period. Maybe you are a great photographer or illustrator, or you know how to generate three-dimensional models. Whatever your skills, you can use them to your advantage and play to your strengths. Other techniques might be new to you, and you may want to challenge yourself. Trying these new approaches is only recommended if you have the time to experiment and explore.

Mehdi Saeedi uses calligraphic artistry to paint a lyrical picture for his poster *The Sunshine Way from Balkh to Konya* (Figure 2.13). His canvas is filled with the poem "Hearken to the Reed-Flute" in honor of Rumi's 800th birthday. A skilled painter, Saeedi transforms the lettering effortlessly into hands delicately playing the reed-flute. His talents as a painter, calligrapher, and designer merge to execute a stunning interpretation of Rumi's writings for this important moment.

Figure 2.13 | *The Sunshine Way from Balkh to Konya* | **Design/Illustration**: Mehdi Saeedi | © Mehdi Saeedi | **Iran** | 70 x 100 cm

The good, the bad, and the ugly

It is not uncommon when beginning the ideation process to have "bad" or uninspired concepts. Never doubt yourself—it is not that you have come up with "bad" work, you just have not yet found solutions. Thomas Edison once said, "I have not failed. I've just found 10,000 ways that won't work." In fact, the only way to fail is not to try. You will be surprised to find that some "ugly" ideas often turn into "good" proposals with a simple or small tweak.

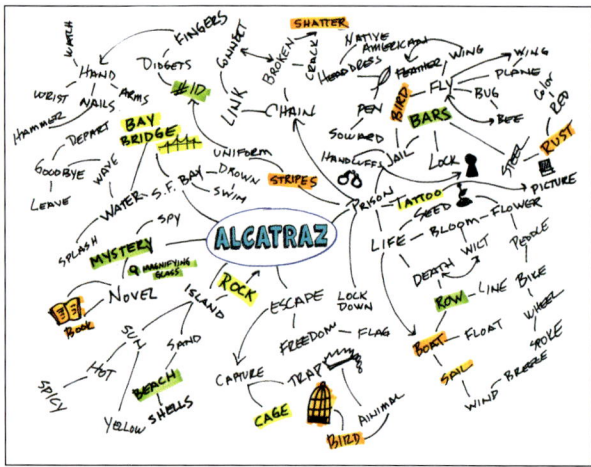

Figure 2.14 | Mind-Map for Alcatraz

Brainstorming

Creative theorist and advertising executive Alex Osborn, of Batten, Barton, Durstine & Osborn (BBDO), conceived the brainstorming technique. It is an informal group technique for creative problem-solving and is an excellent method for developing unrestrained spontaneity. In a group setting, participants are encouraged to communicate freely and without filters about the subject at hand. All suggestions must be considered, and there are no bad ideas. Usually, one person in the group is responsible for writing down all the suggestions made by the group; this person is referred to as the moderator. At the completion of the activity, all the ideas are reviewed and ranked. Working collaboratively provides diverse and wide-ranging insights, forcing connections that lead to new perspectives.

There are a variety of other methods of brainstorming that are not only a group activity but can be modified for an individual—for example, mind-mapping, list-making, and reviewing past materials. These techniques can be used successfully anywhere (even outside of art and design) and anytime there is a need for creative solutions.

Mind-Mapping

Mind-mapping is an excellent tried-and-true technique for problem-solving. The first evidence of mind-mapping dates back to Leonardo Da Vinci; other great minds throughout history like Isaac Newton, Charles Darwin, Albert Einstein, and Walt Disney have also used the technique. It was not until the early 1970s that Tony Buzan, a leader in the field of creative thinking, conceived the term "mind-map." This visual tool still serves as an excellent way to make images and jot down words on a particular topic freely and without judgment. Mind-maps are unrestricted approaches that allow for surprising connections, which may lead to valuable insights that otherwise would have gone undiscovered.

To create a mind-map, simply place a problem or topic in the center of a sheet of paper and draw tentacle-like offshoots to add anything related to that particular category. This may also be accomplished using a tablet with a stylus. From each new visual or word, continue the process. This is a time to have fun and think without consequence. Mind-maps do not need to be beautiful, just imaginative and informative. You will eventually compose an intricate map of thoughts with multiple directions, like the one shown in Figure 2.14. While reviewing your mind-map, start to look for connections between objects and between words and objects. These discovered relationships based on shape and typography become the building blocks for your poster.

Making Lists

Another excellent brainstorming method is making lists. List-making is a theoretical exploration and a tool that shakes ideas loose. In a ten-minute timed session, make a list of forty to fifty possible solutions to a specific problem. The objective is to record all notions no matter how strange or silly they may seem. Even if there are fewer than forty listed, stop after ten minutes. Review the list and identify three to four of the most interesting ideas. Then, in fifteen-minute timed sessions, make new lists based on those selected. In the end, you should have at least two to three strong directions.

An alternative method of list-making is a word bank. A word bank in its most basic form is a list of words usually used as instructional support for vocabulary development to improve creative writing. However, you can apply this same technique to visual development. It is recommended that you set up a list file, whether it be a physical folder in a file cabinet or a digital directory. Building a word bank is not a timed event, so it can continually be added to as your project develops. Although each project generates a new list, it is helpful to look at older word banks for inspiration. Be sure to categorize each word bank for easy reference before you seal it in your vault.

Figure 2.15 | Detail of mood board for the early 1970s

Mood Boards

Mood boards can be a useful tool that helps establish your vision. They are a collage of color, texture, imagery, typography, photography, materials, and stylistic approaches discovered during the research stage. Mood boards may be made up of physical objects, printouts, and other found materials mounted on a board (Figure 2.15). They can also be created using technology. Many useful online tools and mobile applications have been developed for just this purpose. Mood boards are a visual recording of reference material that consists of refined, organized, and cataloged facts discovered while exploring your topic. They serve as an instant recall to the essential aspects of your findings and become a resource as you engage in the design process.

Review Past Work

Reviewing past work can be inspiring. Keeping proper picture files and records of all your previous projects serves as documentation of what you have accomplished, but sometimes, looking at old sketches can also spark new ideas. The traditional method for storing work is maintaining sketchbooks, picture files, tracings, thumbnails, and compositions in filing cabinets and flat files. More contemporary methods may include digital sketching using tablet-based technologies and software, cloud-based online image collections like Instagram or Behance, or third-party modules.

Quick Sketches

A quick sketch starts with a large work area, anything from an oversized drawing pad to a marker board or even a large sheet of scrap paper. On the drawing surface, start sketching any visuals that come to mind related to the specified topic. Working as quickly as possible, sketch your first thought and immediately move on. Sometimes it is necessary to include words that aid in clarifying very loose sketches, like the ones illustrated in Figure 2.16. Rotating the drawing surface, if possible, or even turning the surface upside down often helps in the reduction of redundancies and gives fresh perspectives. Think in an open and unconstrained manner; a free flow of thought should spark new directions. Quick sketches offer the chance to take impulsive leaps, explore divergent views in a non-linear direction, and improvise. Only when the entire page has been filled should

Figure 2.16 | Detail of a quick sketch for a poster on processed foods

you begin editing down to the most successful solutions. Layers of tracing paper can be used to manipulate loose sketches to rapidly combine ideas, rearrange and substitute visuals, and force connections. You never know where lightning will strike! Some of the most famous designs in the world were sketched on restaurant napkins or foggy bathroom mirrors. Make sure you always carry a small sketchbook or notepad or have a recording application on your smartphone so you are prepared to document your thoughts.

Reflection

Regardless of which brainstorming technique is used, reflection is a valuable part of the creative process. It develops cognitive thinking skills and may present new outlooks on existing problems. It relies on personal experiences, observations that shape thinking, and acceptance of new ideas, and it allows you to draw inferences, which ultimately leads to better results.

It is essential to not overthink the concept; coming back days later will help with a fresh and more critical review of your discoveries. Always take time away from the piece. Sometimes it may be helpful to change location during this highly imaginative part of the overall design development. Examining the world around you can be quite inspiring. Go to a favorite place—a park, a train station, a museum, etc.—and actively observe your surroundings. Begin to reflect on the project. Pay attention to sound, color, texture, scent, and other sensory information. This time of incubation will help you feel renewed and revitalized upon returning to the project. Organizational psychologist Adam Grant calls it *vuja dé* and explains, "It is when you look at something you have seen many times before and all of a sudden see it with fresh eyes."[4]

Upon returning, ask yourself why, how, and what: Why did you make the decisions you made, both conceptual and visual? How did you arrive at your solutions? What has inspired you? What was your message? And perhaps most importantly, what have you learned? Reflection is likely to stimulate new perceptions and additional ideas while revealing weaker solutions.

Before you jump onto your computer to attempt to refine your initial quick sketches, it is recommended to use more traditional tools such as pencil and paper while creating thumbnails. This allows for a free flow of thought without the distraction of interaction with technology, the visual iconography that comes along with it, and the limitations you may have using computer applications. Using a tablet and stylus and the appropriate drawing applications can also achieve the same creative flow without distraction.

Once you have completed the ideation process and can start to reduce the number of sketches to just a handful of selected comparables, or "comps," you will need to test your results and get feedback. You can receive feedback from almost anyone—fellow designers and artists, art directors, clients, and even friends; any input helps. Accepting constructive criticism will always improve any vision. A fresh set of eyes may expose a weakness in the design or reinforce your thesis. Feedback is invaluable because it prompts you to rethink a solution until it is fleshed out before moving on to the execution stage of your project.

CASE STUDY

Splendent Sun by Dermot Mac Cormack

Before embarking on this poster, my partner Patricia McElroy and I knew that we wanted this artwork to be emotive and handmade as much as possible. At that time, we were doing a lot of digital work and programming, so we set ourselves a task to create something tactile, something that involved pen and ink, paper, and scissors. The subject for this play revolves around the story of a young man who is born with a set of wings and the subsequent decisions he must make about his "gift." We wanted to imply some of that difficult decision-making process and its inexorable outcome in the physical form of the work. As with most of our design, we put pencils before pixels, sketching many ideas and possible directions. Coincidentally, Patricia at this time was working in Ireland, so we were sending rough layouts back and forth, marked up with comments and suggestions. Ironically, the play also involves the central character flying to and from Ireland across the Atlantic. The handwriting was created using pen and ink, with an old rusted nib. Lots of handwriting attempts and many splashes were later combined in Photoshop for the desired roughness and layout of the type along with blotches of ink. We executed various illustrated options for the bird, but we weren't satisfied with their outcome. Once we stumbled on this particular bird in an old book of illustrations, we both felt that the engraved bird with its bent neck encapsulated the mood of the play. To achieve the desired rip, we tore many printouts of the bird. Eventually one chosen rip was augmented by some Photoshop manipulation to get the desired deckled edge. The final poster contained the energy and motion we were looking for, and I doubt this could have been achieved if the poster had been entirely executed in digital form. The final poster was screen printed in two colors in a limited edition.

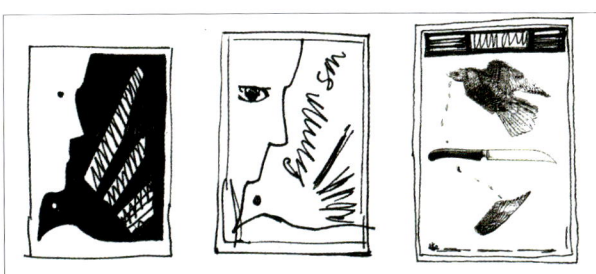

"We knew we wanted the elements to be visceral and evocative of the time period of the play's setting."

Splendent Sun | **Art Direction/Design**: Dermot Mac Cormack, Patricia McElroy
Illustration: Dermot Mac Cormack | **Client**: The Vox Theatre Company, Philadelphia |
© 21x Design | **USA** | 70 x 100 cm

"Since wings are an integral feature of the actual play, we knew we wanted their iconic form to appear prominently in the poster."

Exercise 2.1: Research & Mood Boards
Research a 20th-century decade of your choosing, then make a mood board that communicates the visual style from that decade. Explore fashion design, graphic design, advertising, music, food, color palettes, typography, and technology. Your mood board may be digital or handmade.

Exercise 2.2: Mind-Map
Select a location from column one and a film genre from column two for a three-day, outdoor, midnight film festival. Build two mind-maps, one for the film festival's location and one for the film genre. Generate each mind-map in a fifteen-minute timed session; it must fill an A4 (210 x 297 mm) sheet of paper (or digital equivalent) and may be a combination of words and imagery.

Film Location
Bran Castle, Bran, Romania
Colosseum, Rome, Italy
The Pyramid of the Sun, Teotihuacan, Mexico

Film Genre
Comedy | Animation | Fantasy | Drama | Action | Romance

Exercise 2.3: List-Making
Using the topic of Earth Day, make a ten-minute timed list of all the ways you can express the concept of environmental improvements. At the end of the ten minutes, review your list and remove all the obvious solutions. Next, create a twenty-minute timed list focusing on the successful results from your initial list.

Exercise 2.4: Quick Sketch
Using an A2 (420 x 594 mm) work area, do quick sketches of letterforms based on all seven deadly sins from the list provided. Look for unique characteristics in the letterforms that may visually relate to each sin. Your sketches should communicate the sins and be legible as a specific letterform.

Envy | Gluttony | Greed | Pride | Lust | Sloth | Wrath

Exercise 2.5: Write Your Message
Follow the example topic listed below and develop five messages for each of the topics listed.

Example Topic: Immigration and human rights
Message 1: We need to change the rhetoric of hatred and fear constructed around refugees.
Message 2: Refugees are often victims of physical and verbal abuse.
Message 3: Immigrants enrich their new countries with their knowledge, traditions, and cultures.
Message 4: Borders and walls separate and dehumanize.
Message 5: Nationality is just a word. We are all human beings.

Topics
*Latino Film Competition | World Food Day | Stop Censorship
New mobile cellphone launch | Jazz Festival in Montreal*

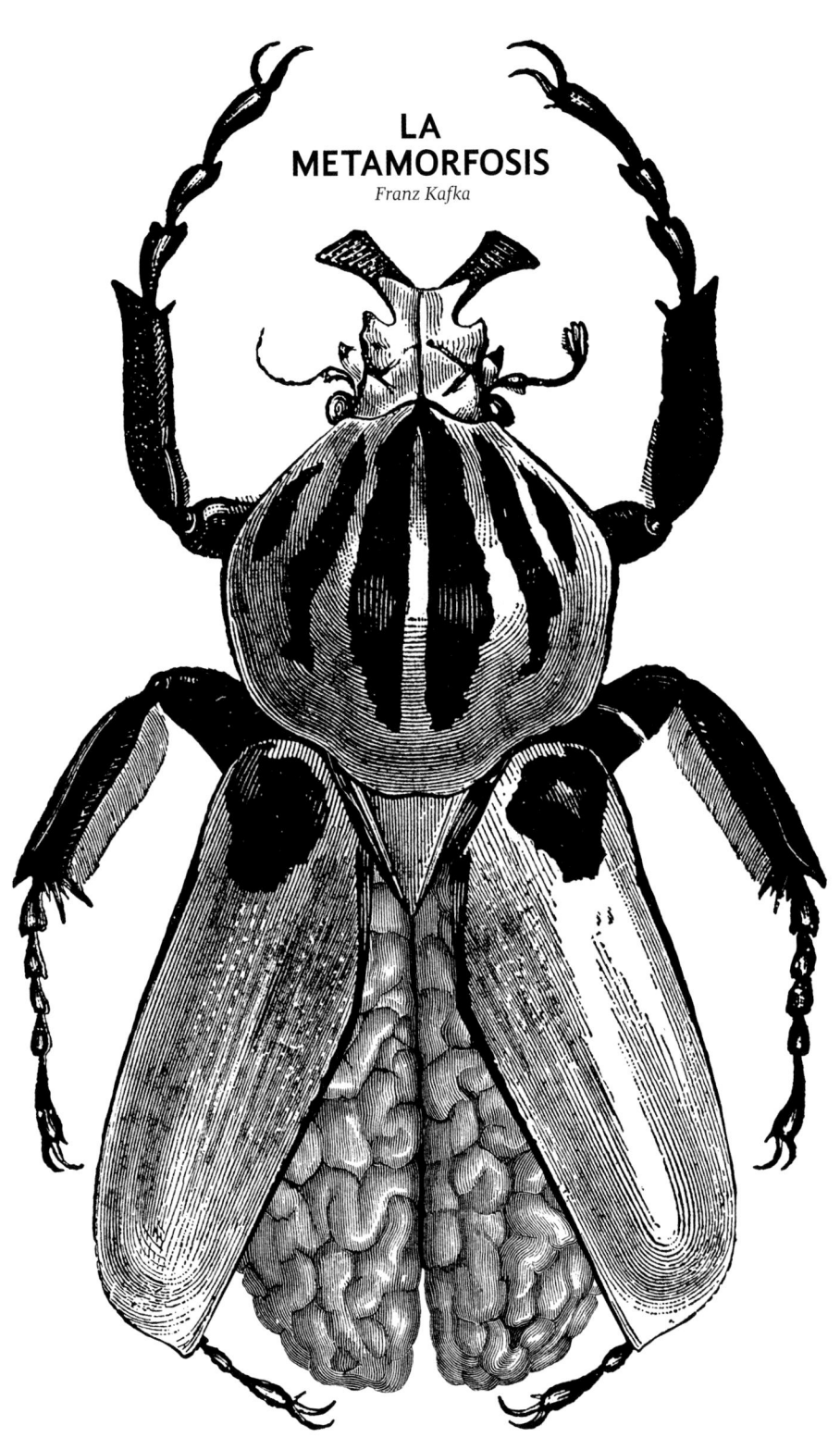

La metamorfosis | **Design**: Miguel Angel Guevara Rangel | © Miguel Angel Guevara Rangel | **Mexico** | 70 x 100 cm

MAKING POSTERS FROM CONCEPT TO DESIGN

Liberté | **Design:** © Moisés Romero Vargas | © Moises Romero Vargas | **Mexico** | 60 x 90 cm

White Tiger Melts | **Design:** Christopher Scott | © Christopher Scott | **Ireland** | 70 x 100 cm

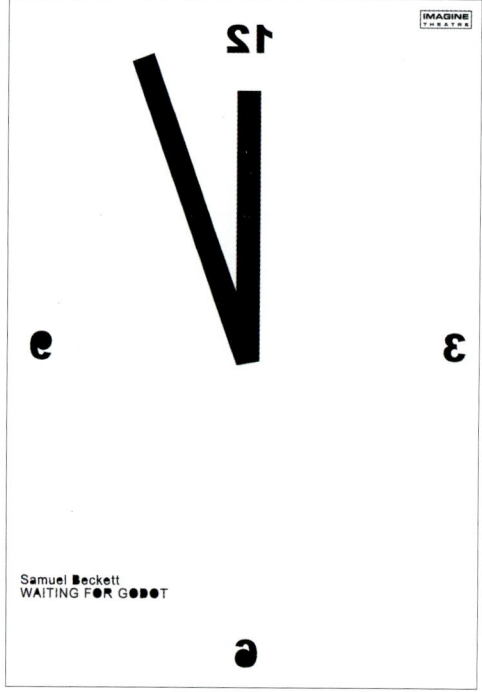

Waiting for Godot | **Design:** Lex Drewinski | © 2000 by Lex Drewinski, all rights reserved | **Germany** | 70 x 100 cm

Previous Page: For Rangel, two key words summarized Kafka's famous novel: "mind" and "insect." He combined the two to illustrate the psychological interpretation of the book.

Clockwise: Simple ideas can fuel powerful designs. Romero Vargas's inspiration came from the lyrics of a song: "Life is a prison with an open door." For Scott, it was the similarity between the stripes of the tiger and the color of the paper, while for Drewinski, it was the concept of time and the feeling of meaninglessness reflected by the play.

CHAPTER TWO CONCEPTUALIZING

Van Gogh 100 Years, 1989 | **Design**: Milton Glaser | © Milton Glaser | **USA** | 61 x 66 cm

Homage to Sonia Delaunay | **Design**: Luis Yañez | © Luis Yañez | **Mexico** | 70 x 100 cm

Hommage Fukuda | **Design**: Benito Cabañas | © Benito Cabañas | **Mexico** | 60 x 90 cm

Clockwise from top left: To celebrate Van Gogh's anniversary, Glaser cross-references a work by René Magritte, a famous Belgian artist, as an inside joke for art lovers who understand the reference. Yañez references Sonia Delaunay's famous "Rythme" painting in the colors and elements of his design. Cabañas bows in respect, paying homage to the optical illusions of designer Shigeo Fukuda.

Mais GMO | **Design:** Tomaso Marcolla | © Tomaso Marcolla | **Italy** | 50 x 70 cm

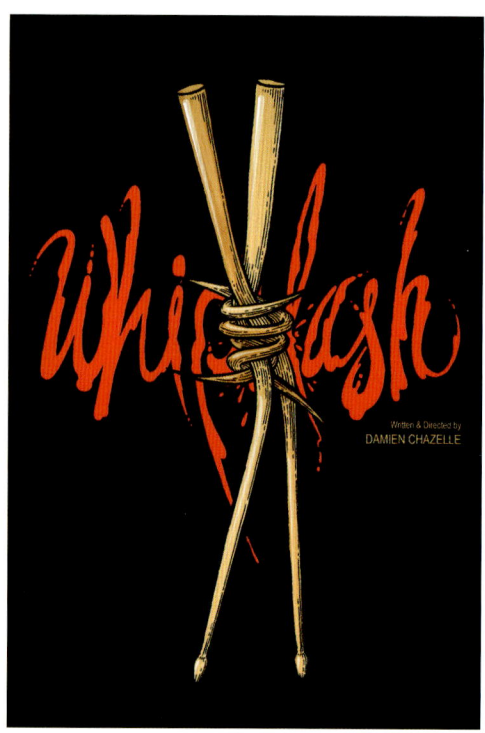

Whiplash | **Design/Illustration**: Elmer Sosa | © Elmer Sosa | **Mexico** | 40 x 60 cm

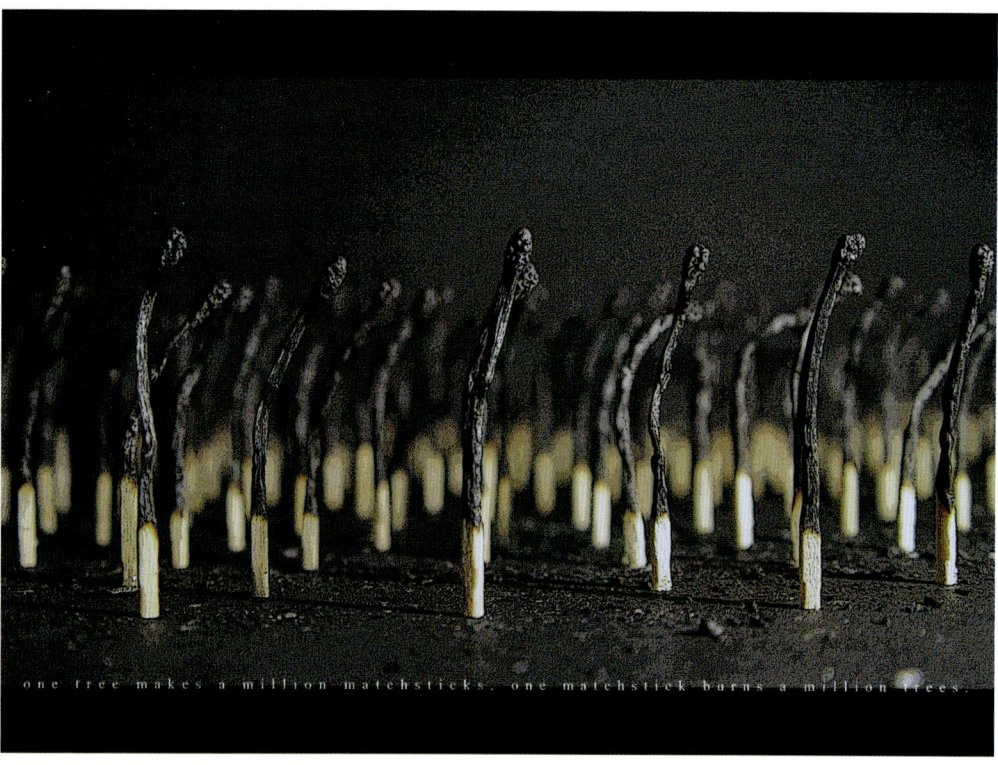

Matchsticks Forest | **Design**: Wesam Mazhar Haddad | © Wesam Mazhar Haddad | **USA** | 70 x 100 cm

Requiem pour les Artistes is a Tadeusz Kantor interplay among the grotesque, the macabre, and the poetic. Contemporary surrealism and Dadaism that are wrapped around the performance become the aesthetic of Batory's work. An image of a skull and crossbones made from a smashed violin and set typography tells Batory's elaborate story of an avant-garde performance nestled inside of a diorama.

Opposite: Inspired by their creators' research, the posters featured on this page communicate a strong sense of menace. Marcolla imagines GMOs as a weapon against humanity, Sosa illustrates a pair of drumsticks intertwined with spikes to represent a passion turned into an obsession, and Haddad tells a haunting story of the destruction that forest fires can cause.

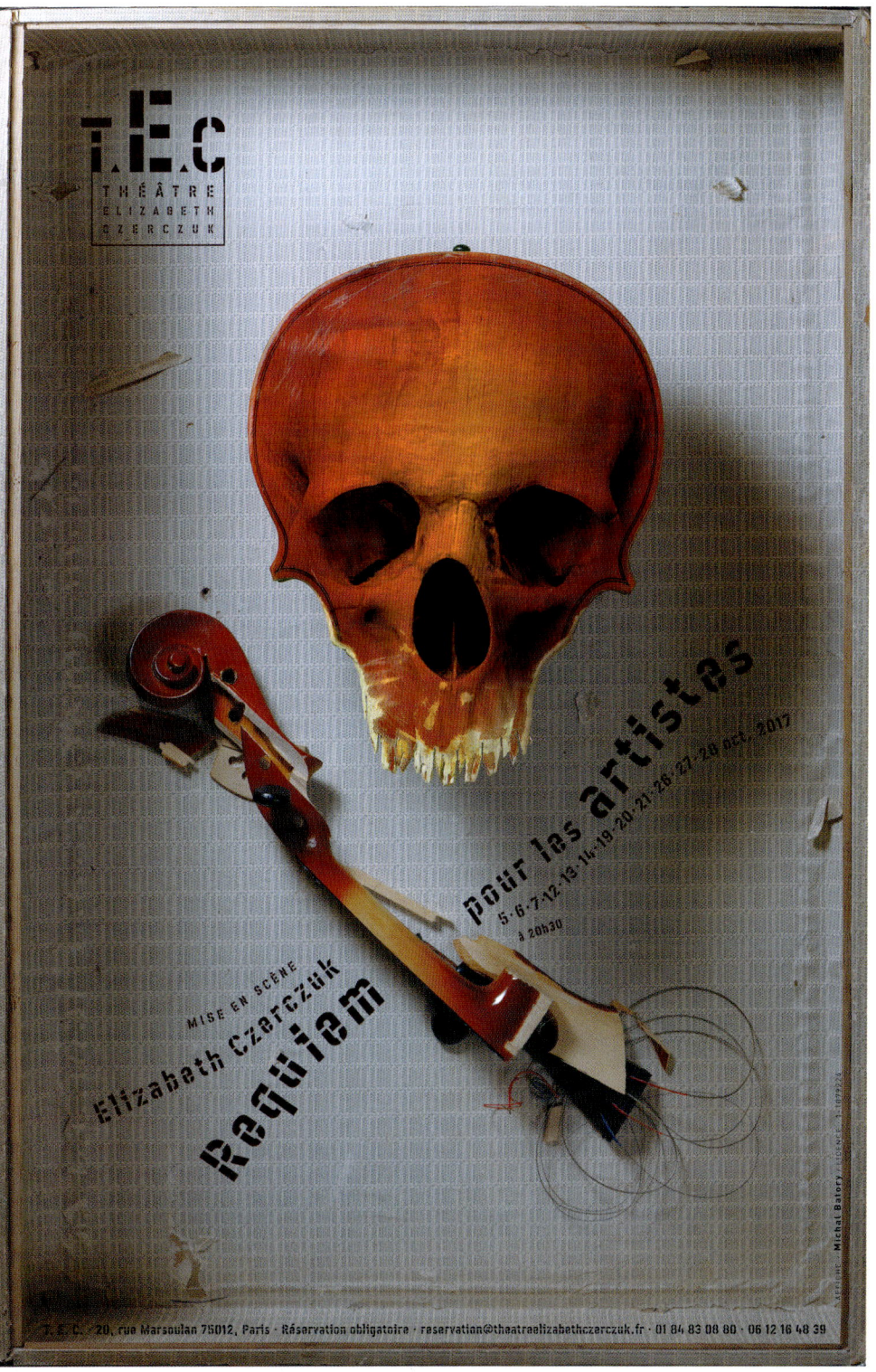

Requiem pour les Artistes (Requiem for Artists) | **Design**: Michal Batory | © Michal Batory | **France** | 70 x 100 cm

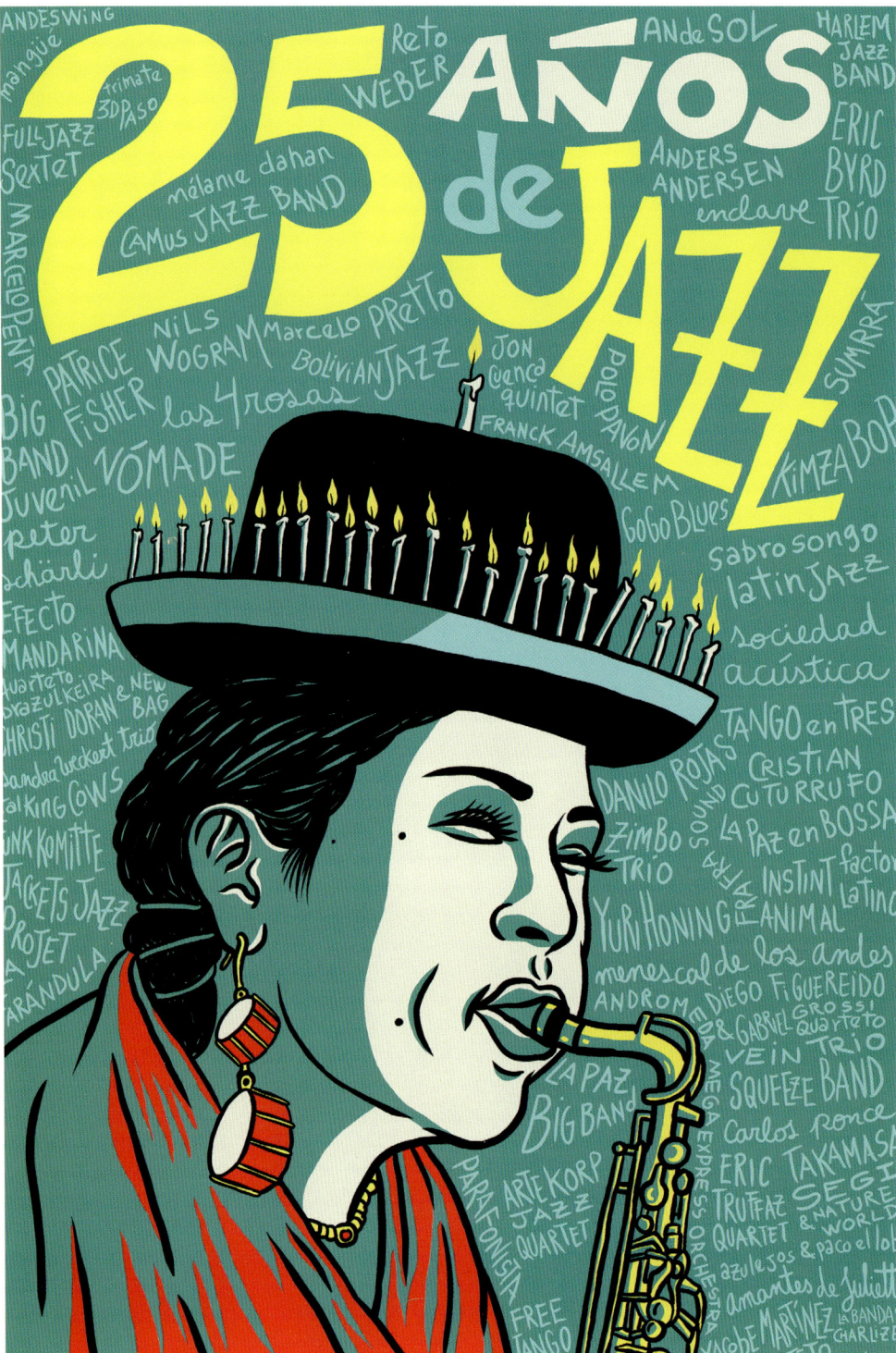

Creating a poster for a music group or event can provide a broad spectrum of possibilities. For the twenty-fifth anniversary of jazz in Bolivia, Marco Tóxico celebrates using symbolic elements like the birthday cake hat and Bolivian outfit.

Opposite: Hill creates a magical world reminiscent of dreams and the subconscious to promote The Sleepers' live concert. With a limited color palette, intricate linework, and whimsical details, Simpson's *Ed Sheeran* poster has a folk-pop vibe reflecting the musical style of the artist. The Heads of State's *Wilco* poster is a combination of a nod to Radio City Music Hall and some of Wilco's themes, while their poster *The Decemberists* evokes the past with an unusual image.

25 Años de Jazz | **Design/Illustration**: Marco Tóxico | © Marco Tóxico | **Bolivia** | 50 x 70 cm

CHAPTER TWO CONCEPTUALIZING

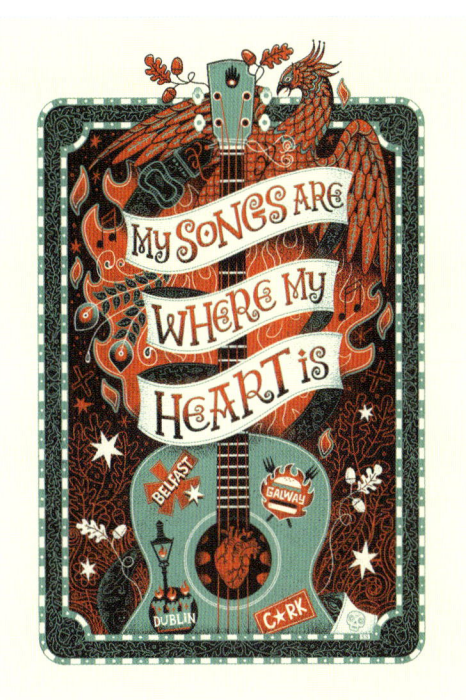

The Sleepers—Forest of Hands | **Design:** Adam Hill | © Adam Hill | **South Africa** | 59.4 x 84.1 cm

Ed Sheeran | **Design/Illustration:** Steve Simpson | © Steve Simpson | **Ireland** | 55.9 x 76.2 cm

45

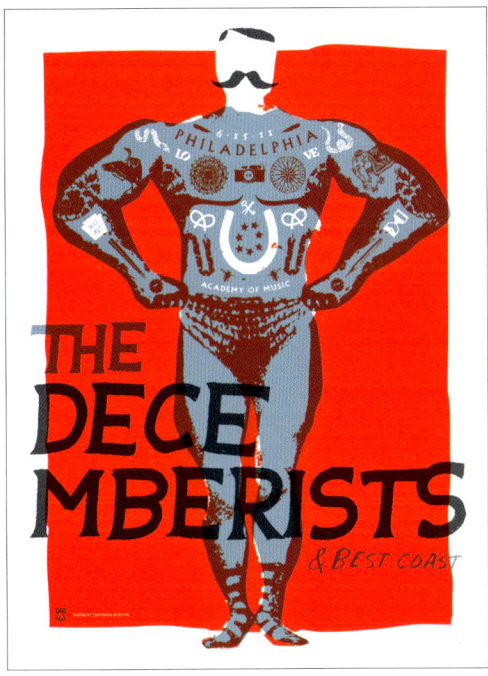

The Decemberists | © The Heads of State | **USA** | 45.7 x 61 cm

Wilco | © The Heads of State | **USA** | 45.7 x 61 cm

MAKING POSTERS FROM CONCEPT TO DESIGN

Digital Medicine | **Design:** Luka Prstojević | © Luka Prstojević | **Serbia** | 70 x 100 cm

The Path | **Design:** Hoon-Dong Chung | © Hoon-Dong Chung | **Korea** | 70 x 100 cm

Inspired by technology, Prstojević's poster blends art and science in a graceful image that communicates its concept of advanced medicine in the computer age. With the philosophy of "contrast is harmony," Chung combines concentration and dispersion with spatial relationships to represent the city of Xiamen as an essential passage for economic and cultural exchanges.

CHAPTER TWO CONCEPTUALIZING

8 May 1945—Victory in Europe Day | **Design**: Lex Drewinski | © 2018 by Lex Drewinski, all rights reserved | **Germany** | 70 x 100 cm

Was/Saw Dyslexia | **Design:** Stephen Doyle | © Doyle Partners | **USA** | 48.3 x 76.2 cm

Clockwise from top left: Words, places, and dates related to your topic can become the core of your concept. Using the number 8 as the smoking barrel of a gun, Drewinski marks the iconic VE Day, when the Nazis surrendered, ending World War II. Doyle cleverly illustrates dyslexia using a rip saw with the word "was" painted on its surface. The back-and-forth motion of *Was/Saw* alludes to the reversal of letterforms a dyslexic person may experience. Playing with typography, Gómez takes the letters from the word "poster" but omits the R and mixes the letters with lines to symbolize a mental jail that the letters escape as they emerge, representing the creative flow of ideas.

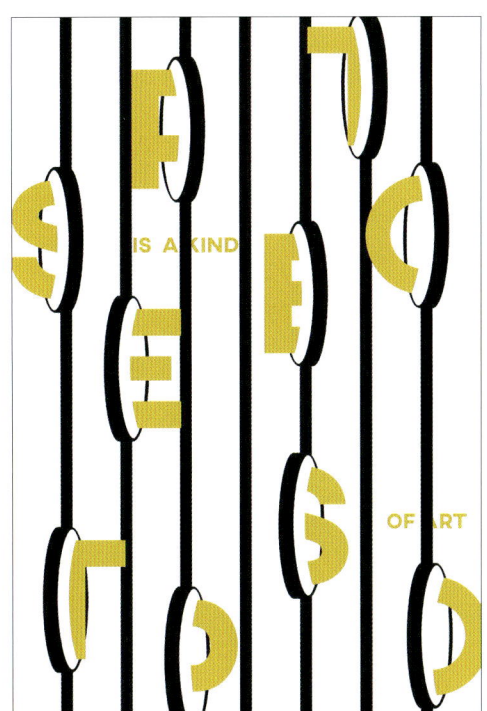

Kind of Art | **Design**: Santiago Gómez | © Santiago Gómez | **Ecuador** | 70 x 100 cm

MAKING POSTERS FROM CONCEPT TO DESIGN

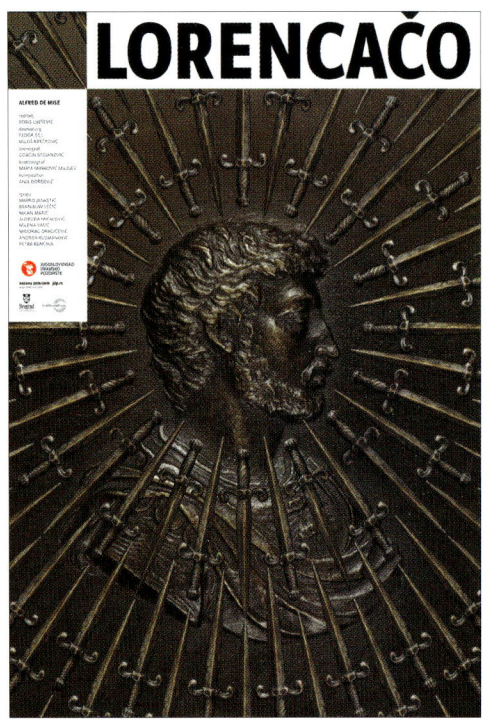

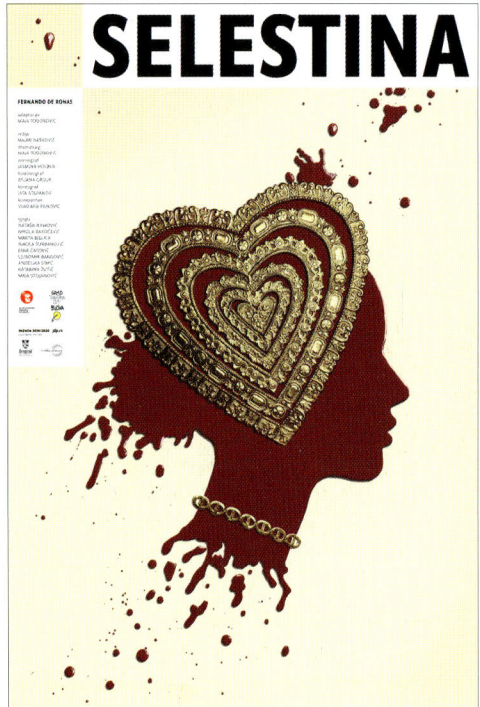

CHAPTER TWO CONCEPTUALIZING

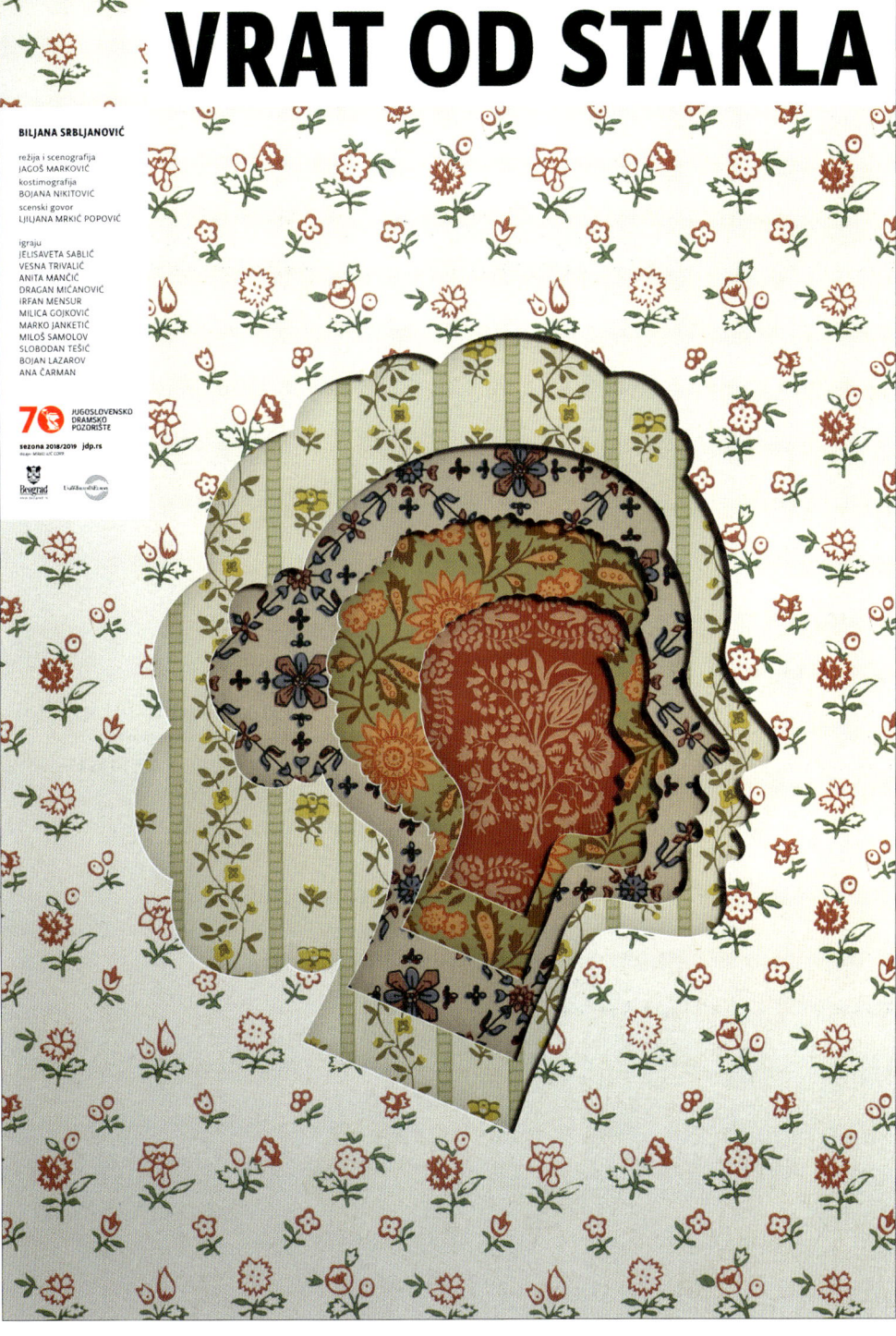

Previously, Ilić had designed posters for the Yugoslav Theatre using a simple, geometric typographic look. For this season, he decided he wanted to do something entirely different. The first play was a story about four generations of females evicted from the apartment in which they have lived for decades. Ilić made profiles of the women with layers of wallpaper, suggesting layers of time. This meant that he would need to apply profiles for the forthcoming plays, a self-inflicted challenge he was happy to take on. To ensure an effective brand recognition for the series, he designed white boxes for titles and credits.

Yugoslav Drama Theatre (series) | **Art Direction/Design**: Mirko Ilić | © Mirko Ilić | **USA** | 70 x 100 cm

"Art is beauty, the perpetual invention of detail, the choice of words, the exquisite care of execution."

- Theophile Gautier

CHAPTER THREE EXECUTION

Like a jigsaw puzzle, design execution is piecing together information that you have gathered while also conceptualizing to assemble a coherent whole. Concepts and execution are interrelated—both are essential to make an effective poster. Implementation of your concepts requires a basic understanding of composition and will rely on your ability to make images, from traditional techniques or digital manipulation, to complete this part of the design process.

The design process resembles an accordion that expands and contracts over and over again. While some techniques allow you to generate more ideas, others help you narrow them down. As you work on your project, you must always keep in mind your message and objectives to avoid getting lost. There is no single answer to a design problem but rather a multitude of creative solutions. The process is not linear; very often you will find yourself testing ideas and developing them before realizing they did not work as you imagined. This might mean going back to conceptualization and carrying out deeper research and brainstorming to come up with new solutions. Writer Peter Reason, professor emeritus at the University of Bath, describes design as a process that grows and develops over time and is often carried out in a constant iteration of analysis, synthesis, and evaluation that continues until you discover an effective solution.[5] While having a model to guide you is important and useful, this model should be flexible, and you should always remain aware of the specific requirements of each case and allow your approach to develop and change over time.

EXECUTION

Illustration: Scott Laserow

Image Making

Image making is often considered one of the unique and quintessential competences of humanity.[6] As humans, we are all born image makers, expressing ourselves starting at an early age by drawing marks in the dirt or sand . . . remember that rectangle with two circles that you called a car? These naïve drawings of buildings, animals, nature, and people were somehow recognizable no matter how distorted or abstract; even stick figures reveal creativity, understanding, and intelligence.

Poster designers use images to grab attention and make connections with their audience. Therefore, the way you make an image has a significant influence on how the message is received. Whereas text takes a moment to read and decipher, the right image can provoke an immediate emotional response that taps into the human psyche. It is essential that you select appropriate visuals that support your concept. When properly executed, an image can transform an ordinary encounter into an exciting and informative experience capable of changing perceptions. This is not to imply that an image needs to be complicated to be communicative; simple imagery can connect and be meaningful. How you choose to make an image is dependent upon your idea, your skill level, and the audience. Poor design decisions will inevitably confuse or distort the message.

Consider exploring some of the fundamentals of art, like color, scale, contrast, value, texture, pattern, and typography, as part of the image making process. How often do you actually examine these basic techniques? Investigating these fundamentals of art and design is a worthwhile exercise that may produce unforeseen outcomes. Russian designer Evdokimov Gosha's *Posters with Letter #A* series (Figure 3.1) is not only a set of beautiful images but also a demonstration of how an iteration of a single graphic can pay off with a remarkable and exciting poster series. Gosha pushes and pulls on his subject, exploring contrast, illustration, photography, texture, figure ground, distortion, flatness, and depth to abstract the letterform A without losing legibility. He challenges himself with the variation of his letterform and places additional typography into his composition for added visual depth and interest. Gosha explores wildly while never forgetting that his letterform is the primary focus. His experimentation with the foundation of image making yields great success.

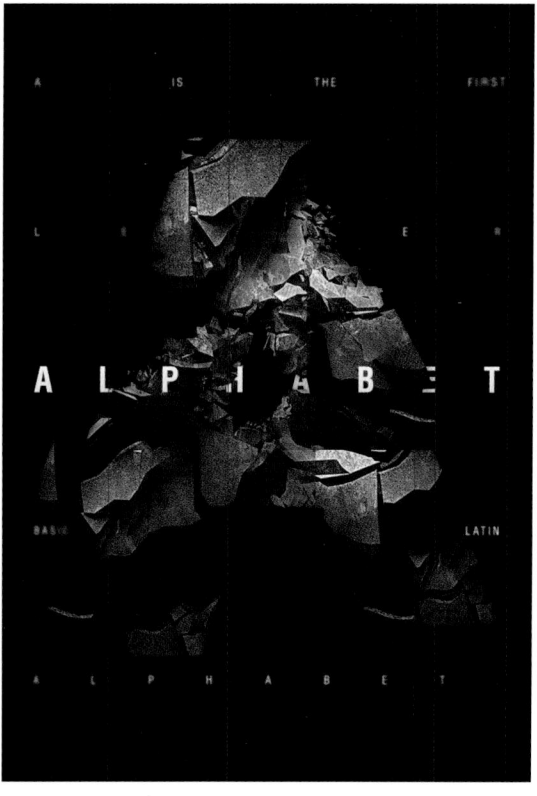

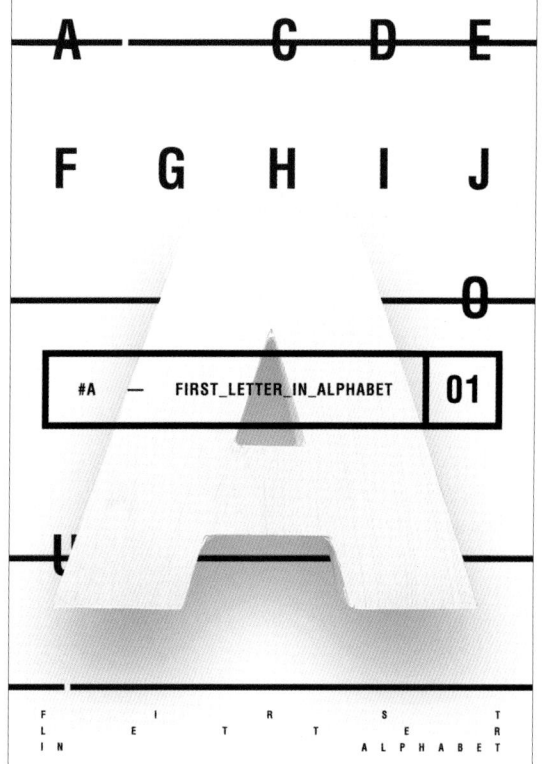

CHAPTER THREE EXECUTION

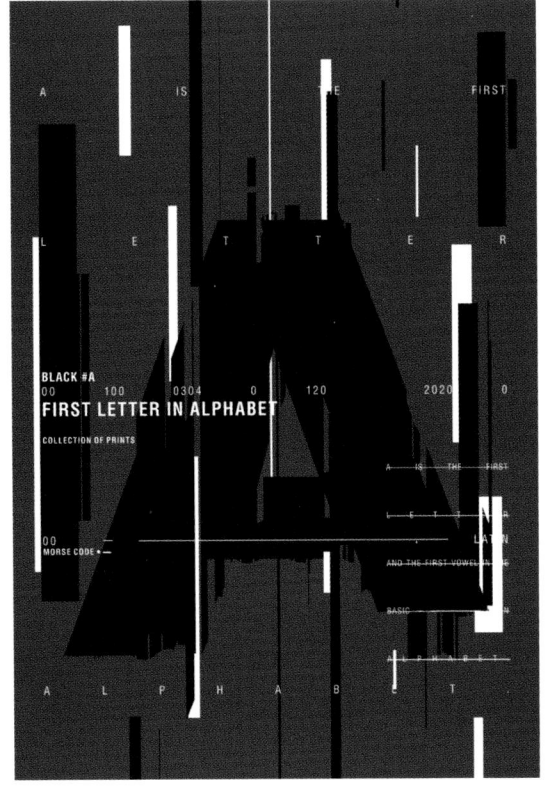
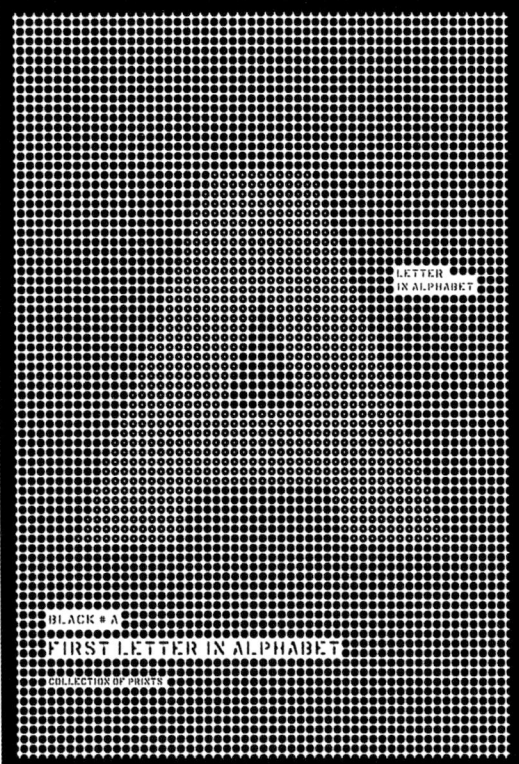
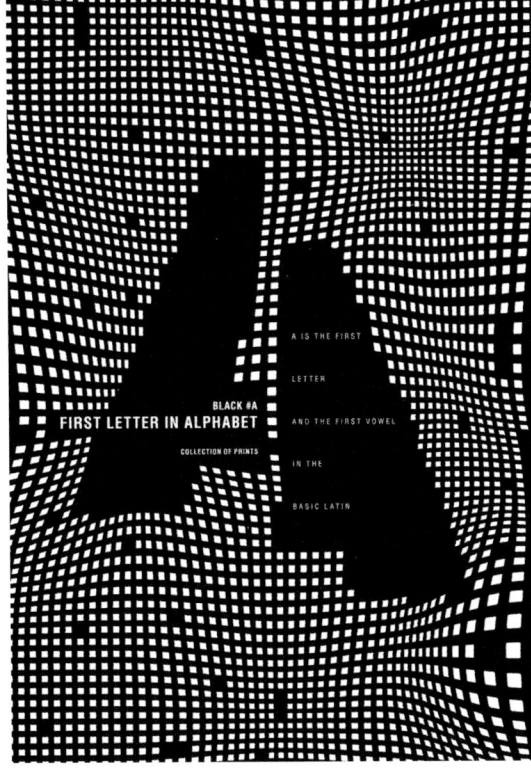
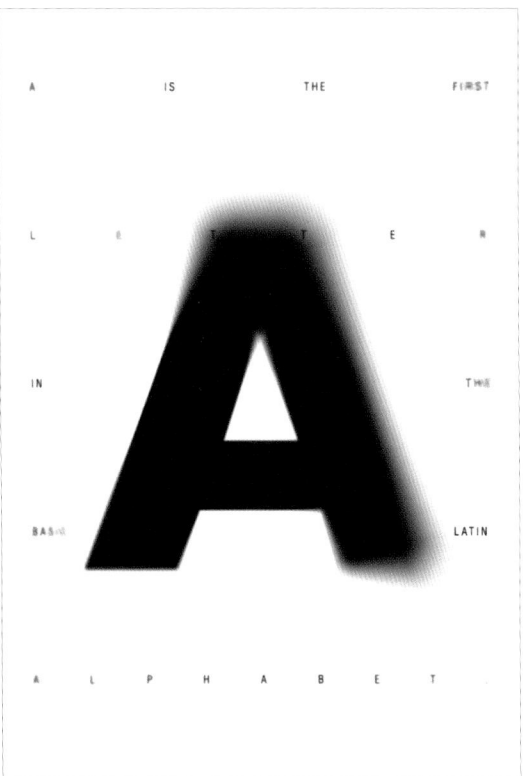

Figure 3.1 | *Posters with Letter #A (series)* | **Design**: Evdokimov Gosha | © Evdokimov Gosha | **Russia** | 70 x 100 cm

Figures 3.2 and 3.3 | *Epitaph #3, Honshu, Japan* | **Design**: Scott Laserow | © Scott Laserow | **USA** | 60 x 90 cm

Poster artists build narratives by making images that provoke. They use everything from traditional media like pencil and paper, pen and ink, watercolor, collage, etc., to emerging technologies, such as drawing with a stylus, capturing visuals, using digital media, and experimenting with numerous digital two-dimensional and three-dimensional applications. Many times, poster artists combine techniques to visually communicate a concept. Therefore, you do not need to be a great illustrator or artist to be a great image maker, be inventive, and work toward your strengths. The methods that you choose to make your image will ultimately determine how the visual is perceived and are as important to your message as the idea itself. For example, if you are designing a poster that requires an emotional response, the way you make an image might be restricted. Although both posters of the Honshu Japan study (Figures 3.2 and 3.3) have identical concepts, composition, layout, and typography, it is clear that Figure 3.3, the photographic approach, is more successful. It relies on a color palette and materials that connect us to the power of nature and its ability to heal. The photographic seedling is tangible and gives hope that Japan will recover and blossom again. In comparison, the illustration of the same image (Figure 3.2) feels cold and emotionless; it lacks the contrast and connection we have with the photographic image.

Line

A line is one of the core elements of design; it is a one-dimensional path that can also define the edges of a shape. It can be horizontal, vertical, diagonal, straight, curved, crisp and graphic, or loose and energetic. It can be thick, thin, delicate, broken, dashed, or dotted—the options are endless. Instinctively, line directs the eyes to relevant information. On its own, line can be quite descriptive and can provoke a reaction. It can appear calming and restful or pleasing and sensual, show movement and energy, and communicate scale and length. When used with other visuals, line and the way you handle it can support a narrative.

A loose line tends to express emotions like nervousness, sadness, or happiness. A graphic line is used more for structure, support, and conformity and tends to be less descriptive than an energetic line. In Figure 3.4, Lanny Sommese uses line as part of the narrative in his poster *Profanity*. The broken vigorous line and the way he chooses to handle the typography by adding a target in the letterform O help interconnect the linework and the concept. Tension is created by the distinct differences between the two figures. The perpetrator is intentionally handled more aggressively by the disparity in height and the sharp downward stroke above the eye, showing aggression, whereas the victim is shorter and the linework below the eye is softer, curved, and more submissive. Sommese uses negative space to form the shape of a yellow rocket being thrust down the throat of the victim, cautioning the viewer about the use of profanity and its explosive effects.

Shape

A shape is an object in space that has two dimensions, height and width, and can be defined by line. It can be stylized or representational. Shapes always surround us; we become so accustomed to them that we lose our appreciation for the beauty of a shape's simplicity. Simple shapes, when used by a skilled graphic designer, can provide meaning. They can command our attention, direct our eye, tell us to stop, or point us in the right direction. As seen in John Rieben's *Jazz Ltd.* poster (Figure 3.5), shape can communicate and begin to tell a story. Rieben's design showcases how shape and color can communicate on an emotional level. His color palette and the lively interaction between contrasting shapes have an improvised, syncopated rhythmic quality that we equate with jazz music. Understanding grid systems allows Rieben to break his grid while still maintaining order in disorder. The large red rectangle forces the eye to the negative space between the gray and gold shapes resting on a baseline. The volume of space aligns with the negative space between the typography at the bottom of the poster. Just as the text rests on a baseline, so too do the shapes, setting the stage for the lively performance above.

Figure 3.4 | *Profanity* (with sketch detail) | **Design:** Lanny Sommese | © Lanny Sommese | **USA** | 50 x 70 cm

Figure 3.5 | *Jazz Ltd.* | **Design**: John Rieben | © John Rieben | **USA** | 50 x 70 cm

CHAPTER THREE EXECUTION

Type as Image

Aside from using objects, graphics, illustration, and photography to make images, poster artists sometimes incorporate typography in clever ways to build a story. Typography is more than a selection of typefaces; it can serve as the expression of an idea when manipulated to communicate a specific meaning beyond the actual word or letterform. The typeface itself is a key influencer, and its selection is as important as any other element in the composition. Designing with typography is no different than creating any other visual, and therefore you should apply the same design principles you use when working with an image.

With no physical manipulation of the typeface, Todd Hart's *Killer Type* poster series (Figure 3.6) demonstrates how typography becomes the visual based on the shapes of letterforms and typographic symbols along with their size, placement, and relationship to one another. Hart selects the perfect typeface for his *Frankenstein Is Franklin Gothic* poster. Not only "punny," but a robust and angular typeface, Franklin Gothic is fitting for a giant monster. *Dracula Is Grotesk* uses Akzidenz-Grotesk's varying weights and widths to paint the

Figure 3.6 | *Killer Type* | **Design:** Todd Hart | © Todd Hart | **USA** | 61 x 81.3 cm

vampire's portrait, while *The Wolf Man Is Helvetica* has fun with one of the most iconic typefaces, Helvetica, for the growling beast. Paying attention to form, Hart selects his point sizes and weights carefully. Choosing organic typographic elements like parentheses and brackets, Hart adds softness to the large, rising chest of Frankenstein and facial structure of Dracula and the Wolf Man. In contrast, the more angular letterforms construct Frankenstein's jaw and the sharp penetrating teeth of Dracula and the Wolf Man. All three posters use spot color and hierarchy to effortlessly move your attention from the playful portraits to the font alphabet below.

Figure/Ground

Our eyes build connections between elements, filling in the gaps so we can make sense of the visual. This is called the law of closure. When engaging with a visual, we distinguish the foreground (or figure) from the background (or ground). Sometimes referred to as positive and negative space, figure/ground balances the foreground, or positive space, and the background, or negative space. Since negative space is never really blank, when used wisely it can not only support the foreground but also alter an initial perception once it reveals itself. Using figure/ground can fool the eye and quickly become mesmerizing as you drift from background to foreground and back again. This illusion presents an opportunity to make a single image with multiple meanings. When using figure/ground relationships, the foreground and background will usually have equal importance. This is best illustrated by the Rubin vase, developed by Danish psychologist Edgar Rubin around 1915 (Figure 3.7). The Rubin vase is an optical illusion where two silhouetted faces in profile face each other, creating a vase out of the negative space.

Yongkang Fu's poster *Living Space* (Figure 3.8) is a Rubin vase with a message. Fu's hypnotic image of fish and bottles continually alters your focus from the figure to the ground. Which do you see first, the plastic bottles or the fish skeletons? Either way, Fu gets his point across—that plastics are destroying sea life.

Figure 3.7 | Rubin Vase

Figure 3.8 | *Living Space* | **Design:** Yongkang Fu | © Yongkang Fu | **China** | 50 x 70 cm

Red is the color with the longest wavelength. It has the property of appearing to be nearer than it is, and therefore it is often used to indicate danger or to highlight something important. Red is associated with fire, violence, and war but also with love and passion. It is known to increase viewers' blood pressure and raise pulse and breathing rate.

Orange is a vibrant color related to health and vitality thanks to the fruit that bears its name. It attracts attention without being as overwhelming as red, and it is also considered more friendly and attractive. In its muted forms, it can be associated with earth and autumn.

Pink represents many qualities often thought of as feminine, such as delicacy, softness, sensitivity, nurturance, and compassion. It is a versatile color; hot shades of pink are vivacious and playful, while the more muted tones represent youth and innocence.

Yellow is considered the brightest and most energetic warm color due to its association with the sun. The yellow wavelength is relatively long and emotionally stimulating, making it psychologically the strongest color. It is linked to positive concepts such as optimism, youth, confidence, and creativity, but in certain shades or contexts, it can also mean betrayal, greed, or warning.

Green is a color often found in nature and therefore commonly used to represent new beginnings, growth, the environment, and rebirth. It is associated with health, freshness, and peace. In its darkest tones it is associated with money and abundance.

Blue is the coldest color. It has a soothing and calming effect that stimulates concentration and can even suppress the appetite. It is the color of clear communication, used extensively to represent honesty, responsibility, and trust. Light blues can be refreshing and friendly, while dark blues are stronger and safer.

Violet or **purple** is an unusual and enigmatic hue that has the shortest wavelength of all colors. It is linked to the worlds of luxury, religion, and sexuality.

Brown is a serious, stable, and reliable color, signifying strength, structure, and support. Brown has associations with the earth and the natural world.

Pure gray has no direct psychological properties. Because of its lack of personality, gray will be significantly affected by the color it is mixed with, toning down the stronger and brighter colors and illuminating the softer colors.

Color

Color can enhance and alter our perceptions and, in certain circumstances, provoke an emotional response. There is a lot of science behind color, often referred to as color psychology, which studies the effects of color on moods, feelings, and behaviors. While our reaction to color can be affected by our personal experiences and cultural background, there are certain cross-cultural generalities that can be applied to the psychological associations and feelings evoked by certain colors and color combinations.[MPR]

Choosing the right color palette is a key aspect of the design process. Colors can significantly affect your designs and how others perceive them. Like shape, color can help you tell your story by reinforcing the message and highlighting emotional or rational elements of your design. However, color can be a double-edged sword; used carelessly, it can have a negative impact, diluting the hierarchy and causing chaos. Therefore, color should always be used strategically and with purpose.

Sophia Talavera Paz created the poster *Como no me iba a enamorar . . . mi Fridita* (*How was I not going to fall in love . . . my little Frida*) (Figure 3.9) for the #TOMMYXMACO student poster competition organized by Tommy Hilfiger, an international clothing brand. Talavera Paz's work was inspired by the pain and strength of Frida Kahlo, especially in the suffering caused by her love for Diego Rivera. While the imagery and text allude to Frida, the color palette serves to connect these items with the brand by applying Hilfiger's iconic blue, red, and white color palette to the design. The result is an explosive image that combines a Mexican theme and imagery with an American brand.

Figure 3.9 | *Como no me iba a enamorar . . . mi Fridita* | **Design:** Sophia Talavera Paz | © Sophia Talavera Paz | **Mexico** | 90 x 90 cm

Composition and Hierarchy

Composition is the placement of elements on the page, their proportions and relationships to one another, and their rhythm. Composition helps lead viewers through your design in a natural way without them noticing. This is known as the flow of the page. Accomplishing flow requires the arrangement of text and graphics, but most importantly, it involves the use of an invisible element created by the blank, empty space. Often, this can be done intuitively by randomly positioning the elements on the page and moving them around until they look good. However, this can be very time consuming and may require years of practice. Composition will allow you to arrange your content clearly by organizing and prioritizing certain elements of your design to reinforce the message you want to communicate. This is referred to as visual hierarchy, a term that originated from the German Gestalt psychology movement, which studied how humans perceive the world. According to Gestalt laws of perceptual organization, we do not perceive our surroundings individually, but rather we try to make sense of them by grouping them as a whole. When an element disconnects from this whole, it stands out, thereby influencing the order in which it is seen.[7] Therefore, as designers, we can use this principle to guide the way in which viewers perceive the information presented.

Using a Grid

A grid is a series of lines that are used to subdivide a page vertically and horizontally into margins, columns, inter-column spaces, lines of type, and spaces between blocks of type and images. The possibilities for grid-based layouts are endless. However, it is crucial to the success of your poster that your chosen grid keep your design aligned and organized. Your grid should work for rather than against you; it should not make you feel constrained. Usually, when creating a poster, designers choose simpler grids, since posters tend not to have a lot of complex information that other layouts like websites, magazines, and catalogs may entail.

A grid structure like the one featured in Figure 3.10 will allow you to align elements, giving order to your composition and creating a feeling of cleanliness. Grids act as a guide to locate the best placement, position, and scale of your design elements. It is not necessary to fill every column of your grid; consider white space when placing your elements. Generally speaking, the tighter your margins, the tenser and more cluttered your design can look, but the wider your margins, the cleaner the design.

Figure 3.10 | *NEST* | © Design Army | **USA** | 43.2 x 61 cm

Figure 3.11 | *Libre Libro 2018 (Free Book 2018)* | **Design**: Maria Mercedes Salgado | © Maria Mercedes Salgado | **Ecuador** | 40 x 60 cm

Rule of Thirds

One of the simplest grid systems is the rule of thirds (Figure 3.11). This system divides a layout into three equally spaced horizontal lines and three vertical lines, then places the focal point on one of the lines or, ideally, on one of the four points where the lines intersect. This technique is prevalent in photography and applies to poster design with great results.

Symmetry and Asymmetry

Symmetry and asymmetry are two simple but powerful design principles that can provide a guiding structure for your design. Symmetry refers to an awareness of harmonious and beautifully proportioned balance. A symmetrical design is equally balanced on both sides of a central axis, either vertically, horizontally, or radially. While symmetry usually refers to mirror-like sides, it does not need to be the same to create a sense of balance and order. Conversely, asymmetry is the absence of symmetry of any kind. A design is asymmetrical whenever the composition consists of visuals distributed unevenly around a central axis point. We can exploit asymmetry, using it to draw attention to certain areas in the design or to convey dynamism or movement.

Symmetry offers an ordered approach to design. The human eye finds the balance brought about by symmetry pleasing—we refer to this as formal balance. As the complexity of a project increases, you will find that symmetric balance becomes increasingly difficult to attain. Rather than trying to force symmetry, you can allow asymmetry in the design and use "informal balance" to achieve an even distribution of elements on either side of a vertical or horizontal axis.

Figure 3.12 | *Creativity Has No Bounds* | **Design:** Umer Ahmed | © Umer Ahmed | **Norway** | 50 x 70 cm

The poster *Creativity Has No Bounds* (Figure 3.12) by Umer Ahmed shows the use of both formal and informal balance. The center image is completely symmetrical, forming a perfect mirror-like reflection on its vertical axis. The enigmatic ink blot is reminiscent of the Rorschach psychology tests, allowing viewers to unleash their imagination and derive meaning. The surrounding information is perfectly balanced on both the vertical and horizontal axes by using a similar size, weight, and placement of the text.

Rule of Odds

The rule of odds asserts that people find the rhythmic harmony of uneven numbers appealing. A common practice among poster designers is to limit their objects to no more than three. Using five or more items tends to create density, and if you are not careful, your design can quickly become busy. If faced with having to use several objects, placing them in three groupings will still maintain balance without causing competition between visuals. Figure 3.13 not only illustrates how the rule of odds creates satisfying unity, but it is also a good example of asymmetry.

Focal Point

One of the functions of hierarchy is to establish a focal point, providing the audience with a starting position and guiding them toward the most important content. Your focal point should be the dominant element in your layout. Before choosing a focal point, ask yourself: If viewers had only a couple of seconds to glance at my poster and take in one piece of information, what should it be? Focal points highlight areas of interest and help emphasize or differentiate specific visuals of your design.

Adding hierarchical emphasis instructs the viewer to digest different parts of your design in order of importance, rather than all the visuals competing for attention equally. Choosing the placement of your focal point is important, and you will want to explore the many possibilities. Placing your focal point at the center of your page is a common strategy. Another accepted practice is placing the focal point in the upper left-hand corner of your layout. This arrangement is derived from the Western standard of reading from left to right and top to bottom. Overall, the placement of your focal point will depend on your content and design.

Figure 3.13 | *Continui* | **Design:** Gary Nicholson | © Gary Nicholson | **England** | 45.7 x 61 cm

The focal point in Marcos Minini's poster *Shaxpeare/Shakespeare/Shagsbere* (Figure 3.14) is dead center and right on the nose. Waiting for you there are a milk mustache and a devilish grin inviting you to a fanciful performance by the Estudio Delírio theater troupe as they pay homage to William Shakespeare.

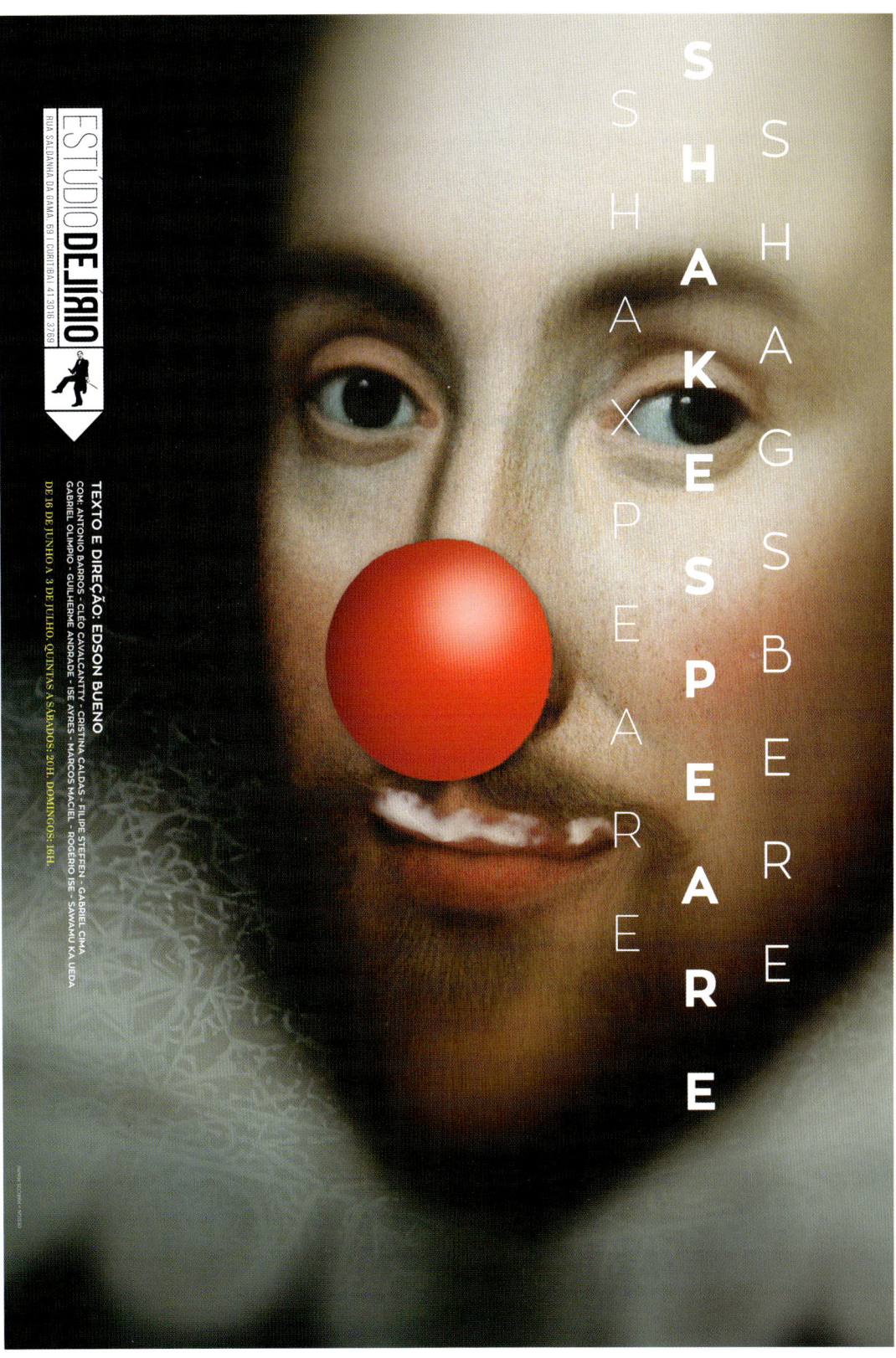

Figure 3.14 | *Shaxpeare/Shakespeare/Shagsbere* | **Design**: Marcos Minini | © Marcos Minini | **Brazil** | 70 x 100 cm

Figure 3.15 | *M for Mantis* | **Design**: Craig Moscony | © Craig Moscony | **USA** | 33 x 48.3 cm

White Space

White space, sometimes referred to as negative space, is the blank space that surrounds the visuals in your composition. White space is not always white; the term is derived from the traditional practice of graphic design where printing was done primarily on a white paper stock. For an untrained eye, white or blank space might merely be considered the background for your design, but its use is actually an important design principle that should not be overlooked.

The more elements a design includes, the more complicated it becomes to organize them within the page. White space can be a challenge for novice designers, who might feel intimidated by projects that involve large quantities of text, images, or other components such as logos from sponsors. A common mistake is trying to fill compositions with artwork, ignoring the impact that white space can have on a poster. Adding white space around a visual can strengthen its weight by giving it room to breathe. Having space makes it easier to separate and organize your design by creating order and balance.

Acting out his inner entomologist mounting and displaying an insect, Craig Moscony uses white space to present his letterform *M for Mantis* from his *Insect Alphabet* poster series (Figures 3.15 and 3.16). By locking up the typography in a ruled grid and placing it at the bottom of his composition, he supports his scientific display aesthetic. His use of white space is not only part of the narrative, but it also helps to increase the significance of the beautifully illustrated letterform and focuses the written descriptive content.

Figure 3.16 | *Alphabet Insectorum* | **Design:** Craig Moscony | © Craig Moscony | **USA**

Creating a Poster Series

A poster series is two or more posters created for a single campaign. This opportunity extends the initial concept beyond that of the individual poster. Each poster created must be consistent with the others without becoming predictable. There are a few strategies you can explore to avoid repetition. Consider executing the same image differently or using different imagery with the same visual style. Change your background colors, alter your color palette, or try contrasting visual styles on the same topic. Consistent font and typographic systems, theme, or composition can make for a harmonious presentation. Regardless of your approach, all the posters in your series must work together as well as stand alone.

Max Rompo uses the traditional Argentinian *verse* (mixing around the letters or syllables within a word), commonly present in tango lyrics, to create a playful take on his series of concert posters (Figure 3.17) for the Orquesta Típica Agustín Guerrero (OTAG). Reversing the initials to spell GATO (cat), Rompo creates a ludic geometric character that acts as the central element connecting his series. Changing the cat's pose allows Rompo to introduce diversity in the series, while the geometric approach and yellow and black color scheme provide the cohesiveness necessary for the posters.

Figure 3.17 | *Orquesta Típica Agustín Guerrero* | **Design**: Max Rompo | © Max Rompo | **Argentina** | 70 x 100 cm

Context

Context is an image's dependence on other visuals, objects, or typography to deliver a message. It reveals the interconnected relationships among the individual elements on the poster that divulge the narrative to the audience. Context can easily be understood by following a simple exercise. Draw a square in the center of a page as seen in Figure 3.18. Now that you have a simple shape, draw the letter B to the left of the square and the letter X to the right of the square. The square transforms into the letter O to form the word BOX (Figure 3.19). It is the context that changed our perception of a shape into a letterform and gave it new meaning; a square became a box. Tomasz Boguslawski's *The Madman & the Nun* (Figure 3.20) illustrates this concept to perfection. Boguslawski starts with a gentleman's collar, which by itself would be nothing more than an image of a collar. He then creates context with the addition of erratic, ambiguous pencil marks, and magically the collar becomes a representation of both the madman trapped in an insane asylum and a nun's habit. Below, he sexualizes the nun by using the collar as the tips of a garter belt to convey the nun's carnal passion and her physical relationship with the madman. Boguslawski continues his theme of madness with the scrawled, manic typography at the top of his poster. Context has changed what appeared to be an uncomplicated image into a twisted story of love, lust, and madness.

Figure 3.18   **Figure 3.19**

Aesthetics

Aesthetics is a philosophical explanation of beauty and taste commonly relating to art. Theoretically, it helps us decipher why we are attracted to a visual. The word "aesthetics" is often attached to an artistic movement, for example, Baroque or Pop. The first connection someone has with your poster is how it looks—it acts as an invitation to seek additional information. A visual with a strong aesthetic will cause a viewer to assume that there is a deeper meaning behind the image and entice them to look further. This cognitive reaction, called the halo effect, is loosely translated as an immediate decree or bias based on how something looks. If it looks beautiful, we presume that it is and that it possesses additional good qualities. Aesthetics may be expressed by an image that evokes a memory or sensation or has a sense of emotional beauty. A specific aesthetic might be conveyed by a minimalistic, clean space or an eclectic blend of organic and inorganic shapes. A poster artist's aesthetic must express style, taste, and accessibility. As they say, beauty is in the eye of the beholder—whether or not we like the viewpoint is less important than if it is working. Because of this phenomenon, people will react differently to the same poster. Any reaction is considered desirable, attesting that the viewer found it captivating and was engaged.

As illustrated in Figures 3.21, 3.22, and 3.23, the play *Macbeth* is explored in diverse and distinctive styles by three seasoned poster artists. All three are strikingly different yet equally successful. Each expertly crafted poster offers a different aesthetic approach that has its own appeal. In Figure 3.21, Hoon-Dong Chung uses emerging technologies to execute an abstracted, contemporary vision of Macbeth. You can clearly see the king's crown covered in blood and a large dagger stabbing through the edge of the composition. The dagger and the crown are recognizable and iconic imagery, and the emotional connection that red has with blood makes Chung's abstraction easy to understand. In the case of Yossi Lemel (Figure 3.22), the composite image in his *Macbeth* poster is a symbolic graphic that pays homage to the play's famous scene "Song of the Witches." Adding details to the points of the crown, Lemel reveals the three witches, while the negative space in the center of the crown becomes the caldron. Using white space and contrast, Lemel delivers a striking image. Finally, Marcos Minini (Figure 3.23) snaps a picture of the tyrannical king melting beneath his crown of blood, his skin turned inside out to show the rawness of the character. Minini's typography emphasizes letterform B, which is a contrasting montage of a quill pen and a sword; this form is where the writer crosses his creation.

Figure 3.20 | *The Madman & the Nun* | Design: Tomasz Boguslawski | © Tomasz Boguslawski | Poland | 68 x 98 cm

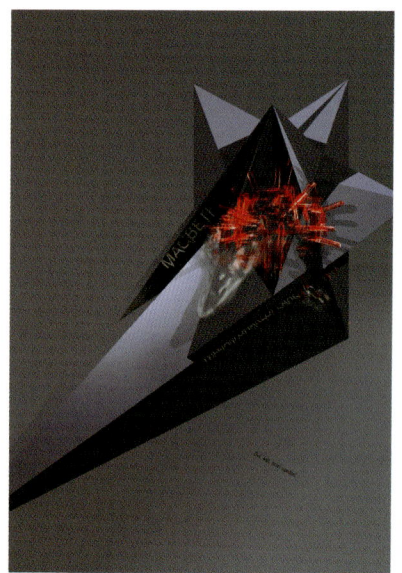
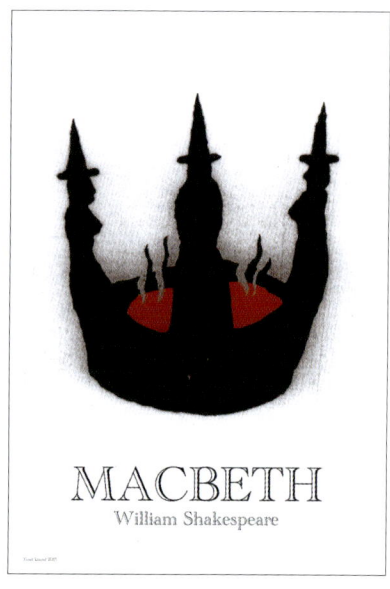
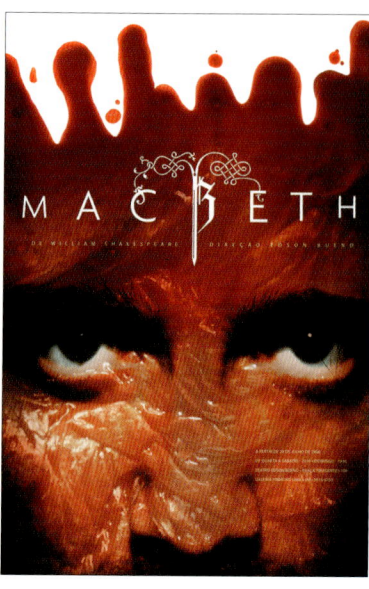

Figure 3.21 | *Macbeth* | **Design:** Hoon-Dong Chung | © Hoon-Dong Chung | **China** | 70 x 100 cm

Figure 3.22 | *Macbeth* | **Design:** Yossi Lemel | © Yossi Lemel | **Israel** | 70 x 100 cm

Figure 3.23 | *Macbeth* | **Design:** Marcos Minini | © Marcos Minini | **Brazil** | 70 x 100 cm

Methods and Materials

Poster designers have an infinite palette of materials and methods from which to choose. New technologies offer additional avenues for designers to investigate and expand their array of techniques. Many further explorations are taking poster artists from a two-dimensional space into a three-dimensional world. Hoon-Dong Chung's *Macbeth* poster (Figure 3.21) demonstrates how emerging technologies have blended with traditional poster design. Chung's use of three-dimensional software works so well because of his understanding of graphic design. He balances his composition by angling his compound image and placing it comfortably within the white space of his poster. His typographic choices and color palette enhance his visual style and integrate well into the image.

Mariana Baldaia's beautifully lush *MÛSÎQÂT 2017* theater promotional poster (Figure 3.24) is an elegant balance of fragile, loose line and painterly strokes. She incorporates the performing arts into the lead performer consisting of a swan, Gambusi, and theater mask. The actor, dressed in red, is sitting above a colorful piano keyboard, playing to the variety of theater performances in the upcoming season. For the finale, Baldaia blends two languages by extending the Persian script to form the letter I in MÛSÎQÂT, allowing both languages to play in perfect harmony.

Becoming more popular in poster design is bricolage, a term frequently used in anthropology, art, and other fields to refer to the act of making something using found materials—whatever is lying around. As Claude Levi-Strauss stated, "The bricoleur, who is the 'savage mind,' works with his hands in devious ways, puts pre-existing things together in new ways, and makes do with whatever is at hand."[8] An important aspect of bricolage is that the visual does not necessarily have a planned or predetermined outcome, but it is a process of "listening" to the materials and allowing them to guide you.

Mohammad Afshar's *The Damp House* (Figure 3.25) demonstrates his knowledge of bricolage. By using found objects and manipulating them, Afshar chronicles the story of a middle-aged woman, sheltered in a house with three other people on a rainy night, who is obsessed with locking doors. Because sound plays a special role in the performance, Afshar chose to use the red headphones as they appeared throughout the production symbolizing fragmented dreams that were carried over into the waking world. Afshar's process of working with found objects, as illustrated in Figure 3.26, shows how careful planning helps to guide the art direction of this story set in magical realism.

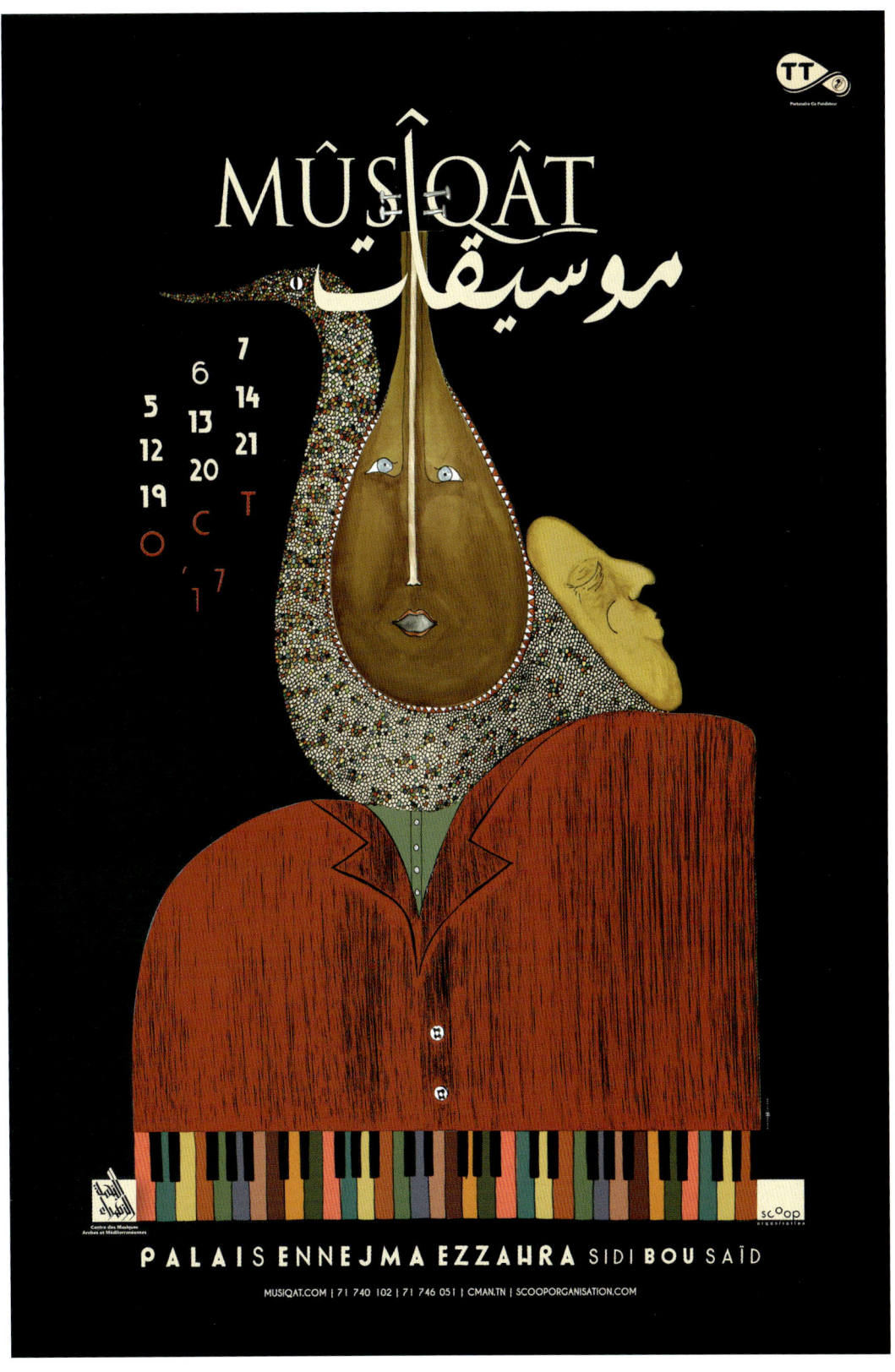

Figure 3.24 | *MÛSÎQÂT 2017* | **Design:** Mariana Baldaia | © Mariana Baldaia | **Portugal** | 110 x 160 cm

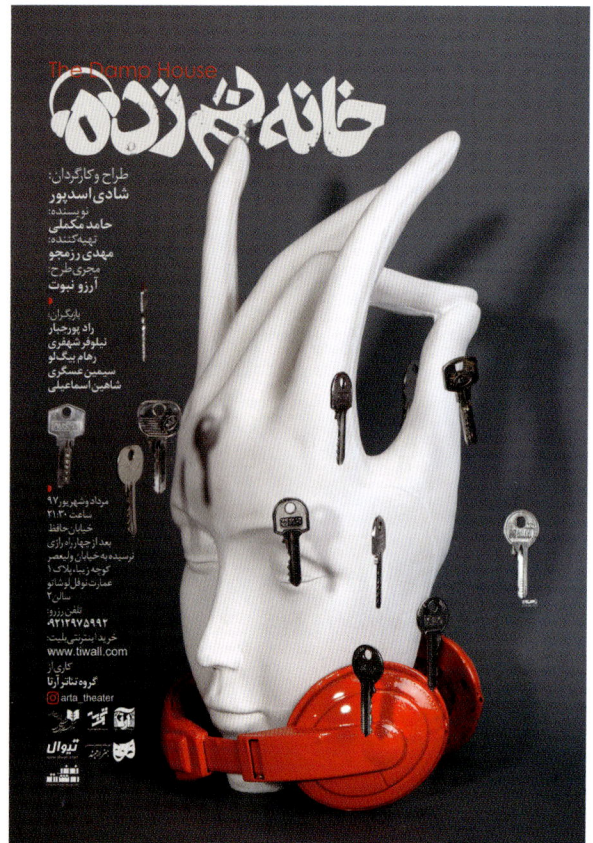

Figure 3.25 | *The Damp House* | **Design:** Mohammad Afshar | © Mohammad Afshar | **Iran** | 70 x 100 cm

Figure 3.26 | *The Damp House* process | Mohammad Afshar | **Photography:** Badri Karamzadeh | © Mohammad Afshar and Badri Karamzadeh | **Iran**

With boundless options to choose from, and given that the execution of your poster is equally as important as the concept and message, it is important to select the appropriate style, methods, and materials. The wrong aesthetic or weak execution can destroy a great design. It is essential that you develop strong skills and have excellent craft. If you are using technology, you must understand how to control the computer application rather than have it control you. If you are making something with your hands, whether it be a drawing, painting, or anything dimensional, it must be well crafted, or it will ruin a great poster. After all, a poor photograph of a beautiful image is still a poor photograph.

Francesco Mazzenga shows us his behind-the-scenes process (Figure 3.27) for his poster *Suelo de Vino*. Mazzenga's poster is for an exhibition celebrating the grape harvest in Valle de Guadalupe, Mexico. The focus of this year's festival is the land the vines grow on, and Francesco took it literally, bringing soil into his studio for an elaborate photo shoot that showcases the connection between humans, earth, and vines. Throughout the process, Francesco lets the elements speak to him, besmirching the feet over and over and playfully adjusting the leaves and grapes to communicate a natural sensation in an artificially built environment. The result is a poster that allows the viewer to imagine an open vineyard where a person walks barefoot, connected with the surroundings in an ancient tradition.

Suelo de Vino process | **Photography:** Francesco Mazzenga | © Francesco Mazzenga | **Italy**

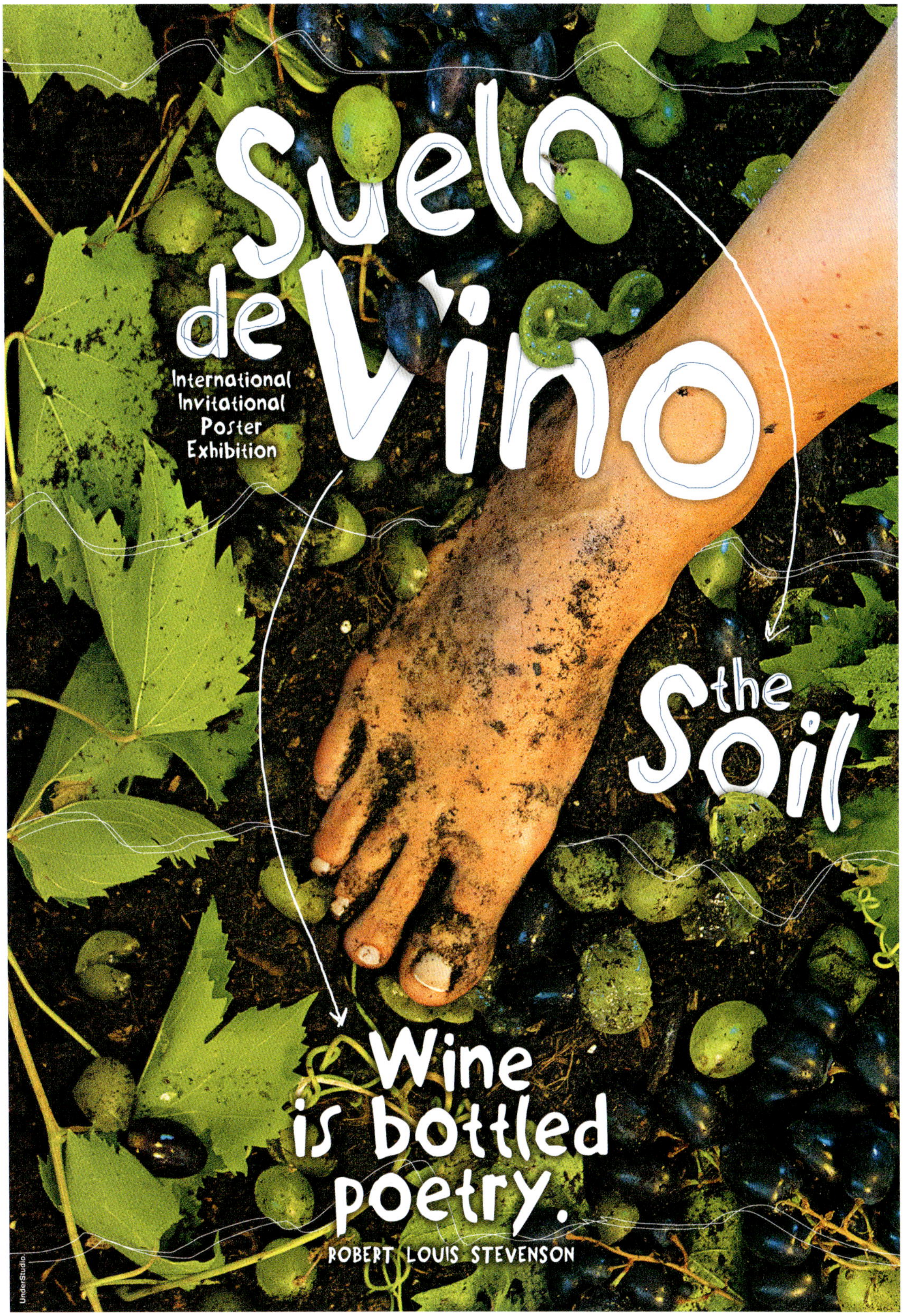

Figure 3.27 | *Suelo de Vino* | **Design:** Francesco Mazzenga | © Francesco Mazzenga | **Italy** | 50 x 70 cm

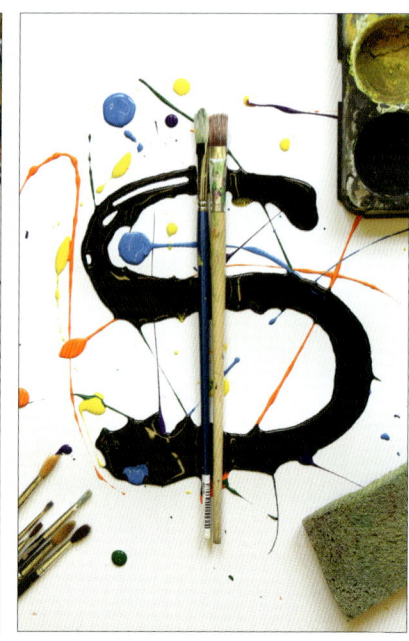

Making Mistakes

Do not be afraid of making mistakes along the way. Making mistakes has always been part of creative exploration. Sometimes, they can reveal what not to do and therefore are a great tool in evaluating visual solutions. Often, mistakes take you in surprising directions. They can expose new paths, help uncover new techniques, and sometimes offer better ways to express yourself by recognizing unconventional solutions. Some of the world's greatest inventions were discovered by mistake. From potato chips, chocolate-chip cookies, and the Slinky to one of humankind's most significant discoveries, Sir Alexander Fleming's penicillin—all were accidents. Never assume that if something you created was not intended, it is unsuccessful. Famed Polish poster designer Stanislaw Zagorski referred to making mistakes as "the lazy designer"; in other words, the designer who does not get caught up with perfecting a visual during the image making process. Trying to get it right along the way may limit your ability to be innovative. It is not uncommon to be initially intimidated by a topic or an assignment. Here is where thorough research can help assuage your fears. However, fear is not necessarily bad, as it can also inspire a concept. The important thing is not to ignore the fear but to overcome it. You must resist your instinct to play it safe, or you may set up a scenario that allows for no mistakes and limits your possibilities.

Figures 3.28 and 3.29 | *Canadian Conference of the Arts* | **Design**: Natalia Delgado Avila | © Natalia Delgado Avila | **Canada** | 45.7 x 71.1 cm

CHAPTER THREE EXECUTION

Figure 3.30 | *Magaloo* | **Design**: Scott Laserow | © Scott Laserow | **USA** | 61 x 91.4 cm

A frequent companion of fear is resistance, which can manifest itself in overthinking. You might find yourself mentally going over an idea again and again, feeling insecure. Sometimes your worst enemy is your inner critic—so stop thinking and start doing! Unfettered image exploration drives your creativity, develops a visual vocabulary, and expands your scope of methodologies for putting things together. So have fun and do not be afraid to fail, fail, and fail again!

From spilled ink to poor scans, some blunders may even find their way into the finished poster. Using mistakes to your advantage requires an understanding of your topic and an awareness of visuals that may support your thesis. Tipping over a pot of paint became the inspiration for the poster *Canadian Conference of the Arts* (Figure 3.28). The topic of the conference was the role of the arts in the economy, so using art supplies was an obvious choice, but it was the visual lure of the paint on the white paper that led to experimentation, ultimately resulting in the dollar sign that makes the connection between art and economy. Having fun and experimenting led to the final solution (Figure 3.29). There can be many good solutions, and while in this case, Figure 3.28 was chosen for the final poster, some people might find themselves more attracted to one of the other proposals.

The following case study (Figure 3.30) illustrates how a mistake can add to the narrative. After printing a black circle onto a textured paper stock, the first unpredicted happenstance was a dust mark in the stock that looked similar to the numeral three (3). Regardless of the imperfection, the printout was then run through an old fax machine to gain added deterioration. The paper stock, which was a bit too thick for the old fax machine, entered the machine late and revealed only two-thirds of the circle upon completion of the copy. Correcting it in Photoshop would surely be a simple fix. Flipping a copy of the scanned mishap and positioning it in place created an objectionable overlap. Given the relationship between the unpleasant alignment of shapes that created a slash across the bloody fishbowl and the uncomfortable message of the poster, this gaffe seemed worthy of keeping. The mistake caused tension on its own, further adding to the emotion of the topic.

Evaluate Your Design

A common phrase in the field of design is that design is never done. A reason for this is that designers are always striving to improve their creations. If we add to the notion of design as a cycle where every iteration brings new knowledge, then the lack of a time limit or deadline can potentially mean that the design process will continue perpetually without ever reaching an end. Therefore, some sort of constraint is necessary. In professional projects, the client, who has specific needs and deadlines, usually provides these constraints. In school, the design instructor who assigns the deadlines and requirements for the projects carries out this role. You can also create your own internal deadlines to move forward with each stage of your project. It is important to schedule breaks as well, as they will allow you to gain a fresh view of your design.

A good thing to try is the squint test. Lean back from your computer or even walk back a few steps and squint until the picture becomes blurry and only the main shapes remain visible. Squinting will allow you to identify the elements that stand out to see how they work within the composition.

Dead Leaf by Christopher Scott

I was in my last semester at the University of Ulster, and for our final project, my professor told us we could do "whatever we want." I was excited but also scared because there were no constraints and no brief. So much freedom was overwhelming.

I had a couple of months to come up with an idea for the project, so I started brainstorming and thinking about things I liked. Growing up in Ireland, I was always climbing trees and felt a strong connection with nature. So my first idea was to make a project about the beauty of the forest. I also liked adventure, and I was always thinking about remote places I would like to visit. Through research, I learned about the Amazon rainforest and decided to make a promotional campaign about the beauty of this land, showing the diversity of the flora and fauna.

I sketched for over a month, but nothing was clicking. I did more research and sketched, but it still wasn't happening; it didn't feel right. I went back to the research and was shocked to learn about the problems of the region, such as drug trafficking, illegal hunting, and deforestation. But there was one piece of information that struck me in particular—if the Amazon rainforest disappears, the whole ecosystem of the world will collapse and everything will die. I couldn't believe the impact that this forest had and how everything and everyone depends on it. So I decided to make a campaign that focused on the deforestation of the Amazon. After four months, I had a sketchbook full of highly detailed and elaborate sketches. I knew I wanted a powerful graphic that the campaign would be based on, but I couldn't find anything I felt strongly about.

To this day, I can't explain what happened next. I went to bed one night and I woke up the next day at 6 a.m. and I *knew* what I had to do. I said to myself, "I've got it!" Even now, I still get emotional telling the story because of how much this image means to me.

I got ten plastic bags and went to a local park. It was around January and all the leaves were dead, so the timing for my concept was perfect. I collected as many leaves as I could fit into the bags and sat down in my pajamas, scanning the leaves one by one. The scanner allowed me to get all the details of the veins of the leaves. I had an image that I drew

on a white piece of paper showing the different spots of deforestation in the Amazon. I selected the best images from the scans and put them together in Photoshop to form the continent of South America. Then I inverted the sketch of the deforestation and burned it so the dots were white and the background black and then switched the black part for the leaves. If you look closely, it is a combination of six different leaves. I didn't do anything else that day. I had many months of incubation and I was eager to finish the image. And by 9 p.m. I was done.

I created the rest of the campaign and was satisfied, but I never imagined the image would take on a life of its own and become so popular. It was my first social project and I don't think I will ever experience something like that again.

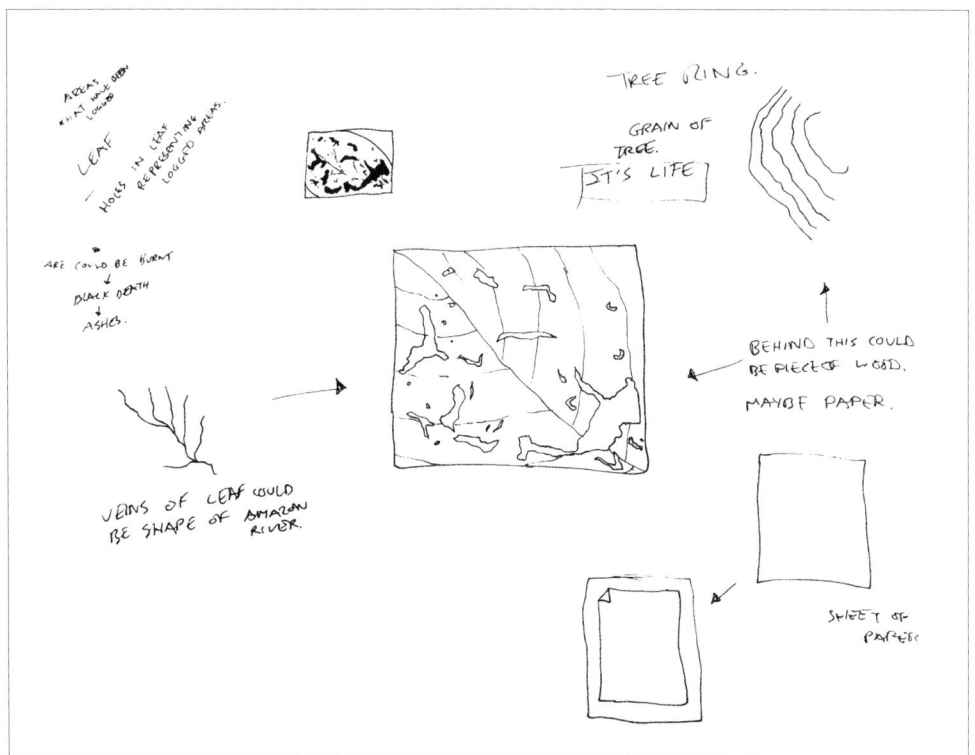

Dead Leaf | **Design**: Christopher Scott | © Christopher Scott | **Ireland** | 50 x 70 cm

Exercise 3.1: Image Making
Part One
Make an image for one of the following terms literally as a symbol. Express your ideas in simple, flat, black and white shapes. Your shapes can be highly stylized or more representational. You can use line, but it must be heavy enough to read as shape. Value can be expressed using a texture of black and white lines. Since you will be working primarily with silhouette shapes of objects, the point of view of the objects you use will be very important.

Angelfish	Car coat	Fish tank	Pig pen
Bed bug	Carpool	Headlight	Ranch hand
Birdbrain	Chairman	Horseshoe	Sawhorse
Birdhouse	Corn dog	House cat	Saw tooth
Brainstorm	Cow pie	House dress	Shoehorn
Bullhorn	Doghouse	Jackrabbit	Spacesuit
Bull nose	Dogwood	Keyboard	Starfish
Busboy	Doorman	Ladybug	Wing chair
Cake batter	Earphone	Nightmare	

Part Two
Using the same word from Part One, create a color version using any medium (it can be dimensional). This should be a completely new solution with no relation to your previous concept.

Exercise 3.2: Type as Image
Part One
Select a letter from the English alphabet and manipulate it so that it expresses a human malady that begins with that letter (A—arthritis, alcoholism, allergies, anorexia nervosa, anxiety disorder, etc.). The malady can be very serious like cancer or not so life threatening like bad breath or insomnia. You can also use phobias (acrophobia, arachnophobia, claustrophobia, etc.). Your approach can be serious or humorous depending on the malady.

Your solution should take advantage of unique shapes found in the letterforms you select. You can also use illustration or other visual elements as part of your solution, but the final piece must be primarily typographic.

Part Two
Using the same malady from Part One, create a typographic illustration using the whole word. This version should be an entirely new solution with no relation to your concept in part one. Using the entire word will present you with new typographic opportunities.

GALLERY

With only shape, Resnick's poster creates an awkward feeling as Resnick tries to fit a square peg into a round hole. Her simple but powerful visual quickly communicates her concept of the difficulty immigrants face trying to fit into another culture.

The Immigrant Experience | **Design:** Elizabeth Resnick | © Elizabeth Resnick | **USA** | 70 x 100 cm

MAKING POSTERS FROM CONCEPT TO DESIGN

Clockwise: Shape, bright color, and high-contrast photography with a dash of exquisite corpse make 1 Trick Pony's poster series playful and fun, reflecting the nostalgic nature of the movies being promoted.

Opposite: Whether delicate, graphic, bold, bright, energetic, concentric, or even spaghetti, line can demand attention and communicate a concept.

Hut Hut, Shoot Out Rock, Samurai, Easy Horse Rider | © 1 Trick Pony | **USA** | Various sizes

CHAPTER THREE EXECUTION

Vilen Künnapu exhibition "Magical Tallinn" | **Designer:** Marko Kekishev | © Marko Kekishev | **Client:** Galerist | **Estonia** | 59.4 x 84 cm

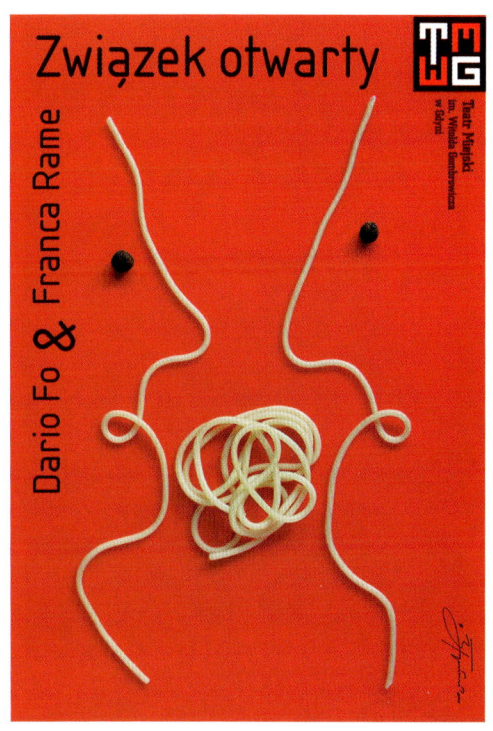

Open Relationship | **Design/Illustration:** Tomasz Boguslawski | © Tomasz Boguslawski | **Poland** | 20 x 29.7 cm

83

Commission for Women 25th Anniversary | **Designers**: Lanny and Kristin Sommese | © Sommese Design | **USA** | 25.4 x 38.1 cm

Xiamen Echoed | **Design/Illustration**: Irwan Harnoko | © Irwan Harnoko | **Indonesia** | 29.7 x 42 cm

5 Years Elmer Sosa & 6 Years Elmer Sosa | **Illustration:** Elmer Sosa | © Elmer Sosa | **Mexico** | 50 x 70 cm

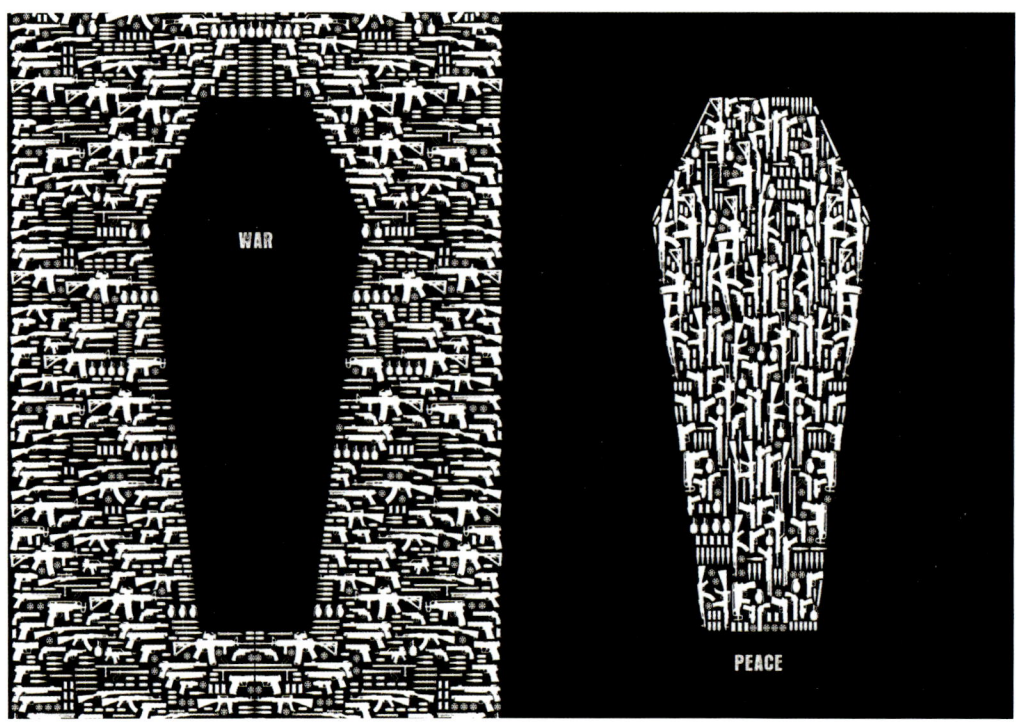

War and Peace | **Design**: Mario Fuentes | © Mario Fuentes—Poster Artist | **Ecuador** | 70 x 100 cm

CHAPTER THREE EXECUTION

The grace of symmetry in Willey and Revell's poster helps create a poignant image of lungs trying to breathe figuratively. The branching lung bronchioles, represented by dry trees, show the suffering of nature surrounded by the cold nothingness of white space.

Opposite top: Symmetry, module repetition, and two colors celebrate Sosa's anniversary as a cartoonist.

Opposite bottom: Fuentes's figure/ground and mirrored reflection show the costs of war.

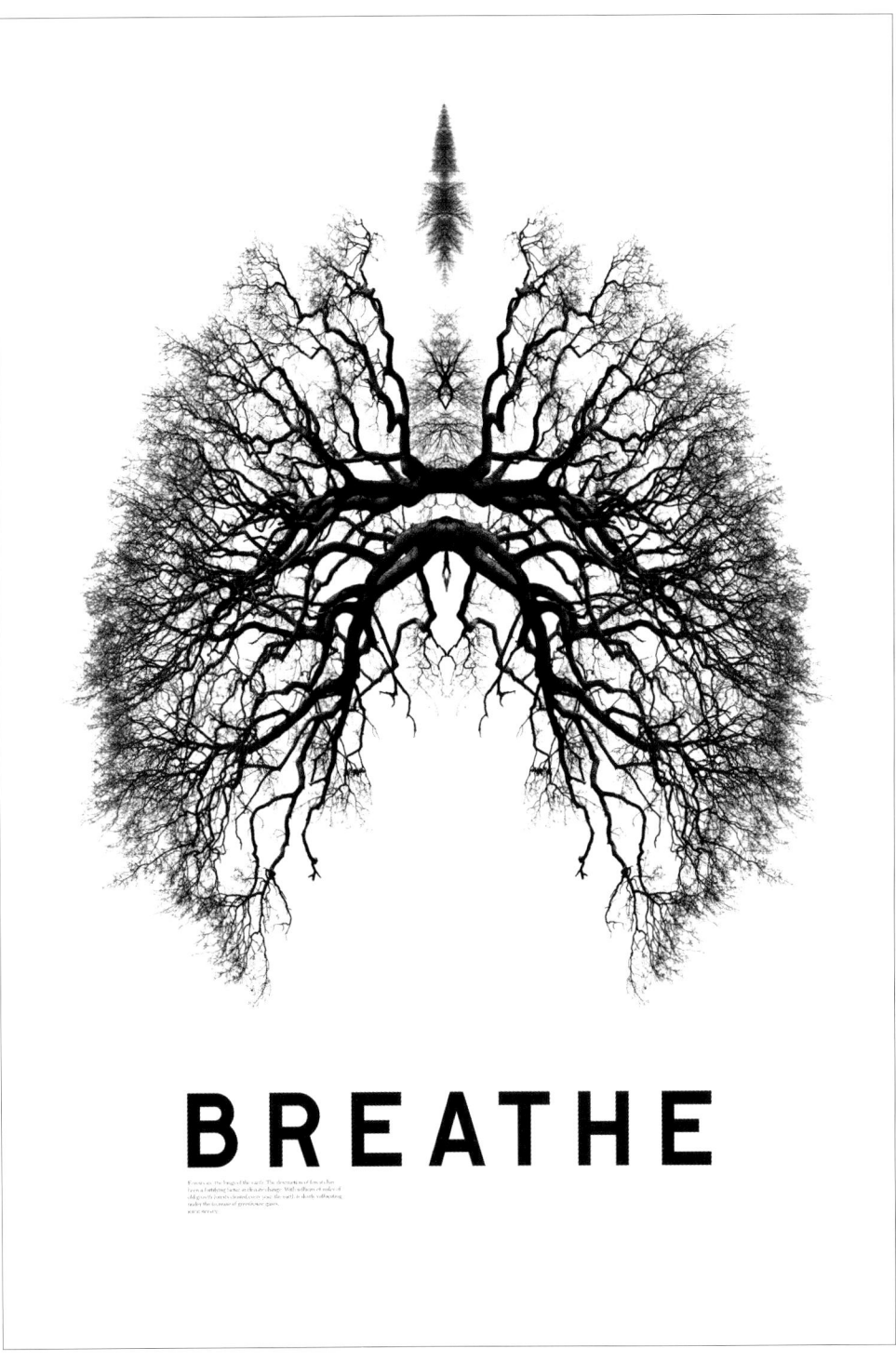

Breathe | **Design:** Giles Revell and Matt Willey | © Giles Revell | **USA** | 84 x 59.4 cm

The Ventures | **Design**: Art Chantry | © Art Chantry | **USA** | 30.5 x 48.3 cm

CHAPTER THREE EXECUTION

Kiss of the Spider Woman | © Design Army | **USA** | 43.2 x 55.9 cm

CO_2 | **Design**: Onish Aminelahi | © Onish Aminelahi | **Iran** | 70 x 100 cm

Clockwise: Whether white, red, or yellow, white space adds an airiness to your poster that helps your audience easily focus on the most important information and quickly move through your design.

Open Artist Studios | **Design**: Benito Cabañas | © Benito Cabañas | **Mexico** | 60 x 90 cm

MAKING POSTERS FROM CONCEPT TO DESIGN

Frankenstein | **Design**: Lanny Sommese | © Lanny Sommese | **USA** | 25.4 x 38.1 cm

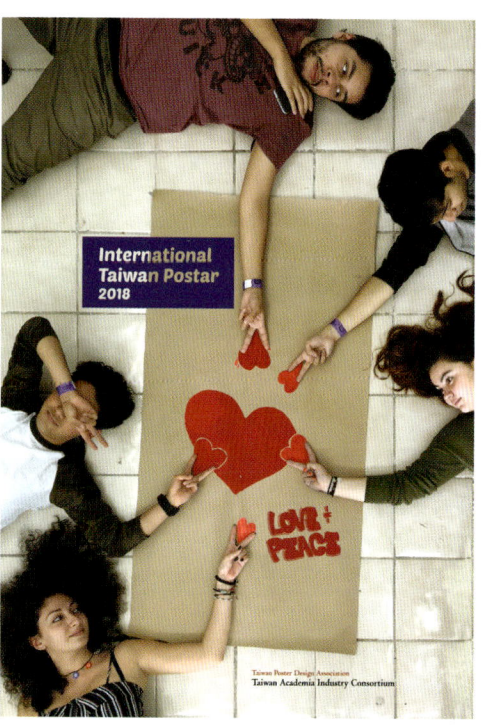

Love & Peace | **Design:** Erin Wright | © Erin Wright | **USA** | 70 x 100 cm

88

Hamilton | **Design:** Nicky Lindeman, Spotco | © Nicky Lindeman | **USA** | 35.6 x 55.9 cm

Festival Outre-Mer Veille | **Design**: Pascal Colrat | © Pascal Colrat | **France** | 70 x 100 cm

CHAPTER THREE EXECUTION

Sycamore Trees | © Design Army | **USA** | 43.2 x 55.9 cm

"M" Fritz Lang | **Design/Illustration:** Rodolfo Reyes | © Rodolfo Reyes | **Mexico** | 45.7 x 61 cm

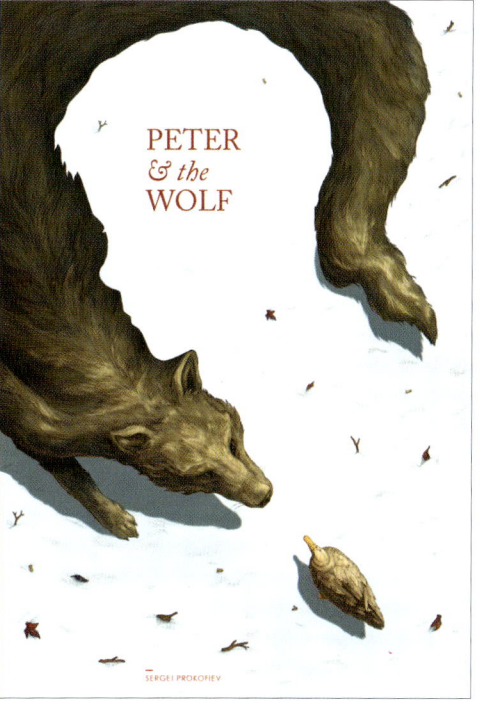

Peter and the Wolf | **Design:** Phoebe Morris | © Phoebe Morris | **New Zealand** | 68 x 98 cm

Opposite: Leading line and focal point are in play, directing you to the center of interest and revealing the story behind each poster.

Figure/ground can be a powerful and straightforward way to communicate a concept. **Clockwise:** The negative space in the broken dinner plate clearly creates a silhouette of a sycamore tree. The shattered dish symbolizes the turmoil and conflict of a post–World War II Jewish-American family. The streetlights in Reyes's cityscape reveal the hidden letter for his *"M" Fritz Lang* poster. *Peter and the Wolf* beautifully illustrates the wondrous tale of Peter (negative space), his nemesis the wolf, and his friend the duck.

89

MAKING POSTERS FROM CONCEPT TO DESIGN

Typography can be soft and subtle, expressive and bold, custom made, and even delicious. These posters display just some of the many ways turning typography into imagery can make a poster powerful.

Ladies and Gentleman, I Represent the New Symbol of Peace | **Artist**: Mehdi Saeedi | © Mehdi Saeedi | **USA** | 120 x 90 cm

Belle & Sebastian | **Design**: Sean Freeman & Eve Steben, THERE IS Studio | © Sean Freeman & Eve Steben | **United Kingdom** | 61 x 45.7 cm

The Decemberist | **Design**: Sean Freeman & Eve Steben, THERE IS Studio | © Sean Freeman & Eve Steben | **United Kingdom** | 45.7 x 25.4 cm

Costumbre Mexicana | **Design/Illustration:** Daniela Merinos Arrieta | © Daniela Merinos Arrieta | **Mexico** | 70 x 100 cm

Parachute | **Design/Illustration**: Peter Bankov | © Peter Bankov | **Czech Republic** | 70 x 100 cm

MAKING POSTERS FROM CONCEPT TO DESIGN

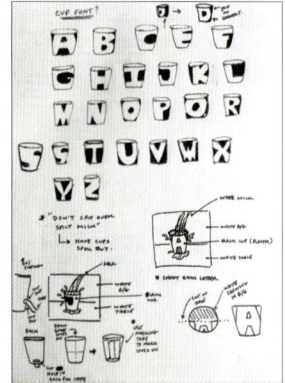

Clockwise: Working from a tight grid, Newman and crew surely had fun staging this photo shoot for *Don't Cry over Spilt Milk*. Weathered background, inventive typography, and typographic hierarchy are laid out on a structured grid, making Hill's concert poster engaging and informative. Kaja's *Teatr Pinezka* (*The Circus Theater Pinezka*) collaged poster is a combination of an original illustration and beautiful typography set on a grid framing the clown.

Don't Cry over Spilt Milk | **Design**: Jon Newman | © Jon Newman is God | **USA** | 61 x 91.4 cm

Andy Lund in NYC | **Design**: Adam Hill | © Adam Hill | **South Africa** | 59.4 x 84.1 cm

Teatr Pinezka (*The Circus Theatre Pinezka*) | **Illustration**: Ryszard Kaja | © Ryszard Kaja | **Poland** | 69 x 99 cm

Perhaps the most fun you will have designing posters is when you get to tap into your inner artist and play with materials to help communicate your vision. Elegant and artful, Boguslawski's poster *Krol Roger* (*King Roger*) is an expertly executed craft paper sculpture that is sure to outlast its original purpose.

Krol Roger (*King Roger*) | **Designer:** Tomasz Boguslawski | © Tomasz Boguslawski | **Poland** | 67 x 98 cm

To make their poster, Freeman and Steben gather a crew of nine to cast plaster molds of each other's hands. For a behind-the-scenes video of how they created *The National* poster, visit www.making-posters.com/thenational or scan this QR code.

There are seemingly endless ways to assemble imagery for a poster that is not only aesthetically pleasing but can also help in communication. Each artist chooses different materials and styles to explore. **Opposite:** From Olivotti's clay figure with googly eyes and Feng's water calligraphy to Colrat's delicate bird of darts and the hand embroidery of Fuentes's *Ethos* poster, each artist on display brings a unique approach to his or her craft.

The National | **Design**: Sean Freeman & Eve Steben, THERE IS Studio | © Sean Freeman & Eve Steben | **United Kingdom** | 45.7 x 61 cm

CHAPTER THREE EXECUTION

Big Brother | **Design**: Sergio Olivotti | © Sergio Olivotti | **Italy** | 70 x 100 cm

Water Is Life | **Design**: Sha Feng | © Sha Feng | **China** | 70 x 100 cm

95

Ethos | © Mario Fuentes—Poster Artist | **Ecuador** | 70 x 100 cm

Platonov Mais | **Design**: Pascal Colrat | © Pascal Colrat | **Client**: Theatre de l'Aquarium | **France** | 70 x 100 cm

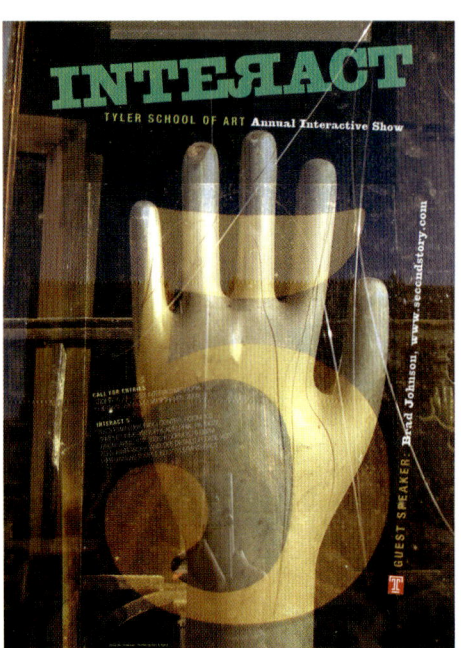

Interact 5 | **Art Direction**: Dermot Mac Cormack, Patricia McElroy | **Design**: Dermot Mac Cormack, Patricia McElroy | **Photography**: Patricia McElroy | **Illustration**: Dermot Mac Cormack | **Client**: Tyler School of Art, Temple University | © 21x Design | **USA** | 70 x 100 cm

This House | **Illustration**: Jacx Staniszewski | © Jacx Staniszewski | **Poland** | 70 x 100 cm

Whether it is handmade or digital, collage or bricolage is one of the more common and attainable ways to assemble your poster. Although the basic methods of these techniques are the same, we can appreciate how each artist applies his or her own style.

Memory Capsules | © Mario Fuentes—Poster Artist | **Ecuador** | 70 x 100 cm

CHAPTER THREE EXECUTION

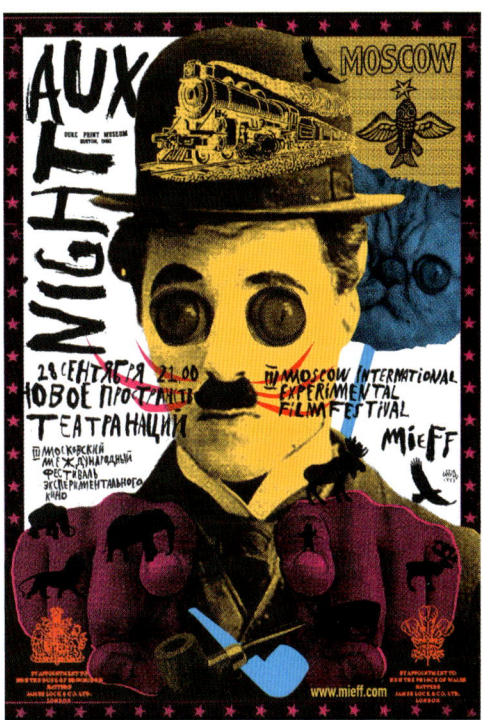

Aux Night and Jaz Ruine | **Illustration:** Peter Bankov | © Peter Bankov | **Czech Republic** | 70 x 100 cm

97

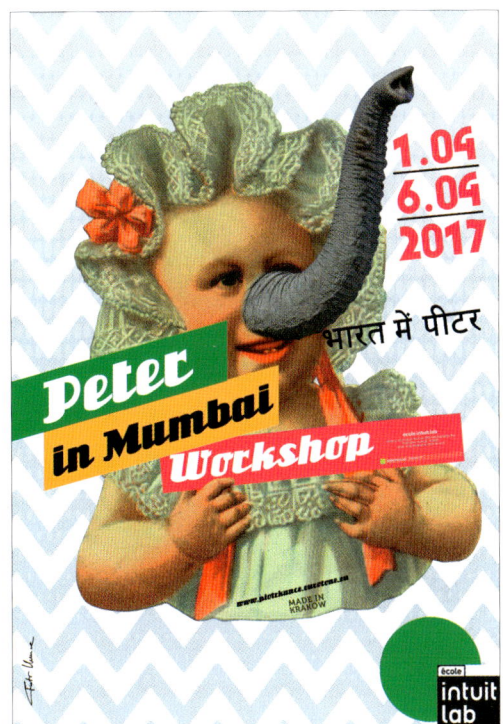

Piotr Kunce Workshop in Mumbai | **Design:** Piotr Kunce | © Piotr Kunce | **Poland** | 70 x 100 cm

Pan's Labyrinth | **Design:** Natalie Harris | © Natalie Harris | **USA** | 27.9 x 43.2 cm

MAKING POSTERS FROM CONCEPT TO DESIGN

Hurricane Katrina | **Design:** Soonduk Krebs | © Soonduk Krebs | **USA** | 45.7 x 61 cm

Clockwise: Krebs's collage is a beautiful epitaph for the victims of Hurricane Katrina. Collected and meticulously assembled, Horkay's whimsical steampunk stylized characters look like they stepped out of a sci-fi movie.

Opposite: Hemmat utilizes bricolage to tell her sorrowful fable about a kidnapped princess locked in a café where she is constantly being objectified and seduced by many men.

DUMBLAND and *After Coronaria-PCI* | **Design/Illustration:** István Horkay | © István Horkay | **Hungary** | 70 x 100 cm

Take Your Umbrella Knight | **Design/Illustration:** Elham Hemmat | © Elham Hemmat | **Client:** Alireza Dastafkan (Kolivare Theater Group) | **Iran** | 70 × 100 cm

CHAPTER FOUR GRABBING ATTENTION

otcha! Now I can start a conversation and share an interesting fact or inform you of an event. Since we live in an environment that is so densely layered with an increasing array of distracting white noise, grabbing attention is one of the most challenging aspects of design that you must address. The endless influx of competing stimuli, whether through social media, television, billboards, print advertisements, etc., makes it impossible to process everything around us; therefore, the focus of our attention is a selective activity. Paying attention requires filtering out other information that is irrelevant at the moment. Because of this, we are continually making unconscious decisions about what to observe and what to ignore. Attention is a limited resource, which means that to connect with your audience, you need to stand out in a sea of information. Since it is widely believed that you have only three to five seconds to grab someone's attention, your poster must pique curiosity and lead to action.

From birth, attention is a primary part of our cognitive system that guides our senses to help us navigate our environment and ensure our survival. We instinctively react and respond to everything—a loud noise might warn of incoming danger, while an attractive color might signal a possible food source. If faced with something blocking our path, we naturally walk around the barrier. This is known as cause and effect; one thing, the obstacle, affects the other, our instinct to avoid whatever is blocking our path. It is so automatic that we often do not realize when it is happening.

GRABBING ATTENTION

(facing page) Illustration Natalia Delgado
(above) Scott Laserow

Figure 4.1 | *ACUD BERLIN (WET in BERLIN)* | **Design**: Luis Rutz | © www.luluiisrsrutzutz.de | **Germany** | 29.7 x 42 cm

In his book *On the Sublime and Beautiful*, Edmund Burke states, "Curiosity is the most superficial of all the affections; it changes its object perpetually; it has an appetite which is very sharp, but very easily satisfied; and it has always an appearance of giddiness, restlessness, and anxiety."[9] Pursuing knowledge and new experiences is an integral part of the human condition. Curiosity compels children to explore and discover new and exciting things with energy and enthusiasm. Our insatiable desire to learn does not stop as we grow older, it just becomes more refined. The power of the unexpected can help you create suspense and intrigue while connecting your message with a relatable experience or story. If the message resonates with the audience, it is more likely to be processed with greater attention. The more they think about the message, the more likely they are to be persuaded.

The Power of Contrast

Contrast is a state of being noticeably different from something else. By placing different or opposing elements next to each other, we can differentiate between them and create a natural hierarchy that is easily followed. This is also known as visual salience or saliency, a quality in our subjective perception that makes specific visuals stand out from their neighbors. Contrasts can be created in different aspects of design: value, color, shape, and scale. The more an element contrasts with its surroundings, the easier it is to see and, therefore, the greater energy the contrast possesses. These elements are additive factors, meaning the more of them you use, the more those elements will draw the viewer's interest.

Like a finely tailored, crisply pressed tuxedo, black and white is a timeless classic. It has been used in art and design for centuries and is the ultimate representation of light versus dark, good versus evil. Black is associated with elegance, secrecy, mystery, and power, whereas white represents lightness, perfection, purity, peace, and innocence. Together, they provide the highest degree of contrast and one of the simplest ways to add pop, create a mood, or build drama. When utilized on a large-scale poster, the combination of black and white can become quite formidable. Luis Rutz's *ACUD BERLIN* (*WET in BERLIN*) poster (Figure 4.1) is bold and stark. Black and white shapes, typography, and image attack the page with force. Rutz maintains balance with white space, trapping the movement and directing your attention to the event title, *ACUD BERLIN*. His poster speaks directly to the experimental arts community of the Acud Berlin theater.

Using Color to Demand Attention

Color can convey a message in an instant, stimulating our senses and fueling our emotions. It can elicit passion; instill anger; make us feel hot or cold, happy or sad; energize us; and even make us hungry. We are predisposed to react to color to ensure our survival; it can point to things like food or shelter as well as warn of possible threats. Color on its own can be quite powerful and an effective means of nonverbal communication.

Allowing just one color to dominate your design can command attention, especially if you choose a color that stands out from the environment. Lex Drewinski's poster for the Imagine Theatre, *Antony and Cleopatra* (Figure 4.2), uses a bold red that cannot be ignored. His provocative design employs the figure ground principle to symbolize the play's most famous scene, where the queen allows a venomous snake to crawl up her body and bite her. The dominance of red captures the dramatic and tragic nature of Shakespeare's play, acting as a symbol of both passion and bloodshed.

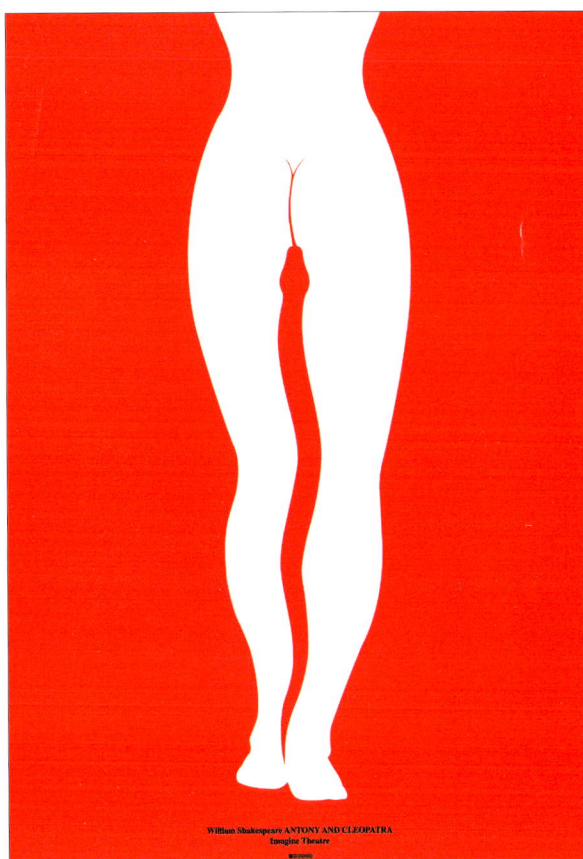

Figure 4.2 | *Antony and Cleopatra* | **Design**: Lex Drewinski | © 1996 by Lex Drewinski, all rights reserved | **Germany** | 70 x 100 cm

MAKING POSTERS FROM CONCEPT TO DESIGN

104

Figure 4.3 | *Un Desierto para la Danza 13 (A Desert for Dance)* | **Design**: Ivette Valenzuela | © Ivette Valenzuela | **Mexico** | 60 x 90 cm

Monochromatic color schemes can use different variations of the same hue. A monotone color scheme is a single hue and its variations of tints, shades, and saturation. This is often used in low-budget productions, as it requires only one color of ink. However, using a fully monochromatic scheme can also backfire by creating a sense of monotony. A way to avoid this is by using focal points that highlight specific areas in your design to naturally draw the viewer in.

Sometimes, value and saturation can have a stronger effect than hue alone. Contrasting a light, bright color with a darker, more muted tone will help highlight specific areas in your design. In Ivette Valenzuela's *Un Desierto para la Danza* (Figure 4.3), the poster's color contrast guides the viewer to the enchanting and unusual trio of dancers placed upon the broad shoulders of the dark angel. The bright yellow tones of the female dancers provide a focal point that attracts the viewer. In contrast, the male figure relies on dark colors, which balances the overall composition. His strategically placed elbow directs you to the title of the performance, while his heel points you to the content where you learn more about the event.

Adjust the Thermostat: Contrasting Temperature

Mixing warm and cool colors can form a powerful contrast and attract visual attention. The poster *Make It Possible* by Moisés Romero Vargas (Figure 4.4) shows an ingenious use of both shape and color to strengthen its message of housing rights. The contrast of cool and warm colors helps emphasize certain elements, such as the roof, which symbolizes hope and the possibility for change. The folded paper draped over the figure reinforces the message that housing rights are basic human rights. Assigning personality to the homeless person makes them relatable and consequently causes the audience to feel empathy. The copy completes the message by placing the responsibility on the viewer to act to make this dream a reality.

Figure 4.4 | *Make It Possible* | **Design**: © Moisés Romero Vargas | © Moisés Romero Vargas | **Mexico** | 50 x 70 cm

Opposites Attract: Using Complementary Colors

The farther away from each other two colors are on the color wheel,[MPR] the greater their contrast. Complementary color schemes use colors from opposite sides of the color wheel, meaning they have the highest contrast, while analogous combinations have the lowest contrast. Due to their antagonistic nature, complementary colors provide a vibrant look that can increase the contrast between the foreground and background or push attention toward a specific element in the composition. However, if complementary colors are not managed properly, they can make your poster challenging to view. For example, when setting typography, you want to avoid using complementary colors, as they tend to vibrate and make the text illegible. A standard solution for this is split-complementary combinations, which use the two colors adjacent to its complement. This color scheme has the same strong visual contrast as the complementary color scheme but causes less vibration.

Figure 4.5 | *Hommage à Roosevelt Douglas/13eme Festival International du Film Black de Montréal* | **Design**: Esteban Jordan | © Esteban Jordan | **Canada** | 61 x 91.4 cm

Esteban Jordon's poster *13th Montreal Black Film Festival* (Figure 4.5) is genuinely electric. Jordan's poster dazzles the eye with bright, complementary colors. Set upon a vibrant yellow background, the contrasting black silhouette of the raised fist punches through the composition, becoming a hole framing the central character. The green film reels attract and direct your eye to the central focal point of the poster. By placing the film reels inside the black sunglass frames, Jordan takes advantage of the sharp contrast between green and red without the vibration generally associated with complementary colors. The *13th Montreal Black Film Festival* poster is bright, bold, and demands to be noticed with a call to ACTION!

The Power of Three: Triadic Color Palettes

Triadic color schemes use three colors 120 degrees apart on the color wheel.[MPR] Two commonly used triads are the primary and secondary color combinations. The primary color triad is made up of red, yellow, and blue; it is a favorite of children's products due to its vibrancy and distinctiveness. The secondary color triad is formed by orange, green, and purple. A beautiful example of this triad is showcased in Sabina Oberholzer and Renato Tagli's poster *Beyond Peace* (Figure 4.6) for the 2018 DMZ Art & Design International Invitation Exhibition. Its bright, bold, and saturated triadic color palette tells the story of harmony between different cultures. Oberholzer and Tagli use the color contrast of orange and purple to represent diversity. They take their colorful embrace and place it on a vibrant green background representing nature, rebirth, and freedom. In this example, color adds a deeper meaning than merely grabbing the viewer's attention. Oberholzer and Tagli's triadic color choice and juxtaposed fingers represent people from different cultural and ethnic backgrounds coming together in peace and harmony. Color plays a valuable role in turning Oberholzer and Tagli's seemingly simple poster into a complex narrative that not only grabs attention but also engages.

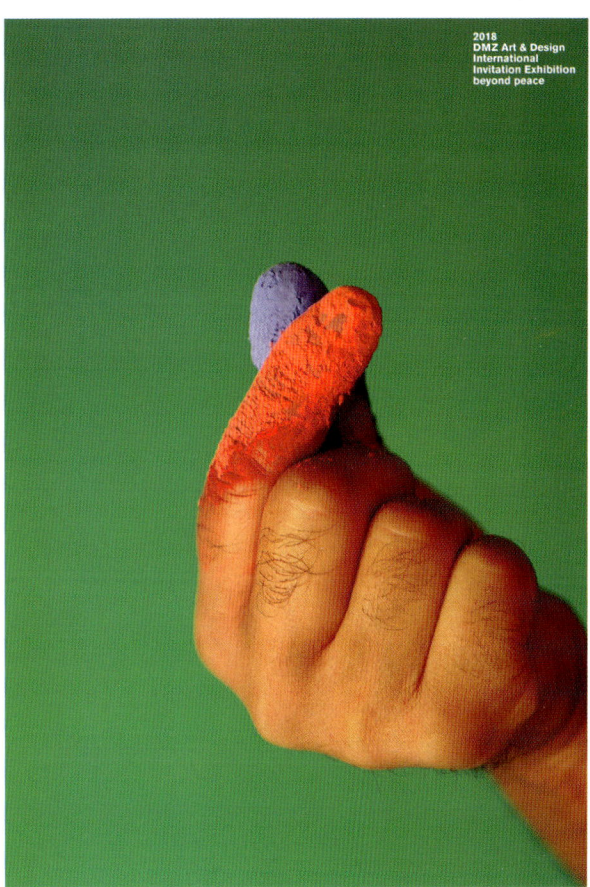

Figure 4.6 | *Beyond Peace* | **Design**: Sabina Oberholzer & Renato Tagli | © Oberholzer–Tagli | **Switzerland** | 70 x 100 cm

A color combination worth highlighting is black, white, and red, which has been used numerous times throughout history in poster design, particularly in protest and social posters. The striking contrast of black and white and the natural energy of red make this a powerful combination, but the reasons for its popularity and use have a fascinating biological and cultural history. Anthropologists have discovered that culturally, human perception begins with three colors: black, white, and red.[10] These colors have been present since the first representations of humanity, and all societies seem to recognize them and their symbolism, which is usually linked to the concepts of light, shadow, and life or blood. In nature, this color combination is aposematic (serving to warn or repel predators), and as a result, we are wired to react to it.

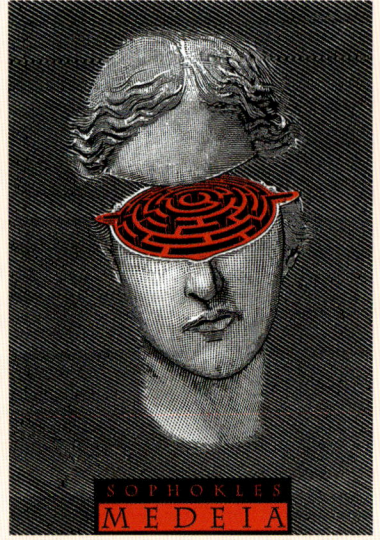

Medeia | **Design**: István Orosz | © István Orosz | **Hungary** | 70 x 100 cm

Man and Nature | **Design**: Andrew Lewis | © Andrew Lewis | **Canada** | 70 x 100 cm

Convergence | **Design:** Mario Fuentes – Poster Artist | © Mario Fuentes | **Ecuador** | 70 x 100 cm

Burst of Color: Using Four Colors or More

There is an abundance of color on display all around us, adding vibrancy and vitality to our world. A broad color palette can add excitement to your poster and help it stand out in almost any environment. Utilizing bursts of color is an effective means of communication and has a way of drawing attention on its own. However, too many colors can result in a poster that is awkward and confusing, ultimately becoming nothing more than a distraction.

Artist Paul Cézanne said, "Color is the place where our brain and the universe meet."[11] This is true in the case of David Plunkert's recruitment poster *MICA SMART* (Figure 4.7). Plunkert paints a vibrant image that uses bursts of multiple colors. If you are SMART, you can see where the maze of information begins on Plunkert's delightfully playful mind-map of inspiration revealing all that the Maryland Institute College of Art (MICA) has to offer the creative mind. Plunkert creates wonderful depth by pointing the leading lines on the bright yellow background to the center of the composition. The large black box containing the written content of the poster also adds to the illusion of dimension. It is no accident that "visionary," "focused," "visual," and "looking" are staring you in the eye. His patina and crackle add a certain authenticity to art's deep and rich history.

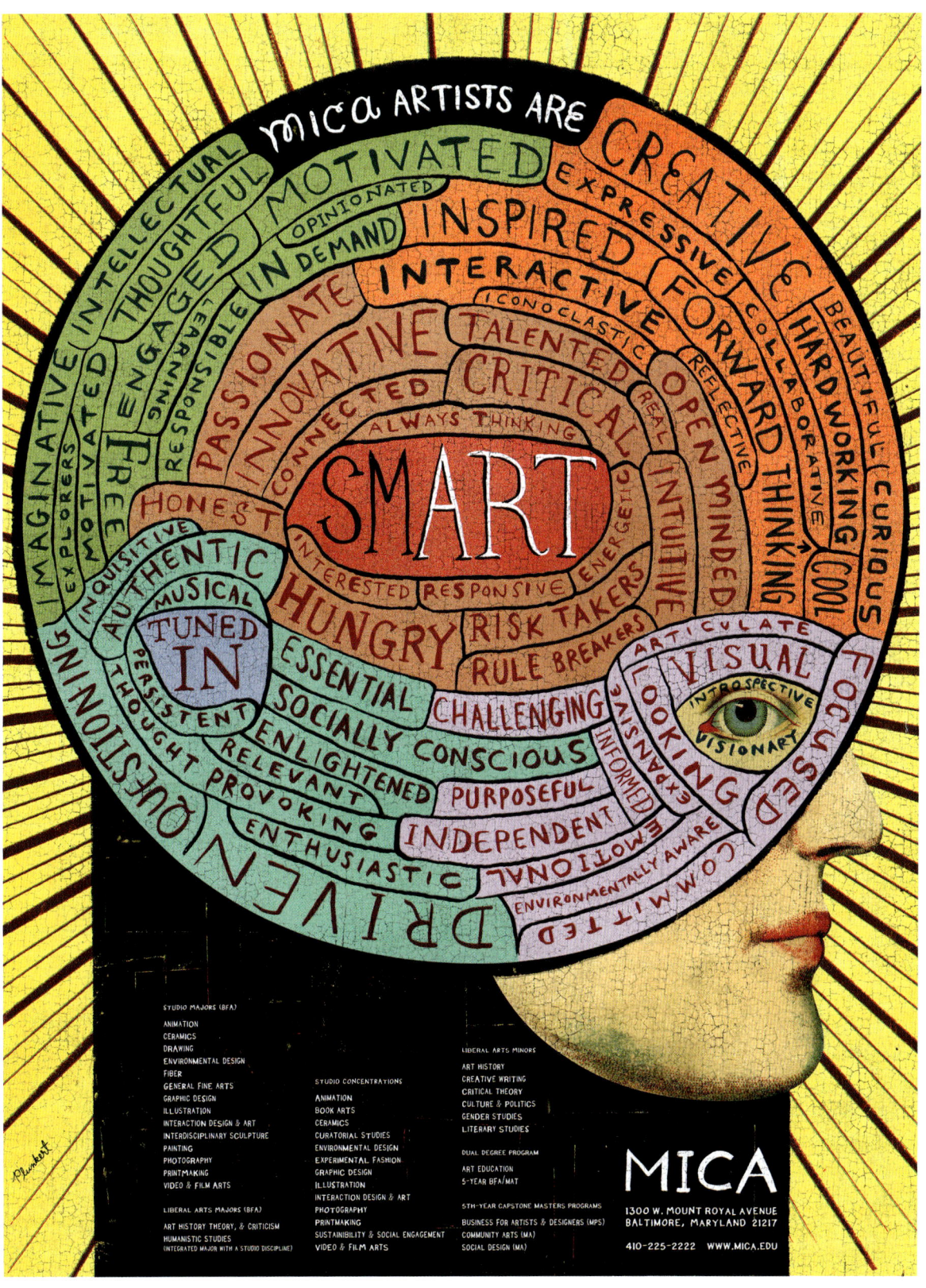

Figure 4.7 | *MICA SMART Recruitment Poster* | **Design/Illustration**: David Plunkert | © 2020 David Plunkert | **USA** | 45.7 x 61 cm

MAKING POSTERS FROM CONCEPT TO DESIGN

Figure 4.8 | *STRIKE!* | **Design:** Christian Nicolaus and Felix Bareis | © Christian Nicolaus and Felix Bareis | **Germany** | 60 x 84 cm

Scale

Scale is the proportional relationships among different objects that are near one another. It can create the illusion of distance based on placement within a composition, making something usually considered small appear to be quite large in comparison or vice versa. A piece of artwork might be termed miniature, small scale, full scale, life-size, larger than life, or monumental. Posters are unique in that they offer initial stimuli from a distance, arousing interest only to reveal themselves upon closer examination. The poster's physical size offers designers and illustrators a larger playing field to explore and sometimes exploit scale, thereby freeing them from the size restrictions of most design projects.

There are different ways to use scale to emphasize features within your design. The simplest way is to establish a hierarchy by changing and contrasting the size of the elements, known as visual weight. The term "weight" provides an excellent mental picture of objects on a scale that you can adjust by deciding how "heavy" or "light" each element will be. The heavier you make a visual, the more attention it will attract. Do not be afraid to fill the frame with your subject, even if it means the subject itself will not fit into the frame. By enlarging an object's size, you can quickly establish obvious importance. Likewise, you can reduce the size of elements to de-emphasize their importance, making them less prominent.

Christian Nicolaus and Felix Bareis's poster *STRIKE!* (Figure 4.8) makes superb use of both the poster's physical size and scale relationships within the poster's composition. Nicolaus and Bareis create an almost audible ear-splitting CRACK! as the bowling pins explode off the surface, revealing the STRIKE typography beneath. The scale and the condensed typeface make it legible by exposing just enough of each letterform even though the pins block most of the typography. Here, the physical size of the poster allows Nicolaus and Bareis to create the illusion of depth and motion with extreme scale shifts. Nicolaus and Bareis use scale, black and white contrast, the rule of odds, and perspective to create a feeling of tri-dimensionality that resembles an optical illusion. Once you are engaged, the poster divulges its message of an educational lecture on design philosophy.

Many times, exploiting typographic scale can have a double impact by presenting typography as a graphic object and helping to emphasize meaning. In Figure 4.9, Coco Cerrella's *Illiteracy* poster, depicting an over-stacked rickshaw and using a massive slab serif font, alerts you to immense weight that must be figuratively lifted by a child. A tremendous force is being visually generated by simple scale, as this poor soul is involuntarily carrying the burden for all of the illiterate children who are being enslaved rather than educated. Your eyes are drawn to the large typography, making it far more significant than the small figure below. Cerrella works with both the size of the poster and scale relationships to convey meaning. The amplified typography on its own may initially grab your attention, but without the context of the tiny figure, the message would be lost.

Figure 4.9 | *Illiteracy* | **Design**: Coco Cerrella | © Coco Cerrella 2011 | **Argentina** | 70 x 100 cm

Rhythm and Pattern

Rhythm is everywhere. We can see it in the spiral of a conch shell, the structure of a snowflake, and the waves that hit the shore. It is the beat of your favorite song, it is why poetry is soothing, and it is the reason meditation begins with breath sensing.[12] Rhythm shows order and organization. It is predictable and inherently calming, making us feel safe, connected, and at ease. Visual rhythm or pattern is formed by these same rules of repeating motifs. A motif is a recurring image, subject, shape, or any other visual component that can be arranged in a multitude of ways. The way our eyes go from one motif to the next can help us move through a composition. When motifs or elements are repeated, alternated, or otherwise arranged, the intervals or overlaps between them can create a rhythm and a sense of movement. If a motif is identical in size and spacing, it creates a regular rhythm or pattern. There are also irregular patterns, like river systems and trees, which branch off and continually replicate into smaller and smaller copies down to tiny rivulets or twigs. Leonardo Fibonacci and Benoît Mandelbrot saw the mathematical beauty of rhythmic motifs and how repetition creates harmony, unity, and movement. In visual rhythm, design motifs become the beat; a particular pattern might take you through the composition in a connected, flowing direction like the slow, steady cadence you hear in music. Other patterns may take you from place to place in an abrupt, dynamic manner, like a staccato rhythm, giving you the impression of movement. At times, simply disrupting the flow by breaking the grid or structure of the pattern of these motifs can grab your

Figure 4.10

Figure 4.11 | *9th DMZ International Documentary Film Festival* | © DMZ | **China** | 45.7 x 61 cm

attention. Our eyes are drawn to the flaw, the odd man out, the anomaly (Figure 4.10). An unexpected break in pattern calls attention and adds interest. This distortion of rhythm can also be accomplished by juxtaposing things that are generally not seen together or depicting scenes that invert or alter the everyday. These aesthetic phenomena instantly give a poster gravitas.

The *9th DMZ International Documentary Film Festival* poster by DMZ (Figure 4.11) effectively breaks the structure by distorting the pattern to give the illusion of a peaceful cascading waterfall, breathing movement and life into the static pattern. The centralized, flattened area gives the illusion of depth and dimension, while the flow of the pattern points directly down to the typography anchoring the composition. Strong figure/ground and black and white contrast combined with a simple application of typography make the *9th DMZ International Documentary Film Festival* poster successful.

Movement

Visual movement is a design principle used to convey the impression of action in a static image or composition. Movement can be suggested visually in a variety of ways using other design elements like space, color, scale, etc. The placement of certain elements can create the illusion of movement, providing a dynamic feeling while also highlighting important information in a design. One way to accomplish this is with leading lines. These can be either physically drawn lines or imaginary lines made visible by the placement of the components on the page. We can think of lines as being either static or dynamic. Straight lines that are vertical or horizontal tend to feel rigid and solid. Directional lines, as their name states, direct the viewer toward a point in the layout. Diagonal lines and S or Z layouts give a sense of movement or imply direction across a design, often from top to bottom and left to right, similar to Western reading patterns. One conventional technique is to use two diagonal lines coming from opposite directions to direct viewers' focus to a single point, known as the vanishing point.

Design by Day's poster *Unspooling* (Figure 4.12) deceives you by using leading lines, an asymmetrical composition, shape, scale, perspective, light, and shadow to unravel a three-dimensional world. Their compelling design slowly draws you into the title and then rapidly slings you down a bright yellow path to the written content maintaining the poster's angular composition. The dark background and the contrasting rich color palette add to the dynamic nature of this poster.

Placement and Direction

A common way to imply movement is by placing objects inside the picture plane to lead a viewer's eye. A running figure in the first third of a poster has plenty of space to run, but placing it on the opposite third gives the illusion that the figure is about to run off the poster. Placing half the figure at each end will thus create the illusion of entering or exiting the composition. Subjects portrayed in dynamic poses or freeze frame create an immediate feeling of motion. This is due to real-life experience, where we know that when a person is in a particular position, some kind of movement will follow. The placement of the subject on a downward (fast) or upward (slow) slope can also

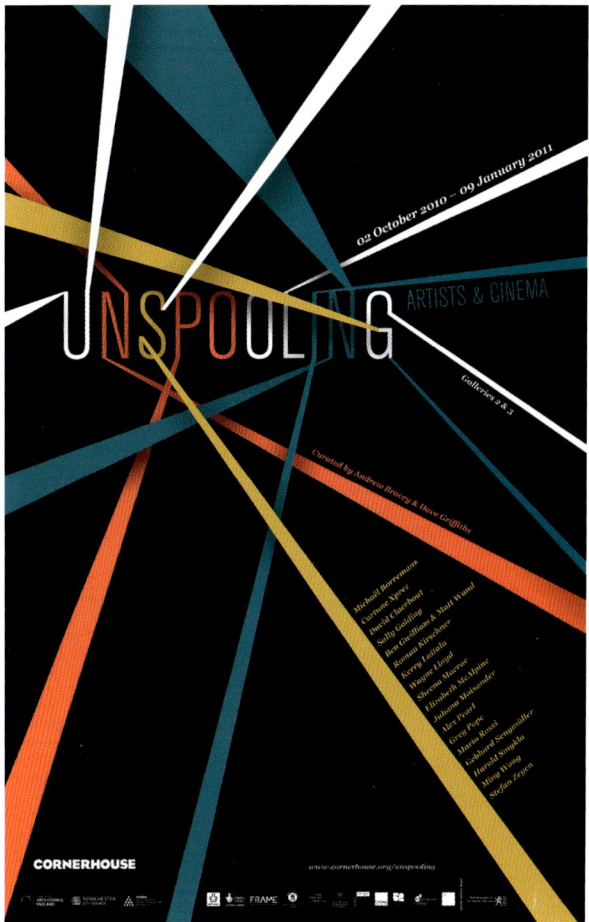

Figure 4.12 | *Unspooling* | © Design by Day | **United Kingdom** | 50 x 70 cm

create a perception of speed. Displaying blurry or multiple overlapping images can produce the impression of motion (Figure 4.13). Because fast objects tend to pass us at high speed, we associate blurriness or indistinct outlines with movement and will naturally react to fuzzy images as we would in real life.

Figure 4.13 | *Diario de un Loco* | **Design**: José Gerardo Almonte Díaz | © Pepo Almonte | **Mexico** | 27.9 × 43.2 cm

Eye Gaze and Pointing

Pointing and eye gaze are social cues and therefore capture attention because of learned associations. Our ancestors used eye gaze to perceive emotions in others and identify the most dominant creature, thus ensuring their survival. In turn, our brains developed mechanisms that automatically detect and follow eye gaze, and when eyes are not visible, we infer their position based on the orientation of the head and body. We instinctively move our eyes in the direction that we see someone else looking. So, if you place a human face looking in a particular direction, the audience will naturally follow the same path.

Ana Luisa Unzueta Arce's theater poster *Periférica* (Figure 4.14) is a haunting image that stares you down. Its gaze, the eyeball gently cradled in the mouth of a bearded man wearing lipstick, is so wonderfully uncomfortable that the viewer cannot help but be focused. The angled grid of contrasting white typography adds a sense of structure. Arce's poster was developed for a gathering of playwrights from La Paz, Bolivia's independent and underground arts scene, centered on uncanny and queer themes. Unzueta Arce wanted to use a powerful, unsettling image that gave an idea of the nature of these plays.

Another way to direct attention is with visual cues. The most common are arrows, or objects shaped like arrows, that point to where we want to lead the viewer's attention. Cues provide a structure and cognitive framework to follow, making information more accessible to assimilate. Similarly, words like "up," "down," "right," and "left" often act as symbolic cues and capture our attention because of experiential learning.

Disruption

Breaking the rules of design with reckless abandonment can provide a path to create an unexpected image. Disruption can re-energize and offer a refreshing view of what is otherwise routine. Taking risks can allow you to refocus, look at things through a distorted lens, and alter a point of view. Throwing a design into disorder with even a subtle interruption can cause tension and grab your audience's focus. Disrupting the ordinary and adding turmoil to a poster will grab attention on its own; however, when layered with an interesting story, the results can become even more powerful. The challenge is to sustain a delicate balance between the rules you break and the ones you follow. Without a strong understanding of layout, composition, and balance, your message may get lost in the disarray, and your poster may ultimately be dismissed and quickly forgotten.

Peter Bankov's theater poster *Typical Story* (Figure 4.15) is a controlled yet chaotic explosion of color, typography, and imagery. Bankov uses contrast to direct you to the center of his poster. There, the focal point—the metallic pipe—leads you to a flame billowing out the dates of the event. Contrast also plays a role in directing your eye to the bottom of the poster with its striking white scrawled title. With complementary color splashes of hot pink and bright blue, Bankov leads you through the visual activity. His color choice, contrasts, and crisp edges add equilibrium to the commotion of the hand-done typography, patterns, and drawn line. At first glance, Bankov's poster may appear to be scattered, but clearly, it is quite the opposite.

Figure 4.14 | *Periférica* | **Design**: Ana Luisa Unzueta Arce | © Ana Luisa Unzueta Arce | **Bolivia** | 50 x 70 cm

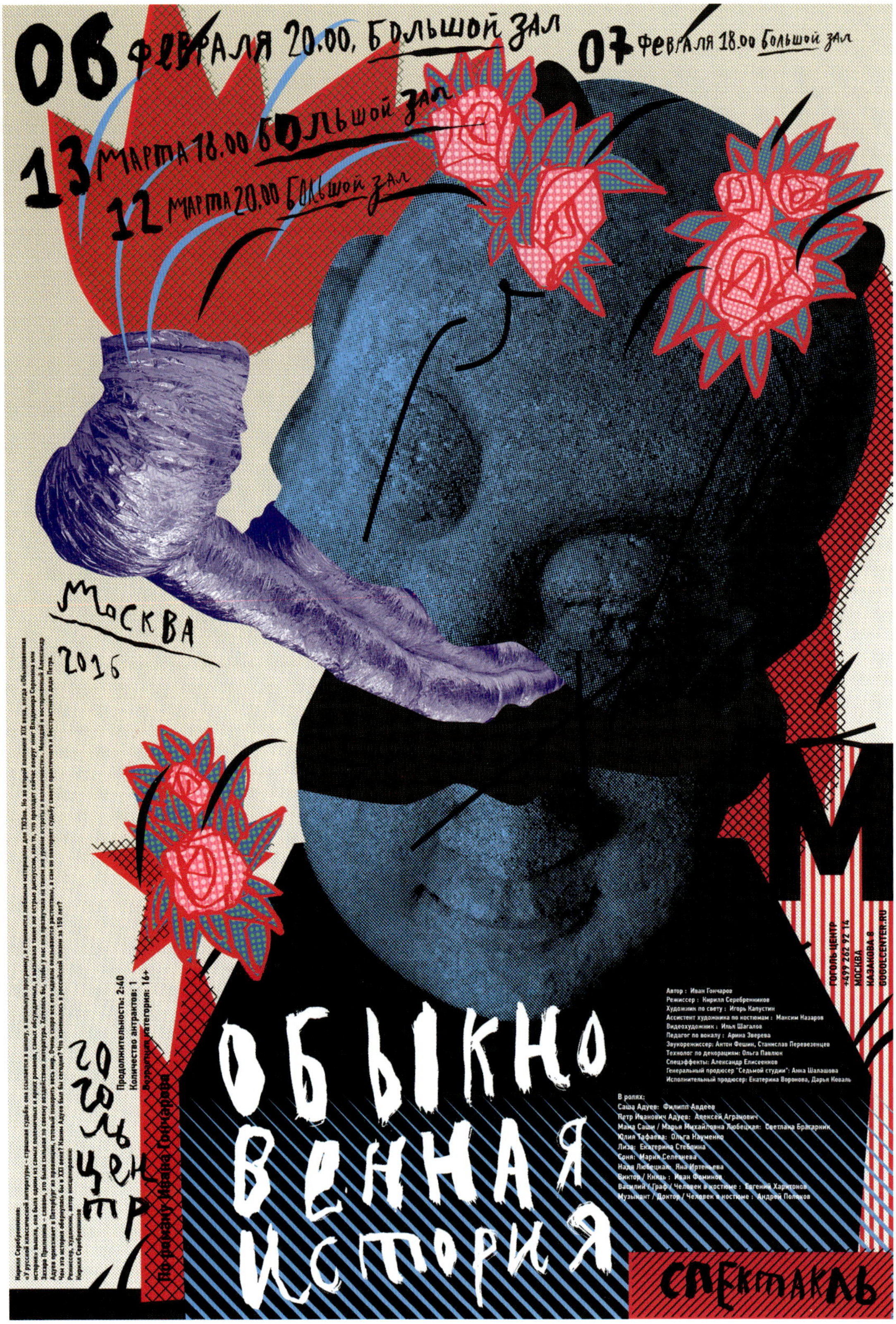

Figure 4.15 | *Typical Story* | **Design/Illustration:** Peter Bankov | © Peter Bankov | **Russia** | 70 x 100 cm

Converse/Marimekko by Andrew Lewis

We work in advertising, so grabbing attention IS OUR JOB! When I look back to posters on the streets of Paris in the late 1880s, I often notice that environment was insanely competitive, and designers were fighting to get their posters noticed first. Leonetto Cappiello introduced red zebras and green hairy monster-people, all of which advertised alcohol. How wonderfully abstract compared to now and the literal and boring marketing we have. Same goes for posters in Switzerland today, which are actually being used on the streets instead of just hanging in galleries and poster exhibitions. The poster must capture your attention; it must stop you in the street. With only two seconds to do so, it better be instantly intriguing to pull you in. Then, after that rush of visual adrenaline, the other factor is having a lasting quality, one that doesn't date itself or, as I said, become stale. And therein lies the true challenge in what I try to do with my posters.

In college, I studied textiles, and because my mother is a fiber artist, I grew up seeing loads of color, textures, and materials, which had a significant impact on my work. I studied color theory in depth, mixing paints and inks for screen printing and learning the science and optics of color. I also love the use of pattern, which contains both design and color elements; it is much more complex than you think. Years ago, I worked with International Wallcoverings in New York. It was such an amazing learning experience developing collections and understanding the various methods of creating patterns from a single design or texture. For each project, I tend to consider what atmosphere and emotional response I want first. I also play with many styles and media (traditional and digital), which opens up many more doors of opportunity and expression. I believe we should constantly experiment and push ourselves, otherwise we become lazy and just repeat our same approach over and over.

Converse/Marimekko | **Design/Illustration:** Andrew Lewis Design © 2018 | **Canada** | 70 x 100 cm

I was working with Baggins Shoes in Victoria, British Columbia, Canada, the largest seller of Converse running shoes in North America. They were looking at some posters I designed for a retail shop in Tokyo and liked the patterns I was using. They then showed me the line of shoes from Marimekko in Finland. The U.S. Converse representative came into the picture and connected the dots, and next thing I know, I am designing a co-brand poster for Converse and Marimekko. Obviously, both brands wanted to show their product in its best light, so I created an image that gave a 50/50 value to each brand.

I first pored through the hundreds of patterns and designs from Marimekko and tried to settle on three to five potential designs that I felt would resonate with a contemporary demographic. I chose the high-top Chuck Taylor Converse basketball shoe due to its having more real estate surface on which to play. My process always begins with pencil drawings and composing a rough format. After photographing a Chuck Taylor shoe at the angle I wanted, I redrew it in pen to create a base template. Working with pattern design, I began to simply play around with placement and scale, just jamming with visuals. I find, if you have a solid initial plan, it is easier to play over top of some kind of structure instead of starting by messing around. I found it much faster in terms of placing patterns inside of shapes. Then I brought the file into Illustrator and tidied it up and finished it off. To be honest, this process from start to finish was about five hours. Sometimes, posters just come together.

Crime and Punishment | **Design**: Ana Pesic | © Ana Pesic | **Serbia** | 50 x 70 cm

CHAPTER FOUR GRABBING ATTENTION

Music Is Oxygen | **Art Direction/Design**: Daniel Warner | © Daniel Warner | **USA** | 50 x 70 cm

Amaranta | **Design**: José Gerardo Almonte Díaz | © Pepo Almonte | **Mexico** | 27.9 x 43.2 cm

121

The power of monochromatic color schemes reveals itself in three very different but equally eye-catching designs. **Opposite:** Pesic's poster *Crime and Punishment* immediately assaults you with a haunting image of a dark, beaked, masked thief, nested into the bold, black, hand-done, gritty typography, set against a stark white background. Using only black and white, Warner creates a stirring image that is as magnificent as it is mystifying. Almonte Díaz's poster for the ska music concert draws from the color and motifs of the traditional red bandana, a trademark accessory of the group's performers.

MAKING POSTERS FROM CONCEPT TO DESIGN

The dramatic force of red, black, and white is combined with the strength of a visual accent to command the viewer's attention.

Opposite: Vibrant yellow dominates these posters, providing strong contrast and vibrancy.

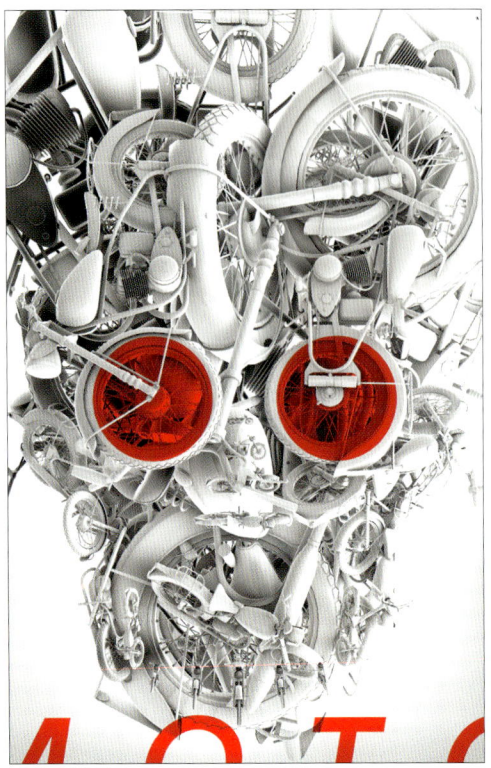

Moto | **Art Direction/Design**: Daniel Warner | © Daniel Warner | **USA** | 70 x 100 cm

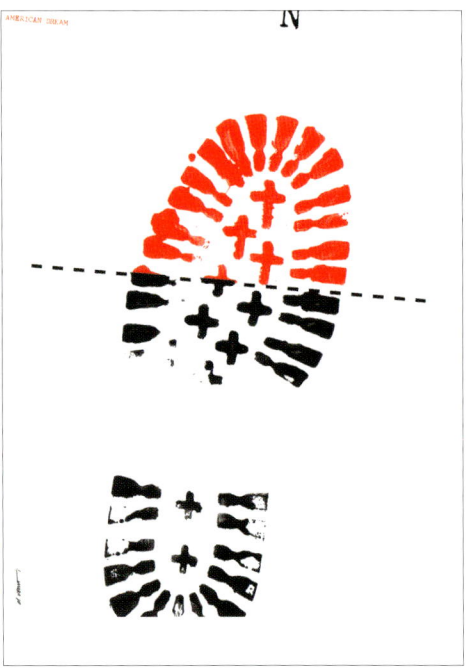

American Dream | **Design**: Benito Cabañas | © Benito Cabañas | **Mexico** | 60 x 90 cm

1492–1992 | **Design**: © 1992 by Lex Drewinski, all rights reserved | **Germany** | 70 x 10 cm

The Nightmare of Edgar Allan Poe | **Design**: © The Heads of State | **USA** | 45.7 x 61 cm

CHAPTER FOUR GRABBING ATTENTION

Upside Down | **Design**: Kelly Holohan | © Holohan Design | **USA** | 27.9 x 39.1 cm

Boofe Koor, The Honoring of the Iranian Writer Sadegh Hedayat | **Design/Illustration**: Mehdi Saeedi | © Mehdi Saeedi | **USA** | 70 x 100 cm

David Bowie 1947–2016 **and** *Lautrec Today* | © Luis Yanez | **Mexico** | 70 x 100 cm

Saturated color, temperature contrast, unexpected imagery, and multiple typefaces allow Salati to create an eclectic, attractive combination that perfectly reflects the spirit of the publication.

Opposite: Hot and cold color combinations will produce very different sensations depending on how they are applied. Plunkert and Morainslie's designs are predominantly cool, giving a sense of calmness and helping the main character stand out, while Marco Tóxico's red dominance stimulates the eye, provoking a stronger reaction. Michalowska's white background softens the contrast, making the blue eye the focal point of the composition.

WITH | **Design**: Michele Salati | © Michele Salati | **Hong Kong** | 70 x 100 cm

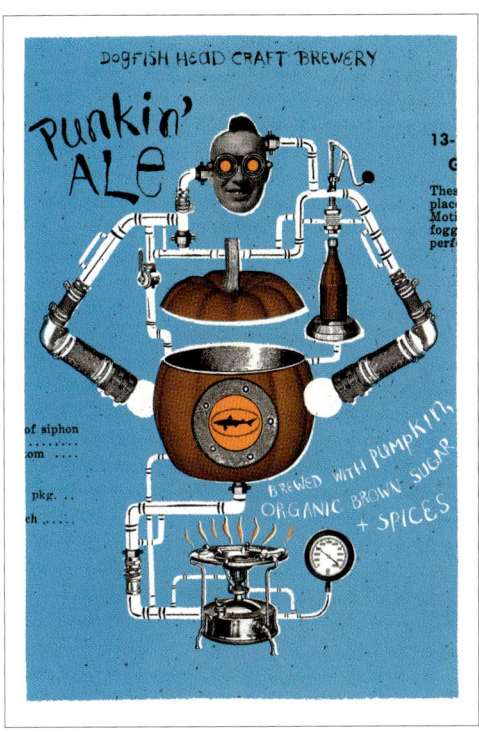

Dogfish Punkin' Ale | Spur Design LLC | David Plunkert | **Artwork** © 2020 David Plunkert | **USA** | 38.1 x 50.8 cm

5th Polish Film Festival, Australia | **Design:** Karolina Michalowska | © Puma Media, Ted Matkowski | **Poland** | 70 x 100 cm

XVIII Certamen Internacional de Cortos, Ciudad de Soria | **Design/Illustration:** Marco Tóxico | © Marco Tóxico | **Bolivia** | 70 x 100 cm

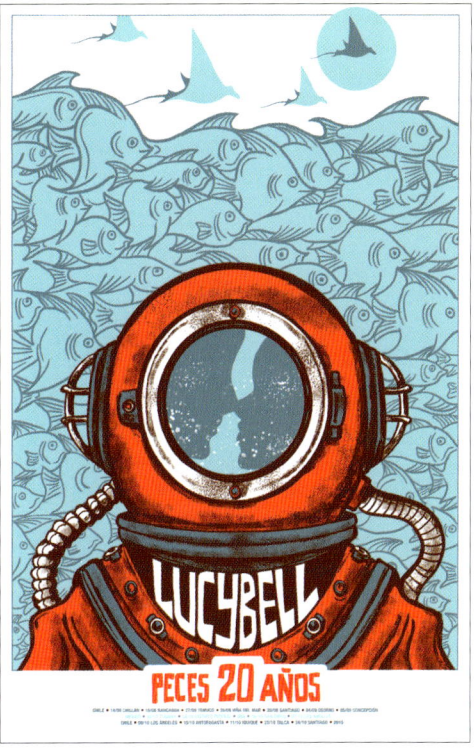

Lucybell—Peces Tour 20 Years | © Gus Morainslie/Mercadorama | **Mexico** | 40 x 60 cm

MAKING POSTERS FROM CONCEPT TO DESIGN

Warner contrasts a sun-like circle with the red background, representing the colors of the Spanish flag. The black figure stands out, and the white horns become the focal point of the image.

Opposite: Marco Tóxico's color triad brings a joyful look for a delicious feast of movies. Lewis unleashes color-contrasting polychromatic patterns to give life to the GQ woman. Chwast creates a radiant illustration reminiscent of the posters from the turn of the century. Glaser uses Art Nouveau with a pop art palette echoing his own *Dylan* poster in his advertising for the *Mad Men* series.

España | **Art Direction/Design**: Daniel Warner | © Daniel Warner | **USA** | 70 x 100 cm

Festival des Films du Monde | **Design/Illustration**: Marco Tóxico | © Marco Tóxico | **Bolivia** | 70 x 100 cm

GQ Magazine | **Design/Illustration**: Andrew Lewis | © Andrew Lewis | **Canada** | 70 x 100 cm

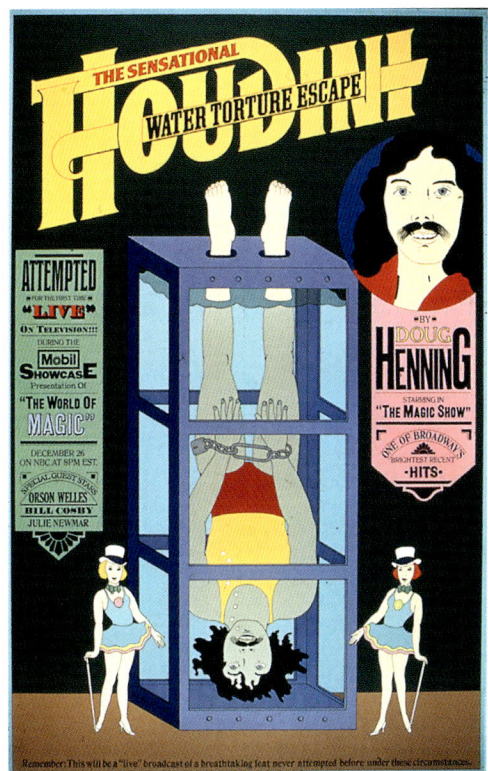

Houdini | **Design/Illustration**: Seymour Chwast | © Seymour Chwast | **USA** | 76.2 x 116.8 cm

Mad Men | **Design/Illustration**: Milton Glaser | © Milton Glaser | **USA** | 61 x 91.4 cm

MAKING POSTERS FROM CONCEPT TO DESIGN

Vibrant colors, bold shapes, and unusual objects become the protagonists of these posters, ensuring you stop to look at them wherever they are displayed.

Opposite: Jenko's green man stares directly at the viewer, creating immediate engagement and a sense of confrontation, while the rest of the posters feature characters staring at a distance, stimulating the audience's curiosity.

Studiolo of Plans, Building Sets Storage | **Design:** Richard Niessen | © Richard Niessen | **Netherlands** | 84 x 118.5 cm

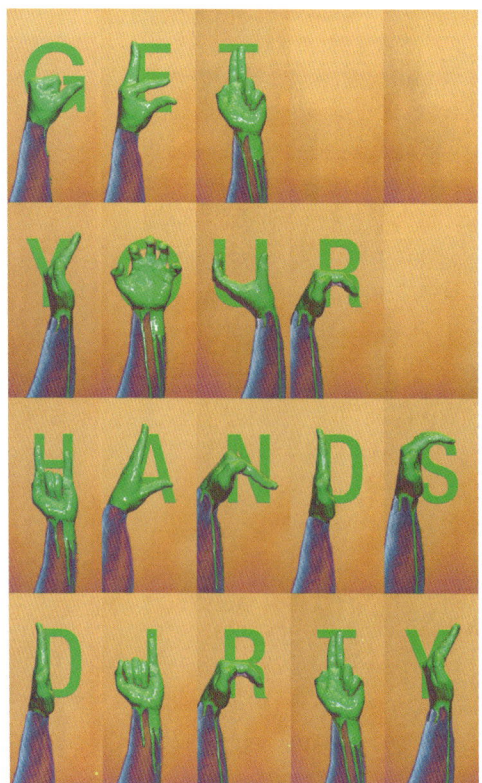

Go Up, Man! Pracownia Plakatu—Doroczna Wystawa 2016 | **Design:** Piotr Kunce | © Piotr Kunce | **Poland** | 70 x 100 cm

Get Your Hands Dirty | **Design:** Jon Newman | © Jon Newman is God | **USA** | 61 x 66 cm

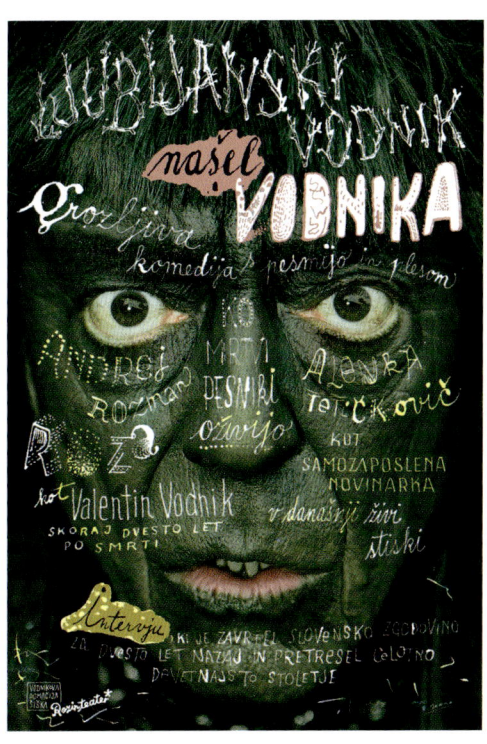

The Ljubljana Vodnik Guide Found Vodnik | **Design**: Radovan Jenko | **Photography**: Dragan Arrigler | © Radovan Jenko and Dragan Arrigler | **Slovenia** | 68 x 98 cm

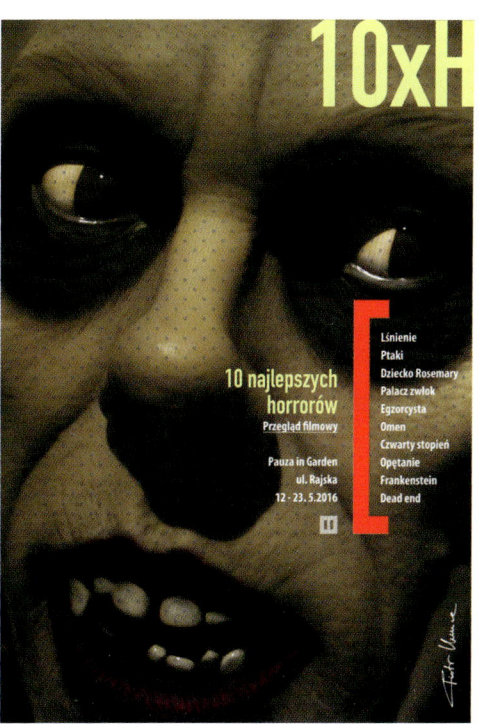

10 Najlepszych Horrorów (10 Best Horror Films Review) | **Design:** Piotr Kunce | © Piotr Kunce | **Poland** | 120 x 180 cm

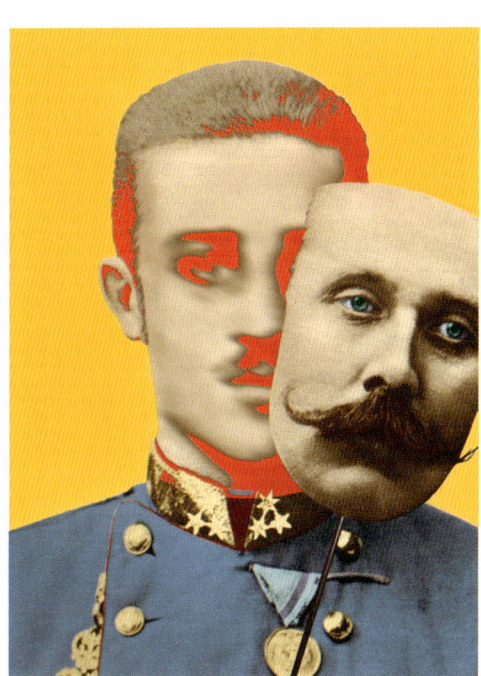

War Unmasked | **Design**: David Jiménez | © David Jiménez | **Ecuador** | 70 x 100 cm

Pierre de Ronsard | **Design**: Umer Ahmad | © Umer Ahmad | **Norway** | 30 x 40 cm

This page and opposite: *Shut Up and Dance* | **Design**: Matthew Bouloutian | © Matthew Bouloutian | **Client**: MANNA | **USA** | 27.9 x 43.2 cm

CHAPTER FOUR GRABBING ATTENTION

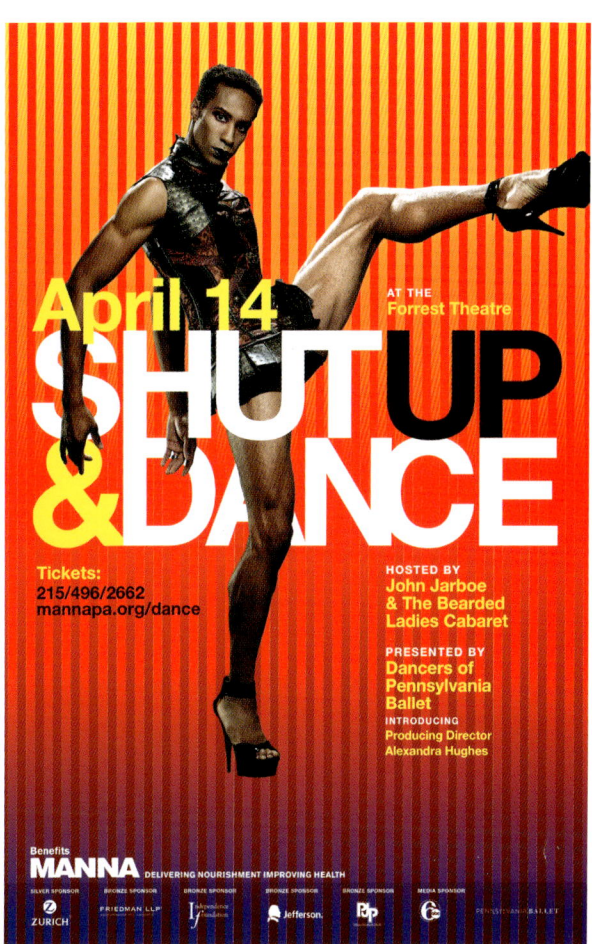

Bright and bold with plenty of movement, Bouloutian's *Shut Up and Dance* posters, made for different years of the event, work together in rhythm and harmony. Typography is an essential part of the composition, keeping the visual system consistent without becoming predictable. The posters create excitement and anticipation, causing you to wonder what will come next.

Museo Nacional de Arte | **Illustration**: Ryszard Kaja | © Ryszard Kaja | **Poland** | 69 x 99 cm

CHAPTER FOUR GRABBING ATTENTION

War Peace, Peace War | **Design**: Yossi Lemel | © Yossi Lemel | **Israel** | 180 x 120 cm

Clockwise: Lemel's poster series shows a superb example of a three-dimensional approach to breaking the pattern. Inspired by the well-known saying "the wolf in sheep's clothing," Wright fills the page with a seemingly endless pattern of sheep that are strategically disrupted by text, allowing you to spot the disguised intruder. Paddeick's poster *Pareidolia* uses the pareidolia effect to communicate its meaning.

Opposite: Kaja's lecture promotion poster employs dazzling geometric patterns and creates an abstract city beneath a volcano.

Era of Disinformation | **Design**: Erin Wright | © Erin Wright | **USA** | 70 x 100 cm

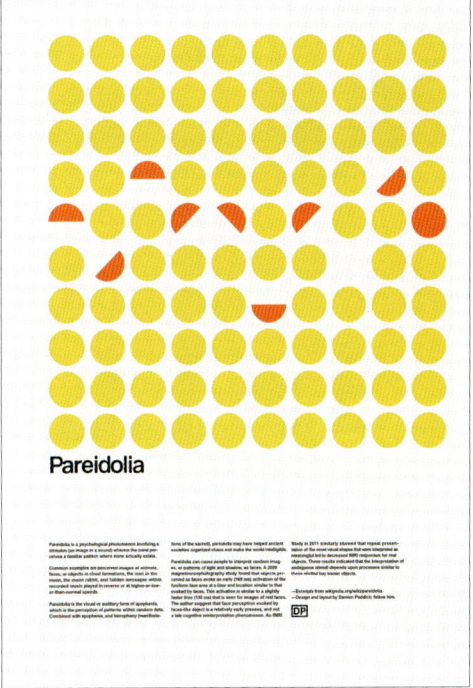

Pareidolia | **Design**: Damien Paddick | © Damien Paddick | **Australia** | 50 x 70 cm

133

MAKING POSTERS FROM CONCEPT TO DESIGN

Der Gott des Gemetzels (The God of Slaughter) | **Design:** Stephan Bundi | © by Stephan Bundi | **Germany** | 89.5 x 128 cm

Decade Kung Fu Exhibition | **Design/Illustration:** Sha Feng | © Sha Feng | **China** | 70 x 100 cm

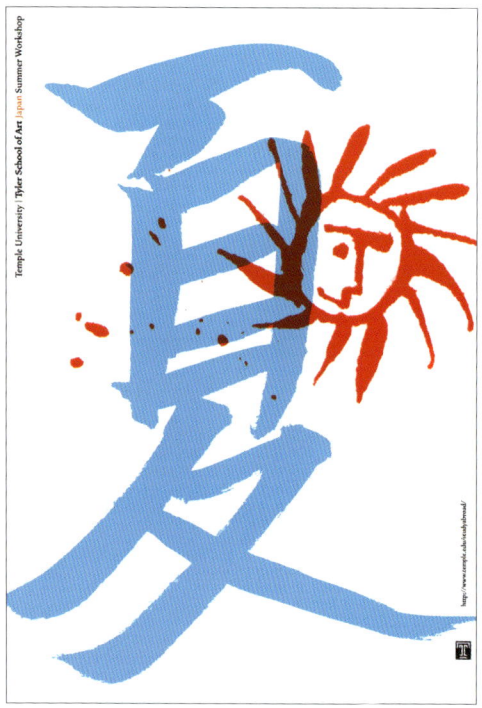

Japan Summer Workshop | **Art Direction & Design:** Dermot Mac Cormack, Patricia McElroy | **Illustration:** Dermot Mac Cormack, Shinubu Ninomiya | **Client:** Tyler School of Art, Temple University | © 21x Design | **USA** | 70 x 100 cm

Hasta la Visa Baby | **Design:** David Jiménez | © David Jiménez | **Ecuador** | 70 x 100 cm

CHAPTER FOUR GRABBING ATTENTION

Ooey gooey, icky sticky, and GROSS—Freeman and Steben worked with real gum and saliva for indie rock artist Mac DeMarco's musical event poster *Homeshake the Garden*.

Opposite: From Bundi's ragged surface to Feng's three-dimensional typography to Mac Cormack's Japanese kanji, prominent characters with bold statements demand the attention of the viewer. Playing with the content, Jiménez takes this to the next level, creating a brilliant twist on one of the most iconic lines in cinema history to transform its meaning and spotlight the topic of immigration.

Mac DeMarco | **Design**: Sean Freeman & Eve Steben, THERE IS Studio | © Sean Freeman & Eve Steben | **United Kingdom** | 45.7 x 61 cm

135

CHAPTER FIVE ART OF PERSUASION

From political awareness and social activism to marketing and sales, persuasion has played a vital role in the world of posters. The origins of persuasive techniques can be traced back to the days of the ancient Greeks, who used persuasion in education and intellectual life. Homer, Aristotle, and many other philosophers studied how rhetoric influences audiences. Today, designers and artists often use rhetorical persuasion when making images for commercial clients. However, the real potential of the poster as a medium for persuasion was originally exploited during World War I, when posters were used to recruit young men. Inspired by Alfred Leete's *Lord Kitchener Wants You* advertisement, James Montgomery Flagg's iconic *I Want You for the U.S. Army* poster (Figure 5.1) is a perfect example of this new type of communication. During WWII, poster production was even more substantial. While most of the images were pro-war, this time also saw the rise of protest posters. During this period, researchers studied persuasion to improve advertising and marketing campaigns.

ART OF PERSUASION

(facing page) Illustration: Natalia Delgado
(above) Scott Laserow

Figure 5.1 | *I Want You for the U.S. Army* Recruitment Poster | **Artist:** James Montgomery Flagg | **USA** | Located in Library of Congress (Photo © CORBIS/Corbis via Getty Images) | 57.2 x 71.1 cm

Visual rhetoric has often been used to identify the most effective way to deliver your message to an audience, especially when there is a need to capture their attention in a short period of time. Using techniques from semiotics and rhetorical analysis, visual rhetoric focuses on the structure of the visual message, its cultural and contextual meaning, and its persuasive effects on the audience. While there is no consensus on how persuasion works, four essential elements are present in many forms of persuasion: the source, the message, the channel, and the receiver. Some of these elements have already been addressed in previous chapters, but it is worth revisiting them through the lens of persuasion.

Source—The source is the person or company who is doing the persuading. Through the evolution of branding, companies have learned how to reflect human-like qualities in all types of communications, including of course posters. Whether the source is a person or a brand, there are specific characteristics that influence its persuasiveness, such as expertise, trustworthiness, and attractiveness. Expertise refers to whether we perceive the source to be an authority on the subject they are addressing. When the audience believes the source of a message is an expert, the message is less likely to be challenged. Likewise, many studies have shown that people tend to be more persuaded by attractive speakers, attaching positive attributes to them and becoming more open to being influenced.

Message—The message is what we want to communicate to an audience to persuade them. A rhetorical or persuasive appeal is a skill that a speaker uses to convey meaning to the audience and provoke a response. In his *Art of Rhetoric*,[13] Aristotle introduces the persuasive appeals, which are represented by the Greek words "ethos," "pathos," and "logos." Ethos refers to the ethical appeal that gives credibility to your message. This means that you should only tell a story about a topic that you are familiar with, and always adapt your content and presentation style to fit your audience. Pathos is the emotional component of your message. It evokes feelings of compassion or heartache through meaningful imagery, which can be an overwhelming experience. Pathos can engage your audience and convey your passion for the topic, forging a connection that goes well beyond the rational. Logos is persuasion by argument and reasoning. Every message should have a convincing argument. Citing facts, using statistics, or referencing history will appeal to viewers' intellect and can be influential in winning them over. Blending these three appeals can help you craft a message so persuasive and impactful that your audience will want to share it with others.

Channel—The channel is the medium by which your message is delivered to the receiver—in our case, posters. The channel you use to deliver your message is as important as what you say. Not every message can or should be delivered with a poster, no matter how dear the cause might be to you. For example, if a lot of information needs to be communicated, you might want to create a brochure or website instead of or in addition to a poster.

Aesthetics are an essential part of the channel. They represent how we communicate our message and carry with them specific ideologies that influence the audience's reception of the message. Therefore, aesthetics should be content-driven, so they are relatable to your audience. Common mistakes include choosing styles capriciously, following fashion trends, or choosing personal preferences rather than focusing on the communication objectives and the interests of the audience. This misjudgment can result in neutralization of meaning or create a conflict between the form and the content.[14] Another essential part of the channel is the context where communication is taking place. After all, we read images seen on the street differently than if they were displayed in a gallery or even in a book. Context can have a strong influence over other elements, so consider it when choosing your channel.

Receiver—The receiver is the intended audience for the message. The Roman philosopher Cicero is believed to have said, "If you wish to persuade me, you must think my thoughts, feel my feelings, and speak my words."[15] We have systemic, social, and personal needs. Systemic needs refer to the automatic responses we have programmed in our brain that are mostly instinctive and out of our control, such as the "fight or flight" response. Social needs address our desire to be liked and respected by our peers. Personal needs relate to our hopes and dreams and how we want to live our lives. When studying your audience, you must be aware of their needs, expectations, perceptions, and cultural values. Take into consideration the audience's personality type, technical level, and operational role. Viewers can have resistance to being persuaded or influenced, and these resistances are continually evolving. Acknowledging opposition can be a tool for persuasion by allowing the audience to choose their response rather than dictating what they should think or do. This freedom empowers the audience, making them more likely to stand by their choice.

Rhetorical Figure

Rhetorical figure is the use of language in a symbolic form to provide emphasis, originality, or clarity by creating a conscious deviation from the literal meaning or the order of a word or group of words. Rhetorical figures provide us with a multitude of ways to say, "This is like this." By looking at similarities and differences, we can communicate meaning. In visual rhetoric, these figures are created with images rather than words, allowing the image to acquire a meaning different from its natural sense. Visual rhetorical figures are often divided into four categories according to the way they operate: amplification (adding elements or exaggerating an aspect), deletion (removing one or more items), substitution (removing one component and replacing it with another), and exchange (making two reciprocal substitutions). Use rhetorical figures in a way that makes the audience understand the information faster and easier. If the picture you use is too complicated, your audience may get frustrated, lose interest, or forget about the message.

Metaphor

A metaphor is the most popular and familiar rhetorical figure. The name comes from the Greek word "metaphein," which means to transfer. A metaphor is a figure of speech where a word or phrase is used in place of another to express a shared connection or similarity between them. A visual metaphor is the depiction of a person, place, thing, or idea by using an image that suggests a particular parallel or relationship that divulges insight and meaning. Both definitions point to a change of perspective that allows us to see the similarities between two unrelated things and therefore can be used to engage and communicate quickly. This resource offers great creative possibilities to transmit a complex idea or message with a single image.

Metaphors create a shortcut to our emotional and mnemonic responses. When we understand a metaphor, we create a mental association that goes beyond our capacity to reason. The ability of the audience to understand the metaphor depends on their knowledge. Nothing is a metaphor by itself; each culture and society establishes its own visual and verbal relationships.

Figure 5.2 | *Victor, Victoria* | **Design/Illustration**: James Lacey | **Client**: Revival Theatre Company | © Dennard, Lacey & Associates | **USA** | 61 x 91.4 cm

James Lacey's poster *Victor Victoria* (Figure 5.2) uses a Russian matryoshka doll as the metaphor to tell the tale of an actress, who is disguised as a female impersonator playing the role of a female nightclub performer. Lacey conveys the account of Victoria shown nested inside her persona of Victor stepping out onto the stage to perform as Victoria. While this poster is contemporary, Lacey uses visual cues, typographic manipulation, color, and graphic embellishments as stage decoration that transport you back to 1930s Paris.

Metonymy

Metonymy and metaphor are often hard to distinguish from one another, as they commonly interact in linguistic and visual expressions. Both are essential tools for making abstract and complex concepts more accessible. Where a metaphor expresses an idea by establishing a relationship of similarity, metonymy is a stand-for relationship, where something stands for something else related to it. We use metonymies when we refer to a man who belongs to a religious order as "a man of the cloth" or a person of importance who steals large amounts of money from a business or the government as a "white-collar criminal." In graphic design and advertising, a common example of metonymy is when an aspect of an object is used to represent the whole object. In corporate branding, color is often used in place of an object. Other times, form is used in place of an object, as when objects are reduced to their outlines or become representational. Visual metonymy is seen when labels, marks, locations, or other objects replace other visuals to bring complex or elusive ideas into a concrete reality that is easily interpreted.

The 20th Toronto Jewish Film Festival poster, *Curls* (Figure 5.3), makes use of metonymy by replacing "payot," the Hebrew word for curled sidelocks or sideburns, with coiled film strips. This metonymic image gains meaning when placed in context with the title of the film festival. The airiness of the white space and the simple use of color communicate the message quickly. This entertaining poster is a true case of less is more and not allowing decoration to get in the way of a great concept.

Synecdoche

A synecdoche is a form of metonymy where a whole represents one of its parts or the part represents the whole. Synecdoches can be conceptual, posing a concept, idea, or material that expresses an object or thing. Synecdoche and metonymy are very similar. The best way to distinguish them is by the relationship between the two halves. With metonymy, the two halves share a relationship but are different objects, whereas with synecdoche, the two halves are in a part–whole relationship, with a portion of an object representing the whole object. Researcher Román Esqueda considers synecdoche to be a way of understanding that focuses on specific semantic content.[16] For example, choosing to represent construction with bricks highlights an aspect of construction that stands in for the whole.

Figure 5.3 | *20th Toronto Jewish Film Festival—Curls* | **Agency:** BBDO—Toronto, Ontario | **Executive Creative Directors**: Peter Ignazi, Carlos Moreno | **Creative Directors**: Nancy Crimi-Lamanna, Deborah Prenger | **Art Director:** Dan Cantelon | **Photographer**: Philip Rostron/Instil Productions | © **Advertising Agency:** BBDO Toronto, Canada **Art Director:** Dan Cantelon **Photographer:** Philip Rostron | **Canada** | 65 x 100 cm

Figure 5.4 | *No Size Limits* | © Jung von Matt/Alster, Hamburg | **Germany** | Various sizes

The campaign *No Size Limits* (Figure 5.4), created by the award-winning agency Jung von Matt/Alster from Hamburg for DHL international shipping, shows a creative use of synecdoche that delivers the brand's message about their large shipping services. Even though the image shows only a rugged texture, the audience can immediately deduce that this is an elephant, making the tag of "no size limits" a comical affirmation of the brand's policy. The material synecdoche uses a key part of the elephant, its skin, to represent the whole. Of course, this presumes that the audience is familiar enough with elephants to fill in the gap and make the connection without having to show the entire animal.

Other Figures

There is a long list of rhetorical figures that have appeared in literature and poetry. While some of them do not translate to visuals, others are extraordinarily effective and powerful and have been used for a long time. Here, we provide a view of some of the most common figures seen in poster design and how they can be used to influence the beliefs and actions of others.

Allusion

Allusion is an expression that makes an indirect reference in speech to something well-known without naming it. Allusion helps us to explain a story and will help the audience to understand your narrative by connecting it to something already known. We use allusion when we say things like "You're a regular Einstein," "Doughnuts are my Achilles' heel," or "Haters gonna hate." Allusions can support metaphors and similes by alluding to something momentous that helps in the communication of the concept.

With a simple typographic design, Ricardo Garla's poster *walk* (Figure 5.5) tells an elaborate story about immigration and makes a stand against oppressive borders that divide us. One of the most exciting aspects of Garla's poster is that it alludes to so many things without referencing them directly. Border security and the border wall have been at the center of the immigration discussion. Garla's divisive point of view is openly opposed to the building of a wall. The rebellious graffiti transforms the word from "wall" into "walk," which suggests freedom of movement between countries.

Figure 5.5 | *walk* | **Design**: Ricardo Garla | © Ricardo Garla | **Brazil** | 25 x 35 cm

Irony

Irony consists of the burlesque expression of something contrary to what you want to communicate. Richard Buchanan describes irony as a mechanism by which we represent an idea through its opposite due to a subtle similarity between them.[17] Irony is often used for its humorous and emphatic effect. It can be a powerful communication tool, but it is tricky to use because you risk losing your audience if they take the meaning literally. Irony should be used only in contexts where you trust the audience's sense of humor. In these cases, irony can be particularly useful, as the audience shares the joy of being in on the joke. There are three types of irony: verbal, dramatic, and situational. Verbal irony is when words communicate a message opposite to what the person wants to say. Think of a typical couple's spat, where both go out of their way to sarcastically state the opposite of what they are thinking, such as, "Thank you for being late again; I had such a wonderful time waiting for you in the rain!" Verbal irony is usually expressed by either overstating or understating the character of something. Dramatic irony is commonly used in cinema and refers to the moment when the audience knows something about the character that he or she does not. Shakespeare used a particular type of dramatic irony, known as tragic irony, in many of his plays, where the fate of one character is revealed to the audience, who then watches as the character plays out the events that will lead to his tragic end. Situational irony involves a discrepancy between what is supposed to happen and what actually happens.

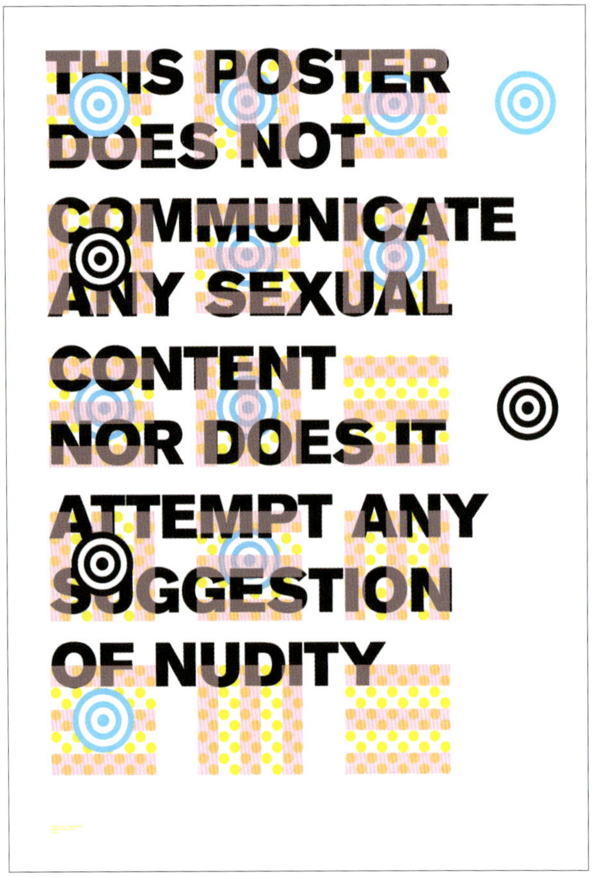

Figure 5.6 | *Rejected Poster* | **Design**: Erik Brandt | © Erik Brandt/Typografika | **USA** | 70 x 100 cm

Figure 5.7 | *Over 1,000,000 Sold* | **Design**: Joe Scorsone and Alice Drueding | © Joe Scorsone and Alice Drueding | **USA** | 50 x 70 cm

Erik Brandt's poster *Rejected Poster* was explicitly created to be ironic. Brandt was invited to exhibit a poster for World Graphic Day in an unnamed country, where the invitation specified as part of the rules that the poster should not have any sexual content or nudity. "How could I resist?" says Erik, who created the typographic poster featured in Figure 5.6, with the ironic text "This poster does not communicate any sexual content nor does it attempt any suggestion of nudity." The poster was rejected for the competition due to the use of the word "sexual" despite not showing any offensive content.

Hyperbole

Hyperbole comes from the Greek word meaning "excess" and is an exaggeration created to highlight a characteristic of an issue. This magnification can be literal, by increasing the actual size of an object, embellishing a concept, or overemphasizing a quality or idea. These overstated images draw attention, as they seem odd and out of place.

Joe Scorsone and Alice Drueding's poster *Over 1,000,000 Sold* (Figure 5.7) is a shocking, hyperbolic image that presents the victim as a commodity being sold in a slaughterhouse. Although this is a clear visual exaggeration, the pain and horror of the image are not. It makes you uncomfortable and queasy. Here, the stark black and white contrast helps in the communication of the concept. Scorsone and Drueding do not allow you the freedom of distraction—they make you face the atrocity head-on.

Figure 5.8 | *Jazz Is Like a Picasso* | © Lindsay, Stone & Briggs | **USA** | 31.8 x 47 cm

Simile

A simile is a comparison between two different things to make a description richer. A simile is another one of the most common forms of figurative language and is used to generate an unexpected connection in the audience's mind. Similes are often confused with metaphors. Metaphors state the comparison directly, whereas similes use the words "like" or "as": "as light as a feather" and "as sweet as sugar," or "Don't just sit there like a bump on a log" and "It fits like a glove." Visual similes serve to establish a relationship between a defining element and what it symbolizes, enabling the viewer to associate the characteristic with a product or service. Using a green color palette and leaves is a visual simile that suggests to the viewer that a product is ecological, natural, or contains natural ingredients.

The poster *Jazz Is Like a Picasso* (Figure 5.8) uses a simile in the header that is supported by an image that also is a simile. Jazz at Five uses an energetic, loose, and expressive line as an homage to Pablo Picasso's famous line work and uses a saxophone as a nose to create a visual somewhat reminiscent of Picasso's abstract works. The fusion of the two Picasso-esque styles on a clean white surface alludes to the improvised rhythmic ideas of jazz, creating a synergistic poster that is "like" a work of art.

Prosopopoeia

Prosopopoeia, also known as personification, consists of attributing human qualities to objects or animals. Most product mascots use this rhetorical figure because it allows the viewer to relate to the message or brand. Research shows that companies using animals as symbols of their brands get better results than the average. Some examples of successful characters include the Kool-Aid pitcher, Tony the Tiger, Joe Camel, and Toucan Sam, to name a few.

The whimsical posters created by Spanish designer Isidro Ferrer for Camper's line of shoes for kids (Figure 5.9) perfectly illustrate the use of prosopopoeia. Animals have been a recurring element in Ferrer's work for a long time. Echoing the characters of his Funny Farm wood carvings project, the creatures of the Camper ads feature fantastic and unusual shapes printed in a woodcut-like style using earthy tones and the iconic red of the brand's logo. The animals playfully engage in human activities such as reading and conversing, all while sporting Camper shoes.

Figure 5.9 | *Camper for Kids Poster Series* | **Design**: Isidro Ferrer | © Isidro Ferrer | **Canada** | 70 x 100 cm

Euphemism

Euphemism is a vague, suggestive term that we substitute for blunt and offensive words or phrases to disguise the harshness and vulgarity with something less unpleasant. Euphemisms are often used to make contentious acts seem less dubious, like when we use the term "collateral damage" for accidental civilian deaths. Euphemisms can also be amusing, like "jumping bones," "pushing up daisies," or "bun in the oven."

Elmer Sosa's nature conservancy and deforestation poster *Ups!* (Figure 5.10) uses a common euphemism for male genitalia, or "wood," to send a humorous message. Sosa's tree is not just any tree; he chooses the arbor vitae, a symbol of the tree of life.[18] The design is compelling on many levels with its black and white image's sharp contrast that demands attention to humor, making his poster appealing without having a moralistic tone. In this case, the euphemism affords Sosa the freedom to use an analogy that would otherwise not be suitable for all audiences.

Building an Emotional Connection

Every perception involves a search for meaning due to our psychological need to understand what we see. Humans experience many emotions. When we perceive without understanding, we may have feelings of uneasiness, boredom, fatigue, or fear. It has been theorized that the creation of emotional experiences is the reason we make art.[19] Emotions play a fundamental role in persuasion and therefore are key components of poster design. From Aristotle and his notion of rhetoric to contemporary researchers, many have studied the role that emotions play in the process of intentionally changing people's attitudes. Emotions are usually regarded as either positive or negative and often affect how we process information. Our emotions can make us trust or distrust what we think and feel.

We connect with images in a different way than we connect with words because pictures are more persuasive and tend to activate our emotions easily. Our limbic system, which modulates emotional responses, is pre-verbal and therefore reacts to images rather than words. Even though a word might trigger a mental image, a picture will usually have a stronger emotional impact, known as "the picture superiority effect."[20] A common example of this is when a lawyer uses photos of a crime scene as a persuasive resource to influence the members of the jury. Despite the beauty of abstract imagery, representational visuals tend to be more effective at making ideas understandable, memorable, and persuasive.

Figure 5.10 | *Ups!* | **Design/Illustration**: Elmer Sosa | © Elmer Sosa | **Mexico** | 70 x 100 cm

Choosing a proper tone for your message will make your poster poignant and relevant. To accomplish this, ask yourself: How do I want to say this? The same narrative can be made happy and optimistic or dark and guilt-inducing. To build an alliance with your audience, you must address their goals, aspirations, and anxieties. Rather than giving them logical reasons, such as statistics or academic concepts, try connecting with their emotions, needs, and desires.

Our past experiences play a significant role in how we react to a visual. When making an image to provoke an emotional response, artists rely on cognitive antecedent. These are learned behaviors shaped by past events that act as a stimulus to cue our emotions. A crying child; a sunrise; a large, dark, and looming shadow all create feelings that can be easily decoded. Presenting unpleasant or sad imagery will surely induce a reaction. Depending on the topic and message, it might very well be necessary. Imagery that tugs on a viewer's heartstrings can be a moving experience. Empathy covers a broad spectrum, ranging from caring for other people and wanting to help them to understanding what the other person may be feeling or making no distinction between yourself and him or her. Being sensitive to other people's emotions and feelings and giving them the ability to share in the experience can be a powerful tool.

Fear and Shock

Disturbing visuals affect us on a psychological level, causing us to react emotionally. According to clinical psychologist Dr. John Mayer, when we see something distressing, "Data from our perceptual system stimulates the part of the brain responsible for emotions, survival tactics, and memory."[21] Our brain is driven to process unsettling information. This sensation is why we cannot look away from an automobile accident. Sigmund Freud referred to this aesthetic as the "uncanny,"[22] or our instinctual attraction to the unpleasant. Aristotle describes this desire with the term "catharsis"—the purging of the emotions of pity and fear that are aroused in the viewer.[23] Poster designers can use the physical allure of jarring images to make posters that stun and startle the viewer.

Figure 5.11 | *Israel Palestine 2003* | **Design**: Yossi Lemel | © Yossi Lemel | **Israel** | 120 × 180 cm

The iconic image of peace, a white dove holding an olive branch, is used in a macabre and shocking way to represent the violent nature of the Israeli–Palestinian conflict, a struggle that has been going on for decades. The symbol of a dove originated with early Christians and has become a universal shorthand for union and tolerance. Yet in Yossi Lemel's poster *Israel Palestine 2003* (Figure 5.11), the dove is submerged in a jar with what appears to be formalin, a substance used to preserve biological and anatomical specimens for scientific study. The jar labeled PEACE preserves the symbol of peace in case it is ever attained.

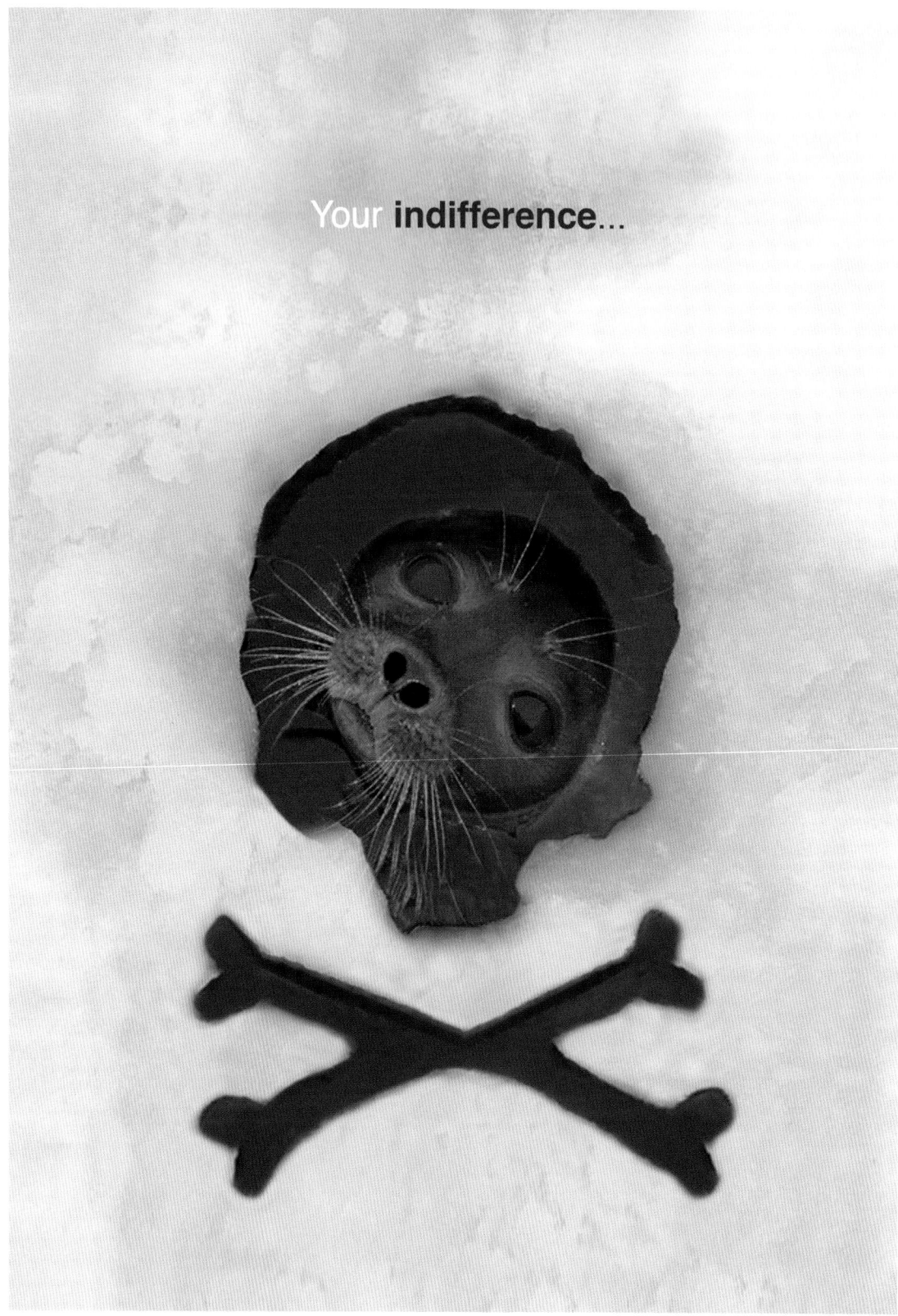

Figure 5.12 | *Your Indifference* | **Design**: Giulia Cavazza | © Giulia Cavazza | **Italy** | 50 x 70 cm

Sadness & Despair

Using animals to evoke emotion, such as depicting a neglected dog chained outdoors in the cold, is a universal resource that makes an instant connection and generates feelings of empathy. Animals are endearing and can appeal to people on an emotional level. Much like children, they represent pure innocence. The World Wildlife Fund's mission is to stop the degradation of the planet's natural environment and to build a future in which people live in harmony with nature. Many people have strong objections to the commercial hunting of wildlife and marine mammals in particular.[24] The heartbreaking poster *Your Indifference* by Giulia Cavazza (Figure 5.12) addresses the controversial topic of the forty-plus-year Canadian harp seal hunt. The poster takes a clear posture connecting the seal with a human skull cut from the ice, contrasting the gloomy death symbol with the cute and innocent face of the baby seal. The seal's stare intensifies the effect by aiming directly at you, the audience.

Jacx Staniszewski's poster HUNGER (Figure 5.13) is a haunting display of cold and hard despair. The poster's focal point of a large, crumbling mouth, disintegrating into a bottomless pit of anguish, is stunning. The dry, dusty, and silent scream is representational and metaphorical. The widening of the mouth signifies the torture and pain of hunger, while the powdered marble symbolizes the desolation of barren lands. Staniszewski directs you to the word "HUNGER" by using the chin of Michelangelo's *David* where the narrative reveals itself. The *David's* peculiar gaze when turned upside-down transforms into an expression of angst and loneliness. Staniszewski's beautifully sad image of helplessness emotes pain that you can feel.

Humor

At the other end of the spectrum are pleasant emotions, feelings of happiness, or a sense of wonderment. The smell of something cooking in the kitchen may bring back a fond childhood memory of a grandparent, or hearing an old song may trigger a particular sensation that strengthens the bond between two friends. Perhaps the most joyful emotional response is laughter. Humor is inherently compelling and can be especially useful when dealing with serious issues. Addressing sensitive topics can lead to depression or despair; however, through humor, we can cope with difficult circumstances

Figure 5.13 | HUNGER | **Design/Illustration**: Jacx Staniszewski | © Jacx Staniszewski | **Poland** | 70 x 100 cm

and see things from a different perspective. Laughter has been shown to reduce stress and provoke the release of serotonin and endorphins, creating a neurochemical reaction that enhances our ability to tolerate the pain and engage in creative problem-solving.[25] By highlighting the comedic or ridiculous side of a topic, you disarm your audience, allowing them to be more accepting of your message and even begin to identify with the problem. Humor provides a sense of control that despite initial apprehension can lead to action.

Handoko Tjung's poster *Climate Is Changing* (Figure 5.14) is an original spin on a grave and challenging topic. The consequences of climate change threaten the survival of humanity on our planet, and yet many people still mock or deny this delicate issue. The topic has been addressed numerous times by designers around the world, many of whom have chosen to use the iconic image of a polar bear on a melting ice cap to represent this problem. However, Tjung uses the polar bear in a new and unexpected way, presenting it as a character fighting for its life and doing whatever it takes to survive. The polar bear is painting his partner as a panda under a bright sunny sky with text that reads "Climate is changing." Tjung manages to make us giggle while still making his point about the grave effects of rising temperatures on the environment.

Arousal

Arousal raises your blood pressure and makes your heart beat faster. It is a physiological state that makes you feel more active and excited. We have developed neural mechanisms to detect arousing events immediately, which is why they are a standard tool of advertising. The two most influential sources of high arousal are threat and sex, including taboo words and images, profanity, and expletives. Using arousing elements will undoubtedly catch your audience's attention, but they can be controversial and off-putting for certain people. A common way to defuse this adverse effect is with humor, which helps to lighten the mood and may be better received by the viewer. Sex can be used to demand attention and create desire, but it can also work against you by distracting the audience from your message. Using sex in advertising creates a degree of resistance from the audience if they consider it offensive. This may lead to the work being susceptible to censorship or boycott. Therefore, using arousal without a good reason is not recommended.

French-Algerian model, designer, and actress Zahia Dehar and famed musician and photographer Bryan Adams, along with People for the Ethical Treatment of Animals (PETA), teamed up to create this alluring poster (Figure 5.15) to promote vegetarianism. Zahia, nude and posing in front of a white background, is what initially draws our attention. There we quickly notice the painted typography on her body equating this seductive beauty to a butcher chart depicting the cuts of meat. The image reminds us of how like animals we are, as we have similar body parts. With her gaze, Zahia points us to the headline, "All Animals Have the Same Parts." The sweep of her body moves us to the tagline, "Have a Heart: Try Vegetarian," which is directly aligned with her shoulder, further anchoring the message of this memorable poster.

Figure 5.14 | *Climate Is Changing* | **Design/Illustration**: Handoko Tjung | © Handoko Tjung | **Indonesia** | 50 x 70 cm

Figure 5.15 | Courtesy of People for the Ethical Treatment of Animals (PETA) | Photo © Bryan Adams

CASE STUDY

Somos de Maíz by Natalia Delgado

I created this poster for a competition about the importance of native corn and the dangers of transgenics in Mexico. I find it very useful and enriching to do as much research as possible to learn about all the aspects of the topic I need to address. The information focused on two critical sides of the issue: the dangers of transgenics and their impact on health, economy, and environment, and the significance of native corn as part of the Mexican diet and identity.

The brief provided a pdf document titled "El Maíz en México en 15 píldoras (Corn in Mexico in 15 pills)," which outlined many essential aspects of the topic. A part of the text (roughly translated here) stood out for me:

> We are made of corn, as corn is our main food. Thanks to the corn we walk, we play, we run, we laugh. Since it is what we eat and it gives us strength, it is said that we are men and women of corn. For our ancestors it was a god, and today we honor him when we bless the seeds, when we sow the cornfield, and when we reap the first ripe corn cob.[26]

This became the inspiration for my design. I loved the feeling of pride and belonging this communicated, and I felt this would create an immediate connection with the audience and therefore make it more persuasive.

I focused on the concept of "Somos de Maíz" (we are made of corn) for brainstorming and imagined different ways to show this connection between grain and human. My first sketches used grains of corn dressed up as people (which actually ended up becoming another poster), but they lacked the attention-grabbing impact I desired.

So I continued sketching and realized that I could use hands as a material and conceptual synecdoche of "us." I bought a couple of cobs from the market and started doing tests. My hands were too small compared to the cob, so I asked my brother, who has big rough hands, to model for me. I painted his hands green to resemble the husks, and we played around with different placements holding the cob. The position acts as a metaphor for the protection humans can provide against the threat of transgenics.

The final design shows the corn with the text that inspired the concept. The A from "maíz" is missing, hiding behind the corn and implied by its shape. The smaller copy reads, "*El alimento básico de México*" (Mexico's basic food), referencing its daily use as part of the Mexican diet. Because the poster was for a competition, I didn't add any additional text. If it were to be used out of this context, I would probably include a small paragraph as an anchor to ground the message for the audience.

Somos de Maíz | **Design**: Natalia Delgado Avila | © Natalia Delgado Avila | **Mexico** | 70 x 100 cm

GALLERY

Immigrant Wall | © Coco Cerella 2016 | **Argentina** | 70 x 100 cm

Cerella applies metonymy to represent migrants by their passports. The mortar, texture, and lighting act as a synecdoche to create the illusion of a brick wall, which is a metaphor for the ban.

Opposite: Metaphor and metonymy can be used in different ways to strengthen your message. Batory's face-painted actor represents the theater. Valenzuela's vulture, a bird of prey, represents the male sexual organ in the context of sexual harassment. Tello's frayed fabric acts as a metaphor for the loss of memory caused by Alzheimer's, Hemmat's nest with different-colored eggs represents different races sharing the same home, and Hemmat's solution of a bird's nest and eggs of all colors and sizes poetically reminds us that people of different nationalities can make the world more beautiful and colorful by coming together.

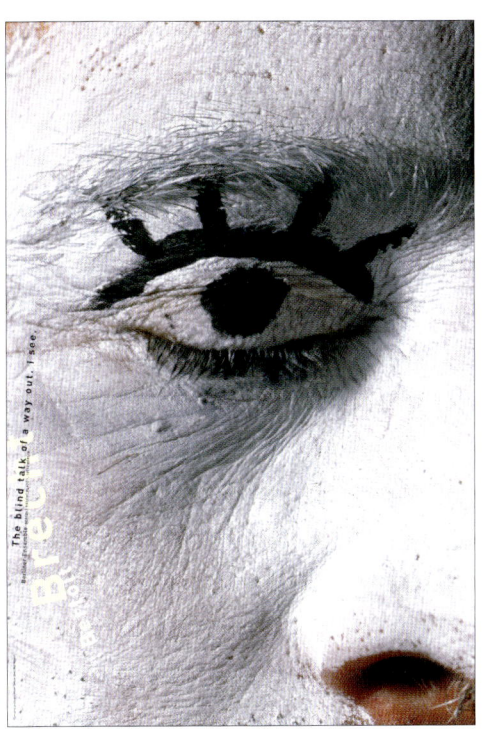

BRECHT | **Designer**: Michal Batory | © Michal Batory | **France** | 70 x 100 cm

No + Acoso Sexual 2016 | **Illustration:** Ivette Valenzuela | © Ivette Valenzuela | **Mexico** | 60 x 90 cm

Alzheimer | **Design:** Claudia Tello | © Claudia Tello | **Mexico** | 60 x 90 cm

Freedom of Movement | **Design**: Elham Hemmat | © Elham Hemmat | **Iran** | 70 x 100 cm

Design Dogs and Depositions | **Design:** Kelly Holohan | © Holohan Design | **USA** | 17.4 x 30.5 cm

Poster Passion | **Design/Illustration:** Sergio Olivotti | © Sergio Olivotti | **Italy** | 70 x 100 cm

Plastic Soldiers Seamline | **Design:** Yossi Lemel | © Yossi Lemel | **Israel** | 120 x 180 cm

Whether it is violence or sex, arousal creates an exhilarating feeling that increases our attention. **Clockwise:** Holohan takes a humorous approach for a lecture by Modern Dog Design at the Tyler School of Art, where the dog/bird chimera acts as a metaphor for the topic of the lecture, including the studio's copyright lawsuit. Olivotti connects it with his passion for making posters, and Lemel's use of arousal addresses the topic of war.

Mermaid Tears | **Designers**: Joe Scorscone and Alice Drueding | © Joe Scorscone and Alice Drueding | **USA** | 61 x 91.4 cm

Rusted Tears | **Design**: Wesam Mazhar Haddad | © Wesam Mazhar Haddad | **USA** | 70 x 100 cm

No H2O | **Design**: Christopher Scott | © Christopher Scott | **Ireland** | 70 x 100 cm

Sometimes, sadness is the best way to address a catastrophic situation. The three featured posters address the topic of water scarcity with a sorrowful view. **Clockwise:** Replacing the body of a mermaid with a waste pipe, Scorsone and Drueding inform us that humans are directly responsible for poisoning our oceans and ultimately ourselves. Mazhar Haddad exposes the ugly truth behind the global waste of drinkable water, and Scott delivers his message using dead fish, emphasizing the lethal repercussions of climate change.

Wright designed this poster to celebrate the 100th anniversary of the birth of Polish writer Witold Gombrowicz. Wright explains, "Many of his writings deal with the idea of immaturity, were filled with sexual innuendo, and had anti-nationalist overtones. The colors of the poster represent the colors of the flag of Poland, and the eagle, from Poland's coat of arms, represents the anti-nationalist overtones. As a metaphor for futility, the eagle is unable to escape even though the cage is open. I also use the cage and eagle in a bit of a subversive dirty joke."

Opposite: Humorous characters help designers to communicate their messages, ranging from newspaper donations to the Day of the Dead, Charlie Chaplin, and a vaudeville-style performance.

Rok Gombrowicza | **Design/Illustration**: Erin Wright | © Erin Wright | **USA** | 70 x 100 cm

Bring Waste Papers—Help Your School | **Design:** Piotr Kunce | © Piotr Kunce | **Poland** | 70 x 100 cm

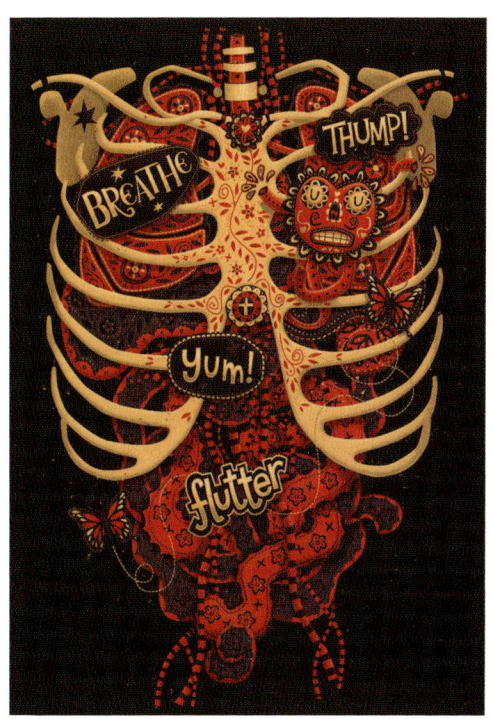

Day of the Dead Anatomical Study | **Design:** Steve Simpson | © Steve Simpson | **Ireland** | 40.6 x 50.8 cm

Chaplin 120 | **Design:** © Manuel López Rocha, 2008 | © Manuel López Rocha | **Mexico** | 60 x 90 cm

Room 17B | **Design/Illustration:** David Plunkert | © 2020 David Plunkert | **USA** | 35.6 x 58.4 cm

Desertification of a Tree | **Design:** Wesam Mazhar Haddad | © Wesam Mazhar Haddad | **USA** | 70 x 100 cm

Access | **Design:** David Jiménez | © David Jiménez | **Ecuador** | 70 x 100 cm

We're Not All Well-Born in the Maze | **Design:** Eva May Chan | © Eva May Chan | **France** | 85 x 115 cm

An ironic view of unemployment shows a typical text encouraging job seekers to apply for a job under a hammer, a metonymy of work, that has been perforated with nails all along its handle, making it impossible to grab.

Opposite: Hyperbole can be used to magnify the possible consequences of the effects of a problem, allowing the audience to understand its importance. Mazar Haddad portrays a tree stump as a desert, while Jiménez and Chan show the desperation and chaos of healthcare inequality by exaggerating the difficulty of access.

Now Hiring! | **Design**: Gus Morainslie | © Gus Morainslie | **Mexico** | 50 x 70 cm

MAKING POSTERS FROM CONCEPT TO DESIGN

Using diseased skin and hair as a synecdoche, Serve Marketing Inc.'s delightfully disgusting campaign *Nothing Punny* masterfully persuades the viewer to use protection to avoid catching an STD.

Opposite: Feng employs metonymy for his series *A Bite of China* by combining Chinese characters with elements of traditional cuisine to illustrate the unique flavors from diverse regions of the country.

Nothing Punny Campaign | Ignorance Is Blisters, What's the Warts That Could Happen, His and Herpes | © 2019 Serve Marketing Inc., All rights reserved | **USA** | 320 x 693.4 cm

CHAPTER FIVE ART OF PERSUASION

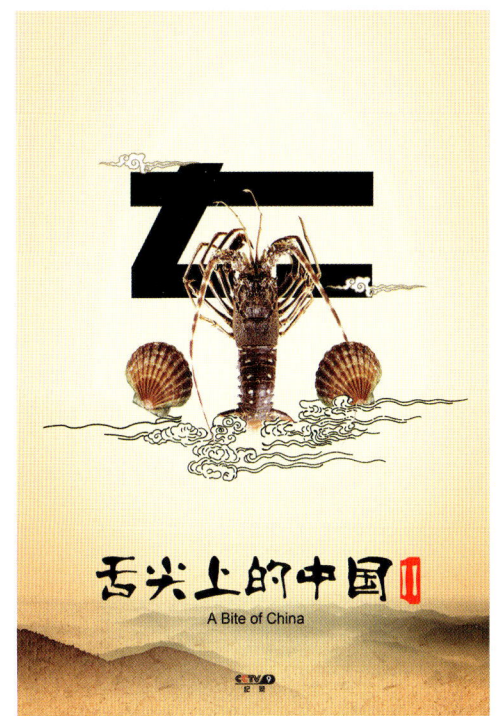

A Bite of China | **Design**: Sha Feng | © Sha Feng | **China** | 70 x 100 cm

CHAPTER SIX STORYTELLING

"Once upon a time" and "long, long ago, in a faraway land," inevitably stir up bedtime story memories. According to the Oxford English Dictionary, the phrase "once upon a time" has been the go-to standard since the 1380s.[27] It has been translated into over ninety languages and is known throughout the world. When we hear this classic introduction, we are instantly transported back to our childhood and await a fascinating tale. Stories have always been integral to human culture. A good storyteller captures imaginations by weaving a rich tapestry of pictures and words that pass wisdom from one generation to the next, help craft culture, and make sense of the world in which we live.

STORYTELLING

(above and facing page) Illustrations by Jess Lin

From an early age, we are told bedtime stories, fairy tales, and fables. Although they entertained and even scared us at times, they were shared mainly to condition and teach lessons—"the moral of the story." These micro adventures have a linear structure: a beginning, a middle, and an end. Their storyline offers information about events, settings, and characters. Before written language, images functioned to record knowledge using a narrative. Throughout history, narrative art has performed a vital role in different cultures, capturing a snapshot in time or depicting facts, hopes, and dreams. According to director George Lucas, "Narrative is one of the oldest and most important impulses in art. It is also the most popular form of art. Tracing the arc of narrative art reveals how culture is created, reinforced, and then compelled to evolve."[28] Early evidence of storytelling dates back to the Upper Paleolithic Age of humankind as our first documented means of communication. Through narrative art, we get a glimpse of how our ancestors shared stories about their lives and their relationship with the world (Figure 6.1).

Initially, narratives were arranged in an unorganized, unstructured manner. This then developed into the use of lines of text and later to a sequence of pages in books, ultimately leading to the linking of images to tell stories in the way that we are familiar with today. Images have played an essential role in our culture and have become more pervasive. Because our brains process visuals much faster than text, we comprehend more information when it is presented as a narrative. Visual storytelling simplifies complex ideas and gives them form.

The characters are what first captivate the audience and introduce the plot. The plot creates the structure, direction, and conflict, which should start a dialogue that requires engagement and thought. The story then builds toward the point of greatest interest, where the most significant elements of the narrative are revealed—this is called the rising action. It is at this point that the story starts to conclude as the conflict is resolved. This ultimately leads to dénouement, the end of the narrative where all the components of the story are pieced together for a final resolution. Many times, a story is direct and focused and finishes predictably. Other times, a story can take dramatic leaps, rise to a crescendo, or fall off into silence. In much the same way, a poster can tell a story. This can be accomplished with a strong concept and simple imagery or by layering information for a more profound and fuller experience.

Figure 6.1 | *Three Horse Riders with Swords, a Scorpion and a Leopard in Shelter Nº 8 at Bhimbetka Caves* | **Photography:** Anders Blomqvist | © Anders Blomqvist/Getty | **Contributor:** Frédéric Soltan

Creating Your Visuals

There are two types of imagery: denotative and connotative. Denotative imagery consists of straightforward representations of objects and things. By themselves, they offer little additional meaning other than what they represent. A connotative image has multiple layers of information beyond what the image itself may initially convey. Before written language, humans made images to communicate, to record, and to tell stories using denotative imagery. Today, these types of images are still commonly used; for example, the iconography on smartphones is denotative (Figure 6.2). The camera icon stands for nothing more than a camera. Although at times these graphics may be executed with a bit of flair, in the end, they are just cameras.

Figure 6.2 | Typical camera graphics for handheld devices

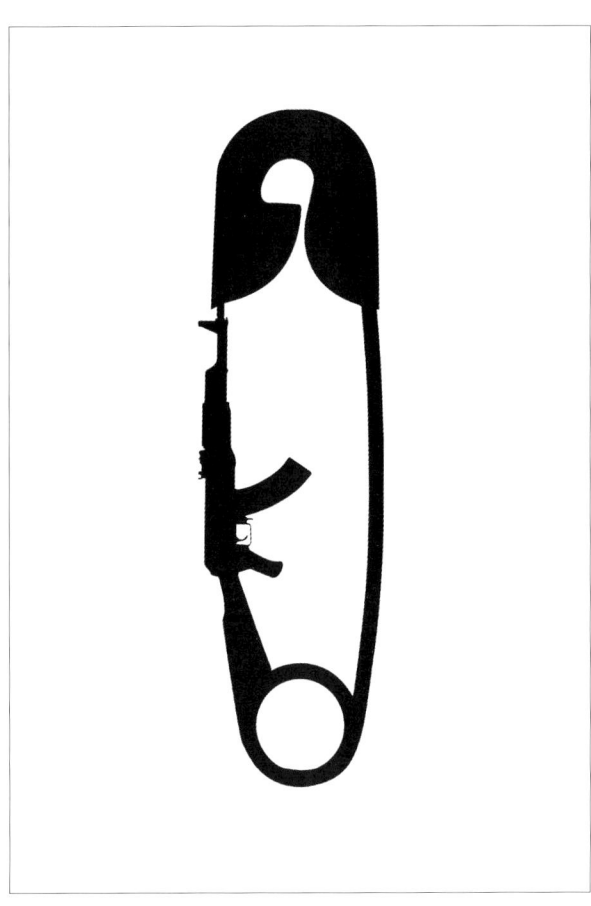

Figure 6.3 | *Safety against Violence* | **Design**: Christopher Scott | © Christopher Scott | **Ecuador** | 50 x 70 cm

This, however, does not mean that denotative imagery cannot communicate beyond what it alone represents. In the hands of a talented poster designer, denotative images can be manipulated to carry a narrative. As seen in Figure 6.3, Christopher Scott makes good use of our connection with familiar images by subtly altering a safety pin to build visual impact. In his poster *Safety against Violence*, an easily recognizable denotative image of a safety pin allows Scott to exploit and alter the object, quickly turning it into a connotative image while still maintaining its core meaning of "safety." His image is so identifiable that no typography is needed to support his point. The simplicity of his image creates more than just a powerful poster. It is symbolic and has become a logo for his cause of safety against violence.

Having a deeper meaning than denotative images, connotative images offer broader perspectives that help your story by building more profound connections. Connotative images are usually made up of many visuals that work together to form one strong message or multiple narratives within a single poster. Stephan Bundi's poster *Terror* (Figure 6.4) also uses a denotative image of a safety pin. Placing the safety pin over two concentric circles and a series of twelve equally spaced lines gives context and displays the image of a clock. This connotative image of a clock warns of impending doom as time runs out and we are no longer "safe." Bundi anchors his poster with bold, black typography that does not interfere with the rest of the composition.

MAKING POSTERS FROM CONCEPT TO DESIGN

170

Figure 6.4 | *Terror* | **Design:** Stephan Bundi | © Stephan Bundi | **Switzerland** | 70 x 100 cm

Structuring Your Story

Before you begin, ask yourself:

- What is my story about?
- Who am I telling it to?
- How will I attract my viewer?

There are many ways to structure the same story by using different narratives. Rearranging the order of events can change the manner in which a story is told, but it should never alter the underlying message. Exploring alternate storytelling approaches will lead you to discover the most reliable solution. Just as a spoken narrative has flow and direction, so does a poster. By applying visual hierarchy, you can direct the viewer to read your poster as intended. When you are crafting your narrative, it is important to remember not to allow an artistic style to dictate the story. Choose a technique that helps support the narrative rather than one that competes with it.

Scorsone and Drueding's poster *Beware* (Figure 6.5) is thought-provoking and an excellent example of how a visual metaphor can be used to tell a story—in this case, a wolf in sheep's clothing. Scorsone and Drueding's choice of metaphor is perfect and plays on our past experiences. The clergy appear kind, caring, and trustworthy (the sheep in their story), when in reality, sometimes the lure of safety and comfort is exploited for the most diabolical of acts: sexual abuse (becoming the wolf in their story).

Scorsone and Drueding's poster uses sharp contrast, a strong graphic, and spot color to grab attention. Making excellent use of positive and negative space, the image comes alive at the wolf's neck, which connects to the body like a Lego snapping into the priest's collar. Its evil grin directs our focus to its transformation as it starts to expose its true self, a wolf in sheep's clothing. The image furthers its insidious intentions with the addition of spot color to the eye and the slithering tongue. Its nose is arrogantly pointing up in the air, directing your gaze to the typography. The display typeface, Ironwood, has pointed ends that reflect the wolf's razor-sharp teeth and support the medieval theme, furthering the narrative of the barbaric behavior of pedophilic clergy. BEWARE is easily understood and quickly connects with its audience, creating an immediate dialogue.

Figure 6.5 | *BEWARE* | **Design**: Joe Scorsone and Alice Drueding | © Joe Scorsone and Alice Drueding | **USA** | 61 x 91.4 cm

Nostalgia and Reminiscence

When used in conjunction with typography and graphics, color can further deepen the narrative. It can instill happiness and joy, cause tension, or make something feel old and nostalgic. For example, a decade can be symbolized by a specific color palette representing that moment in time, from the deep hues of the 1920s and the pastel tones of the 1950s to the electric and vibrant colors of the 1980s.

MAKING POSTERS FROM CONCEPT TO DESIGN

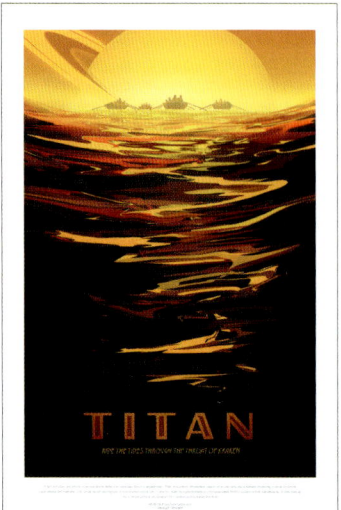
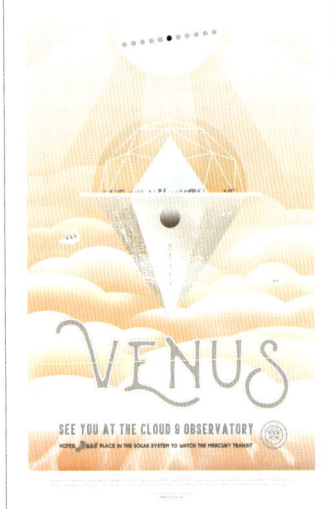

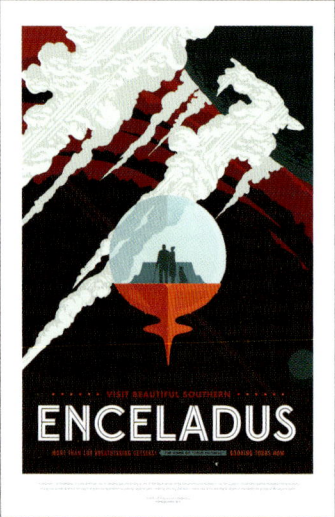

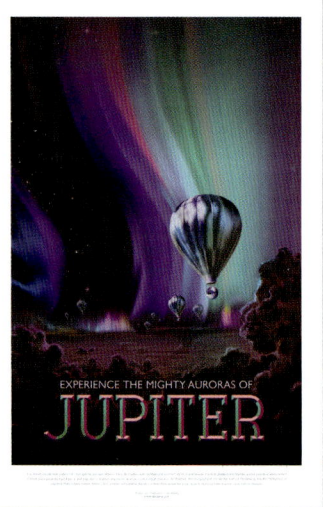

Figure 6.6 | Visions of the Future | **The Studio** Creative Strategy: Dan Goods, David Delgado | **Illustrators**: Liz Barrios De La Torre (Ceres, Europa), Stefan Bucher (Jupiter Design), Invisible Creature (Grand Tour, Mars, Enceladus), Joby Harris (Kepler 16b, Earth, Kepler 186f, PSO J318.5-22, Titan), Jessie Kawata (Venus), Lois Kim (Typography for Venus and Europa), Ron Miller (Jupiter Illustration) | Courtesy NASA/JPL-Caltech | **USA** | Various sizes

The NASA Jet Propulsion Laboratory's set of *Visions of the Future* travel posters (Figure 6.6) uses nostalgic color palettes and typography to tell stories of faraway planets and moons. Each poster is unique and utilizes color in a retro or retro-futuristic aesthetic. Each color palette recalls a period in time and is used in a very sophisticated manner so as not to cross the line from retro to dated. Notice how the color in the posters focuses the eye on the introduction of the story. In *Enceladus*, your attention is directed to the red platform of the flying bubble, offering a glimpse of what life would be like on the moon Enceladus. A cool color palette plunges you deep into the icy waters of Europa, where you can safely view its wonders through a portal, whereas in *Kepler-186f*, yellows and reds portray a hot and desolate planet. The *Venus* poster's pastel color palette is soft and comforting, inviting you to float among the clouds and offering a sense of relaxation.

Along with the intense use of color to set a mood in individual posters, the NASA poster series continues its narrative across fourteen retro-futuristic utopian societies. Depicting the planets in this fashion sends a clear message of exciting and exotic new worlds as possibilities for humanity as we continue to explore the universe. In each case, these imaginary travel locations speak to different personality types. If you are a thrill seeker, travel to HD 40307g Super Earth, or if you are searching for a more romantic getaway, Jupiter or PSO J318.5-22 may be more to your liking. All these posters are beautifully designed with careful consideration of typography and color that results in a successful setting of the mood. When seen together, they compose an almost breathtaking, surreal event, as they rise to a crescendo and captivate completely. NASA's travel poster series makes you wonder about the future and wish you could be alive to witness it.

Telling Your Story with Type

Typography can communicate by both what it says and how it says it. This is usually done with simple and bold typography that makes itself important. It is huckstering and calling to you, demanding your attention. Since the typography is also part of the visual, it is important that it has a strong aesthetic. There are many ways to achieve this, starting with the appropriate typeface. Choosing wisely is half the battle; the font itself can provide a lot of information. For example, an organic playful typeface introduces your story as fun and unassuming, while layers of typography can create depth, texture, and form.

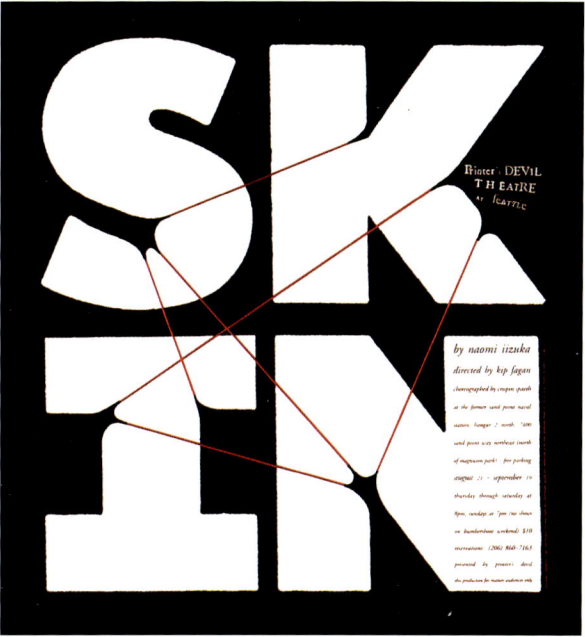

Figure 6.7 | *SKIN* | **Design**: Art Chantry | © Art Chantry | **USA** | 50.8 x 50.8 cm

Art Chantry's theater poster *SKIN* (Figure 6.7) immediately grabs your attention with its large, unsettling, and bound typography. A tormented and fractured relationship is woven together by a taut string of bondage and sexual tension. Chantry cleverly sees opportunity to stack a single word to help communicate separation, perhaps between the two main characters of the play. It also allows him to make use of scale to stun his audience. He pulls and tugs at the red string, creating a fleshy, soft feeling in the typography. He is so successful that the typography itself becomes skin and a clear metaphor for emotional agony. It is disturbing and beautiful at the same time, allowing a peek into the play.

Chantry creates typography that's both sturdy and frail, possibly alluding to typical male and female archetypes. The addition of the red string and the way it is used form a powerful and destructive bond that could possibly represent the tension between the play's anti-hero and anti-heroine. Chantry magically creates this painful yet poetic beauty and rhythm within the structures of the typography and the red string. His gutsy, weathered, rough, and textured typography and strong use of black and white help set a mood of an aggressive urban society, where this play takes place.

MAKING POSTERS FROM CONCEPT TO DESIGN

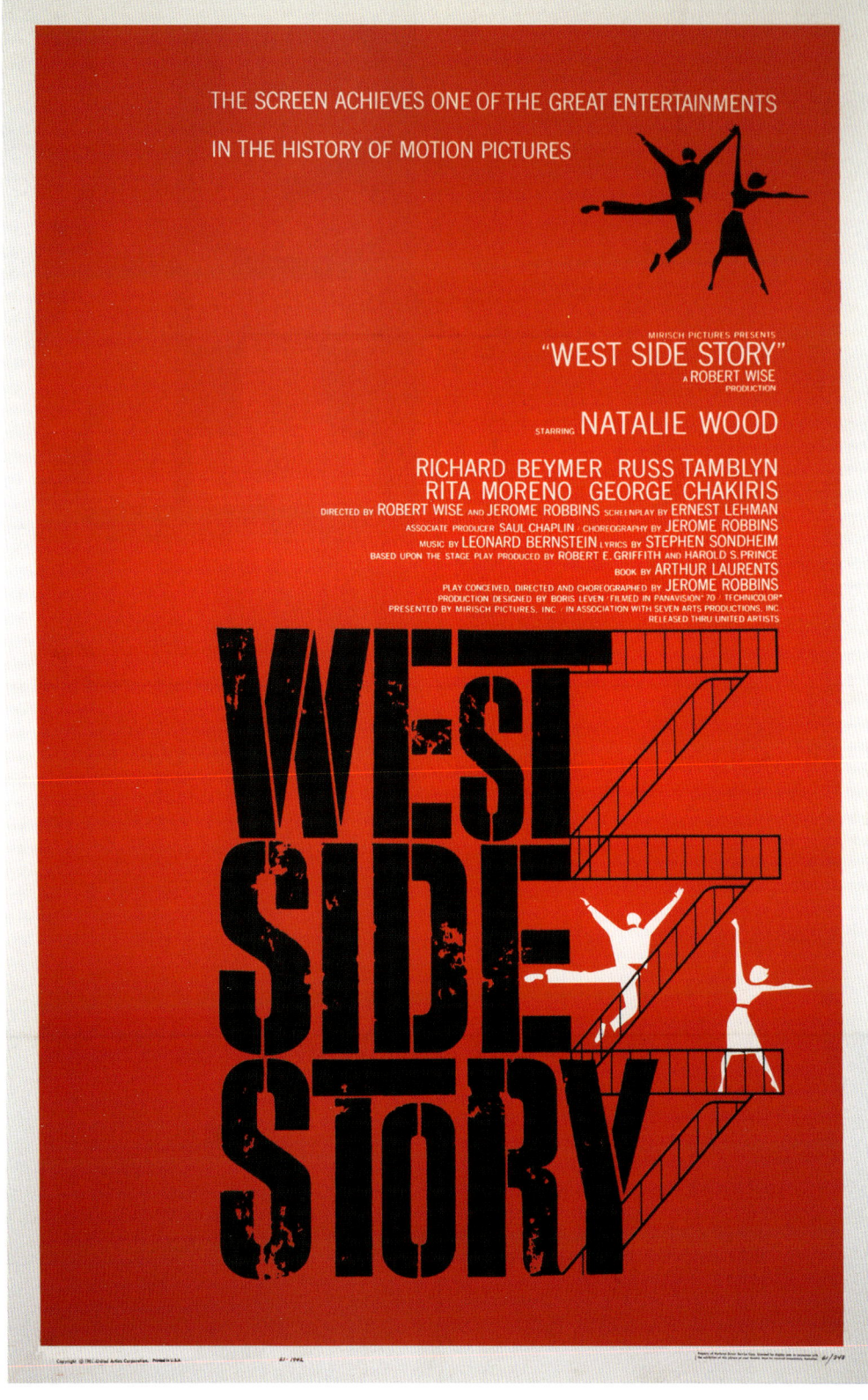

Figure 6.8 | Film poster for *West Side Story*, directed by Jerome Robbins and Robert Wise (1961) | © ™ UNITED ARTISTS | **Designer**: Joseph Caroff | **Photography**: Movie Poster Image Art/Getty Images | **USA** | 68.6 x 104.1 cm

Multiple Narratives

Sometimes stories are told using layers of information balanced throughout the composition. A series of shorter stories embedded into the foundation of the main story offers the storyteller additional ways to tell the same story. Multiple narratives often add more interest and can command greater attention. In literature, multiple narratives use devices such as alternating narrators, telling a story within a story, or bringing together multiple story arcs to enhance the theme, create a stronger story, or deepen characterization. Multiple narratives are also commonly used in fine art and photography, where images are presented in diptychs or triptychs. By presenting different images or variations on the same topic as a cohesive collection, you can strengthen your message and present a grander tale.

One of the ways to create a multiple narrative is to tell a story from different perspectives. A way to accomplish this is to have multiple narrators telling fragments of the same story; another common strategy is to show a single incident from the perspective of different narrators, points of view, or even points in time. A multiple narrative can also include multiple storylines that intersect through some evident connection, such as a similar theme or shared characters. Multiple narratives challenge the more traditional linear approach of poster design and bend the rules by telling a story from any point within the composition and still leading to the same conclusion. Telling the story from alternative points of view allows the individual to participate in the story differently each time and even perhaps have a different experience than someone else. This type of narrative is particularly useful when trying to depict movement or change, especially time related. Multi-narrative posters can be used successfully regardless of topic or type. They have a rich history and have appeared in everything from advertising to safety to theater posters.

We can see an example of layered storytelling by looking at the work of master designer Joseph Caroff (Figure 6.8), who is well known for his involvement in the film industry as the designer of the James Bond 007 logo. Caroff's *West Side Story* movie poster relies on typography as an integral part of the narrative. He creates structure and mass by using a strong, bold typeface. Then, by contrasting it with a thin line, he creates a building with a fire escape. He continues to manipulate typography by extending the bar of both T letterforms and reducing the point size of the letterforms below, giving the illusion of a doorway or window. The weathered typeface implies that this story takes place in a blue-collar, metropolitan neighborhood. Caroff continues his narrative by adding simple silhouettes of a young couple dancing on the fire escape. Knocking out the dancers to white is a smart choice. Not only is the contrast engaging, but it also draws attention and foreshadows what is to come. The bottom of the composition is the only logical placement for the typography; otherwise, it would be difficult for it to read as a building or structure. This is where the story's action rises. The strong typographic foundation allows our eyes to rise up toward secondary typography with valuable information about the movie. There we discover a shorter story within the overall narrative. Dancing atop the subheader is the same couple from below, only this time they are no longer reversed out to white. However, by using the same graphics, he also informs us that they are the same in almost every way other than ethnicity. Using duplicate graphics helps us believe they are of the same age with the same passions, same dreams, and same desires. In a relatively short time, Caroff quickly engages us and introduces some of the main characters, as we initially notice the two performers dancing on the fire escape next to the bold typography. He then creates conflict by inserting the additional two actors at the top of the poster, which leads to the conclusion.

Narratives across a Poster Series

Individual posters in a series can have different aesthetics and yet still tell the same story. Changing the visual but staying on script will reinvigorate the initial feeling someone gets when they see something for the first time. Reinforcing an idea through a series of posters creates a memorable experience and is an ideal way to influence a viewpoint and change minds. It is important to note the difference between a sequence and a series of images. The former refers to a group of images taken in succession, such as stop-motion animation, while the latter implies a group of images with similar composition or related content.

Figures 6.9 and 6.10 | *Bring in 'Da Noise, Bring in 'Da Funk* | Courtesy of Pentagram Design | USA | Various sizes

Paula Scher's *Bring in 'Da Noise, Bring in 'Da Funk* poster series (Figures 6.9 and 6.10) tells a similar story with two different visual approaches to the same narrative. They were both created the same year, and both use typography as an energetic element to convey movement but in different ways. In Figure 6.9, Scher's use of hand-done typography radiating out of the high-contrast photograph of the sole of a tap shoe communicates the impactful story of *Bring in 'da Noise, Bring in 'da Funk*—a musical performance told through tap dance set to hip-hop and funk rhythms. Figure 6.10 takes a more playful approach to Scher's narrative by showing the joy and dynamism of the performer. The sharp, contrasting angles of the blocks of set typography along with the leaping dancer create a beautifully awkward composition that breaks the norms of a conventional gridded layout, perhaps suggesting that the show, like the poster, is different and unexpected. Both posters publicize a high-energy event and communicate the stunning, electric, and explosive experience the audience will encounter at this theatrical event. How will you tell your next story?

The End

CASE STUDY

Storytelling by Joe Scorsone and Alice Drueding

A poster is a compact piece of visual theater, a compressed narrative designed to expand and resonate in the viewer's mind. The more powerful the experience, the longer it will linger in memory and influence the viewer's perspective. Whether framed as comedy or tragedy, the expressive power of dramatic storytelling plays a decisive role in a poster's impact.

The purpose of most of our posters is to raise or renew awareness of sociopolitical and environmental issues and ultimately to provoke a reaction. Whether seen in public or private spaces or on the internet, they are designed to grab your attention long enough to plant a message before you move on. The message you take away may inspire various responses that include seeking additional information, changing personal habits, voting, working for a cause, donating to an organization, or spreading the word to others.

While most of the subjects we address in our work are serious, humor can be an effective messenger. Comedy's exposure of human weakness is tempered by laughter and the possibility of positive outcomes. Its belief that the viewer is smart enough to get the joke is inviting and inclusive. The experience of recognition and pleasure when a juicy little bomb of wit explodes in the mind leaves a persistent afterglow and the greater likelihood that the viewer may retain and heed the message.

In the poster *Use Your Head*, the target audience is young people, primarily young men who are likely to filter out yet another ominous message about the dangers of unprotected sex despite their awareness of the potential consequences. We poke fun at them by visualizing the verbal metaphor of men "thinking" with their penises, in other words, not thinking at all. The playful style of the bold, hand-drawn image captures the spontaneity of a sexual encounter, while the double meaning of "use your head" drives home the joke without overstating it. Unexpected humor disarms the viewer, making him—or her—more receptive to the message about "smart" sex.

In sharp contrast to the humorous approach in *Use Your Head*, *Fistula* tells a deeply tragic story that is unfamiliar to most viewers. In the developing world, a fistula is an injury that results in a million or more women and girls being ostracized and left to fend for themselves on the periphery of family and community. The visual narrative for this complex subject refers to the devastating physical, psychological, and

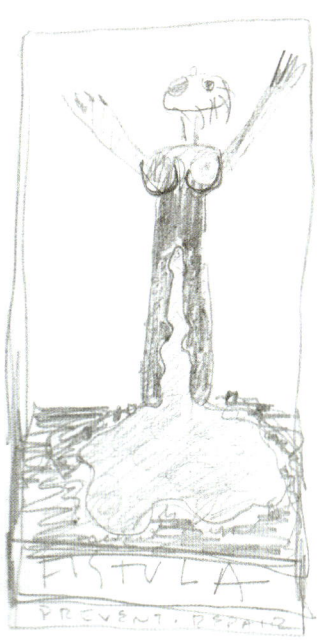

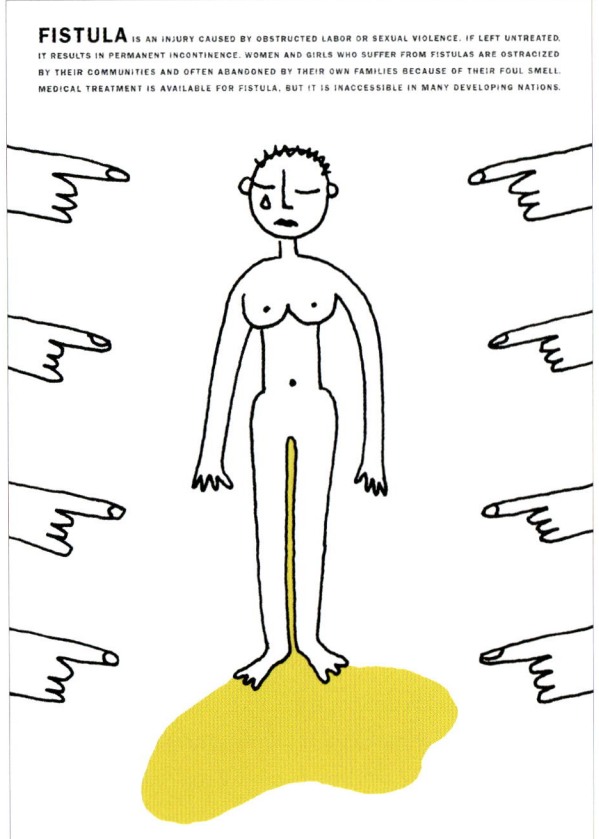
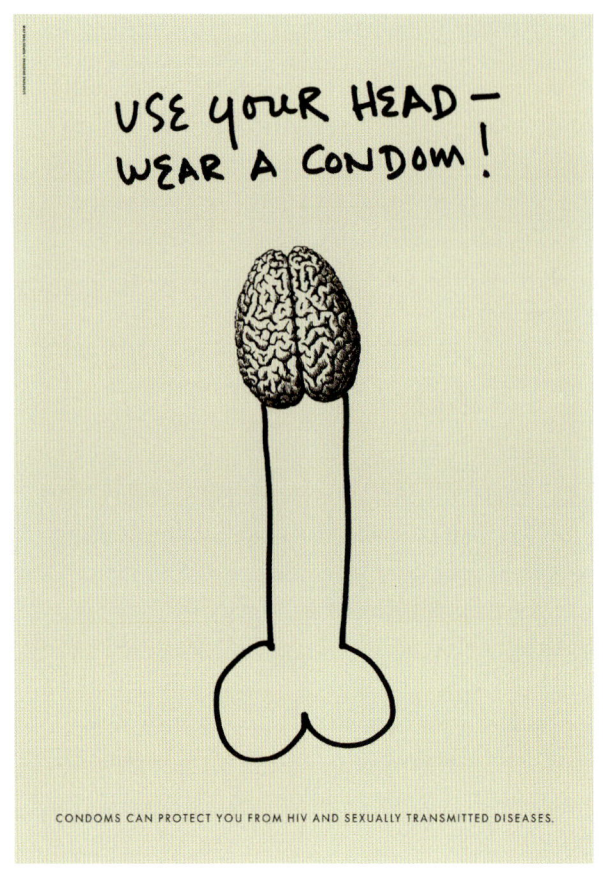

Use Your Head and *Fistula* | **Design**: Joe Scorsone and Alice Drueding | © Joe Scorsone and Alice Drueding | **USA** | 61 x 91.4 cm

social consequences of a medical condition that is brought on by sexual violence or obstructed childbirth. The poster's candor and empathy, along with a powerful degree of discomfort, are intended to inform and resonate in the viewer.

The image is a painfully intimate icon of suffering. With intended irony, the female figure with a downturned gaze is centrally placed in the composition and is anchored in gold while illuminated by radiating shapes, all to echo the images of the glorious virgins of Western art. Innocence and humanity are conveyed through the simplicity of the drawing. The viewer's eye is inevitably drawn to the only shape and color on the page—the yellow stain that depicts the perpetual state of incontinence caused by a fistula. The impulse to look away is thwarted by the pointing hands that isolate and accentuate the figure. The immediate visual impact is reinforced by textual information that elicits both outrage and hope: though access to medical care for this treatable injury is currently limited, the problem has a solution.

The conceptual approaches to *Use Your Head* and *Fistula* are driven by serious subject matter. In an effort to create a lingering emotional and intellectual effect, the respective power of comedy and tragedy tailors each of these visual narratives to their intended audience and specific message. Whatever the method, the goal is to reach into the viewer's mind in the most effective way possible and never let go.

GALLERY

Fiddler on the Roof | **Illustration:** Ryszard Kaja | © Ryszard Kaja | **Poland** | 99 x 69 cm

Posters for the stage and theater offer some of the greatest opportunities to craft a narrative, as they come with a story already built in. Kaja's poster is an enchanting image of an exaggeratedly tall fiddler . . . on the roof. The fiddler is a metaphor representing the families living in a small village below. By poising an oversized figure on the tip of a rooftop, Kaja creates tension that reinforces the show's underlying theme of balancing tradition with trying to survive a life of uncertainty.

West Side Story | **Design/Illustration**: István Orosz | © István Orosz | **Hungary** | 70 x 100 cm

Gardi Hutter | **Design**: Stephan Bundi | **Client**: Theater Orchester Biel Solothurn | © by Stephan Bundi | **Germany** | 89.5 x 128 cm

Tales from the Vienna Woods | **Design/Illustration**: Natasha Shendrik | © Natasha Shendrik | **Russia** | 67 x 97 cm

Clockwise: Orosz's interpretation of Bernstein's musical illustrates a modern version of *Romeo and Juliet*, the story of a fatal love bond between children of two hostile families. The architectural environment communicates openness and closeness at the same time and hints at the tragedy to come.

Shendrik's color palette and use of monochromatic imagery creates a solemn mood to tell the story of an innocent young girl caught up in love and heartbreak in a dark comedy about the lower middle class during the rise of Nazism in the 1930s. The play's title and alternating pattern doom the young girl to face her fate.

With a snip and a stitch, Bundi sews together the story of *Gardi Hutter: The Tailor*, a joyous solo performance of physical comedy and mime.

CHAPTER SIX STORYTELLING

Emigrate or Die | **Design**: Matthew Bouloutian | © Matthew Bouloutian | **USA** | 70 x 100 cm

The Pianist | **Design**: Nina Ninkovic 2016 | © Nina Ninkovic | **Bosnia** | 70 x 100 cm

Clockwise: Black and red dominate the composition with an explosion of action, forcing your eye directly to the violence and aftermath of the Armenian genocide (1915–1923). But it is the scale that tells the story, as the gigantic figure stomps out the life of the tiny, feeble, and innocent in a horrific bloodbath.

Ninkovic's high-contrast, black and white image of a birdcage is a metaphor visualizing her interpretation of *The Pianist*. The birdcage, representing Nazi control, and piano keys work perfectly together to help tell the story of a Polish-Jewish pianist playing live on the radio during the Nazi invasion of Poland and his escape to freedom.

Freeman and Steben present a raw image of a homemade tattoo being inscribed onto a fist, giving us a peek into white nationalist subculture, for their movie poster.

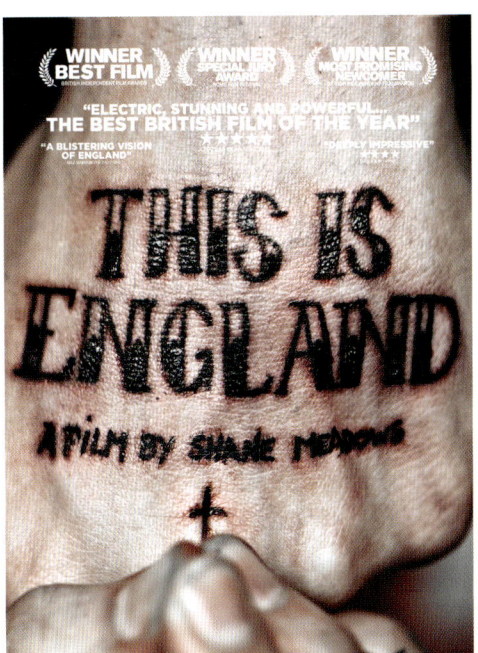

This Is England | **Design**: Sean Freeman & Eve Steben, THERE IS Studio | © Sean Freeman & Eve Steben | **United Kingdom** | 45.7 x 68.6 cm

MAKING POSTERS FROM CONCEPT TO DESIGN

With the right image and the proper execution, telling stories with pictures can take viewers into other worlds and magical places where they can be frightened or charmed.

Eyolf (*Something in Me Is Gnawing at Me*) is a vision of heartbreak. It is a fraying representation of a nine-year-old boy, who is fascinated by a strange and symbolic woman with rats. Colrat's narrative of an empty, deteriorating red hooded sweater is emblematic of Eyolf's fascination with the woman and his mysterious death—his body was never found.

Eyolf (Something in Me Is Gnawing at Me) | **Design**: Pascal Colrat | © Pascal Colrat | **France** | 120 x 176 cm

CHAPTER SIX STORYTELLING

I've Been Compromised | **Design**: Mark Sposato | © Mark Sposato 2019 | **Client:** Houndstooth Studios | **USA** | 33 x 49.5 cm

Clockwise: "Our protagonist struggles with a fractured psyche, so I chose to cut up an image of our haunting opening shot in a way that's reminiscent of a document sent through a paper shredder. This treatment set the right mood for a retro-inspired spy thriller. I decided to fracture or 'compromise' the title treatment as well for a more cohesive look and maximum visual impact."—Mark Sposato

Materials, a deep color palette, and a Turkish-inspired illustration style become part of the narrative to help tell the tale of a harem ruled by a cruel sultan and his fate at the hands of the scorned women. A new take on a film classic can let an artist like Staniszewski apply his unique style to construct an unexpected vision of the movie *The Shining*.

Pardekhane | **Design**: Elham Hemmat | © Elham Hemmat | **Client**: Shima Asadi | **Iran** | 70 x 100 cm

183

The Shining | **Design**: Jacx Staniszewski | © Jacx Staniszewski | **Poland** | 70 x 100 cm

Aldriglandet (Neverland) | **Design/Illustration**: Gitte Kath | © Gitte Kath | **Client**: Teatret Moellen | **Denmark** | 60 x 85 cm

Visual stories can also be told using classic themes of storytelling like tragedy and drama.

The journey to Kath's *Aldriglandet (Neverland)* begins in a dusty and magical world of adventure and discovery. With a blend of romance, Kath's poster is a snippet in time; we catch the arrival of Peter Pan, who is darting from window to window, perhaps in search of his shadow. The layering of texture and newsprint caps reflect the new universe this story takes place in. This is not the brightly colored and joyful interpretation we have been accustomed to seeing. Instead, this version is a raw, real, and grayer tale.

CHAPTER SIX STORYTELLING

Documentary | **Design/Illustration:** Mohammad Afshar | **Photography:** Sadri Karamzadeh | © Mohammad Afshar and Sadri Karamzadeh | **Iran** | 70 x 100 cm

Cradle of Tortured Peace | **Design**: Wesam Mazhar Haddad | © Wesam Mazhar Haddad | **USA** | 70 x 100 cm

185

Túlsúly | **Design:** Kristóf Szabó | © Kristóf Szabó | **Hungary** | 70.7 x 100 cm

Clockwise: Afshar's poster *Documentary* tells the story of a person whose imagination and thoughts are exposed to others who pirate them. Haddad's poster is a painful reminder of Aylan Kurd, the three-year-old Syrian boy who was found dead on the beach. His image becomes a story representing the more than 12,000 children who have reportedly been killed as a result of the Syrian civil war. Szabó's poster about the ongoing war in Donbas, Ukraine, is a simple but poignant narrative. The central figure is under siege by the Russian army. The silhouette of the tank anchors the poster, giving rise to the infantry rifles acting as the tread of the vehicle.

MAKING POSTERS FROM CONCEPT TO DESIGN

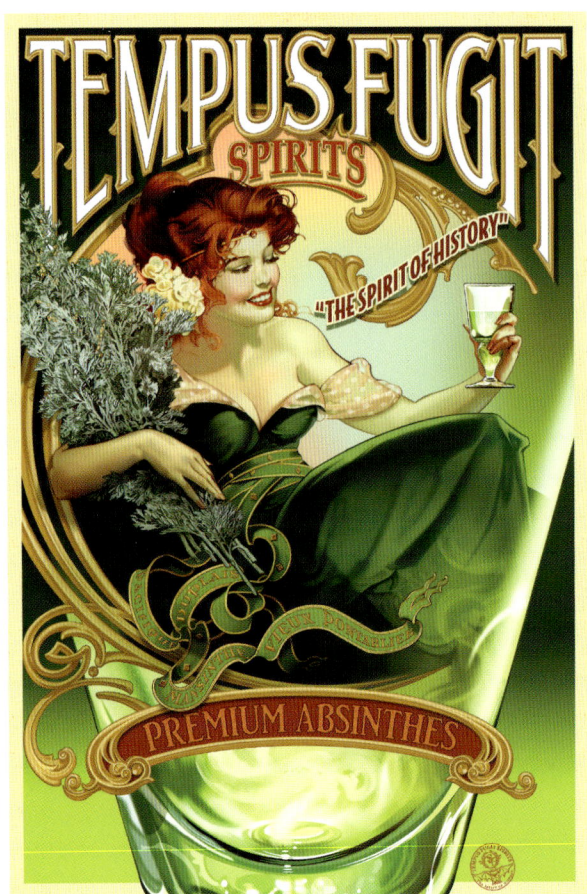

Green Fairy | **Design/Illustration**: Robert Rodriguez | © Tempus Fugit Spirits | **USA** | 41.9 x 61 cm

Katla Vodka | **Design/Illustration**: Rodolfo Reyes | © Rodolfo Reyes | **Mexico** | 45.7 x 61 cm

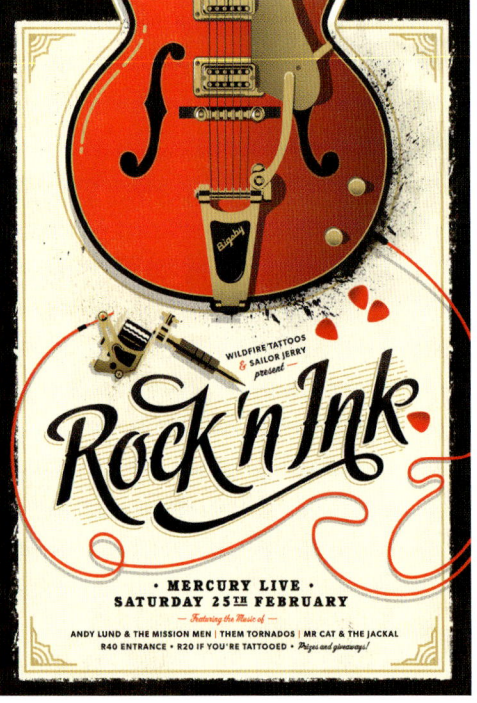

Rock'n Ink | **Design:** Adam Hill | © Adam Hill | **South Africa** | 59.4 x 84.1 cm

Clockwise: Vintage or retro, this aesthetic will instantly help to create a mood and place your poster in a time period attracting a targeted audience. Rodriguez's exquisite *Green Fairy* for Tempus Fugit Spirits takes us back to the turn of the century. Reyes channels his inner A.M. Cassandre while executing his poster.

Hill's *Rock'n Ink* poster is an excellent example of connotative image making with a narrative. The red Streamliner center block double-cutaway guitar conveys the blues-inspired style of music that will be performed at the event. Hill's choice of stout and sturdy calligraphic typeface reinforces the retro aesthetic of his poster. Tossed guitar picks, splattered ink, and torn edges are all part of the design, adding a grittiness to the Wild West concept.

CHAPTER SIX STORYTELLING

World travel, meeting new people, or enjoying *Cardenal Mendoza Solera Gran Reserva Brandy* with a friend: Simpson's poster is an explosion of multiple narratives that are blended into one powerful visual.

Golden Week | **Design/Illustration**: Steve Simpson | © Steve Simpson | **Ireland** | 63.5 x 86.4 cm

MAKING POSTERS FROM CONCEPT TO DESIGN

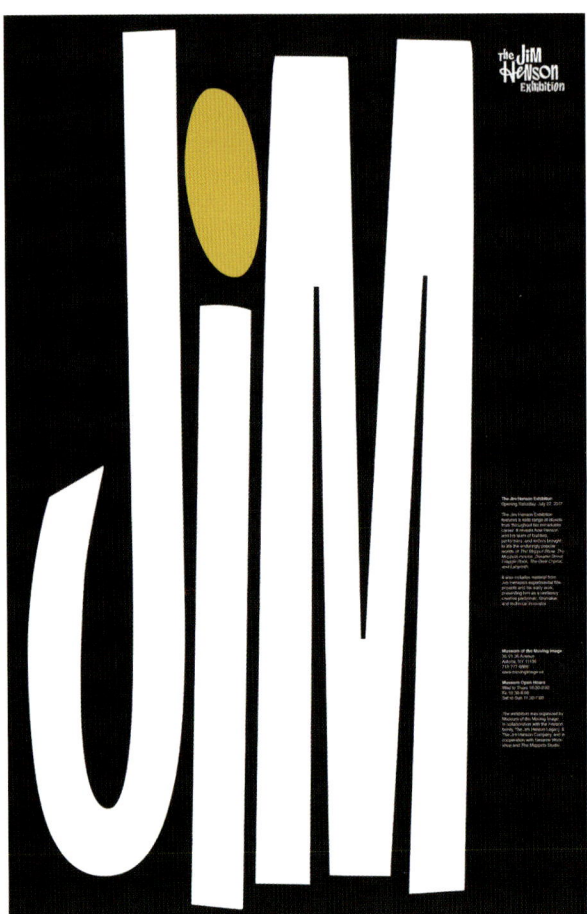

Jim Henson Exhibition | **Design firm**: COLLINS | **Lead Designer**: Caroline Bagley | **Chief Creative Officer:** Brian Collins | **Senior Experience Designer**: Clay Kippen | **Business Manager:** Antonia Lazar | **Chief Creative Officer/SF**: Matt Luckhurst | © Collins + Partners LLC | **United Kingdom**

Playful and plush, long and lean, Bagley's poster is a study in typography and scale. Bagley's graphic choices and lively composition help us recall the joy the Muppets brought to our childhood. Her selection of a lighthearted, condensed, sans-serif font and mixed-case letterforms creates a typographic caricature of the Muppets. The spot color of gold turns these delightful letters into something almost figurative, as they bounce off of their baseline with glee.

Sometimes how you execute a poster becomes part of the narrative. Olivotti adds layer upon layer of stamped typography, of panic and terror in his poster. The rubber stamp represents how bureaucratic control can devour our freedom.

Bureaucracy Kills Good Work | **Design/Illustration**: Sergio Olivotti | © Sergio Olivotti | **Italy** | 70 x 100 cm

CHAPTER SIX STORYTELLING

Chekhov Lizardbrain, sketches below, poster series above | **Design:** Matthew Bouloutian | © Matthew Bouloutian | **Client:** MANNA | **USA** | 45.7 x 61 cm

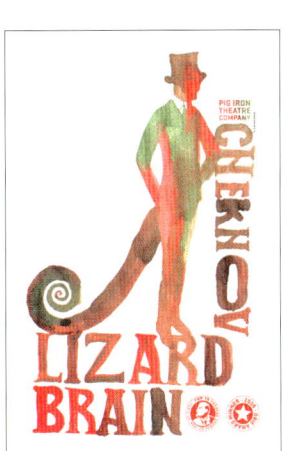

Bouloutian creates a poster series employing multiple narratives to tell one story: Pig Iron Theatre Company's *Chekhov Lizardbrain*. Each poster is an allegory of a lonely, mildly autistic botanist trapped in his "reptilian" or "lizard" brain, where primal survival instincts are expressed.[29] However, each poster has a different narrative. One poster focuses on the top hat to hold your attention. The hat creates an inner space containing a swaying lightbulb made from multiple figures, which is a visual metaphor for Dmitri's lizard brain. The other poster relies on the interrelationship between the central character Dmitri, his lizard brain, and their inner dialogue.

MAKING POSTERS FROM CONCEPT TO DESIGN

Doyle of Doyle Partners turns the written word into sculpture in his School of Visual Art's *Art Defies* subway poster series. Although each poster stands on its own as a beautiful image, when they are grouped, you can truly appreciate Doyle's vision.

2017 SVA Subway Posters | *Art Defies Expectations, Art Defies Logic, Art Defies Gravity* | **Design:** Stephen Doyle | © 2017 Visual Arts Press, Ltd. | **USA** | 76.2 x 116.8 cm

CHAPTER SIX STORYTELLING

neighboring lines of text, creating an aerial network of language, turning texts into synapses and circulation. Though originally intended as a satire for the idea of hypertext, I soon realized that these three-dimensional diagrams seemed to have a poetic power of their own, recontextualizing language and ideas into sculptural form."

—Stephen Doyle

"The posters, showing works created from pages of books, are part of a series of sculptures that I've been working on for years that I call 'Hypertexts.' I first started when 'hypertext' was a novel term for a novelty of the internet, showing a line of text that was blue and underlined, meaning that it linked to another document elsewhere in the cyber world. This linking from one text to another, even mid-sentence, seemed to me to be rather Dada in intent, abstract, somewhat random and capricious. Intrigued, I wondered what it would look like if a book's own lines connected to other lines elsewhere in the book. I created sculptures where the lines of text shook off the shackles of the page and leapt up, out of the book, and started conferring with their

191

"The art challenges the technology, and the technology inspires the art."

— John Lasseter

CHAPTER SEVEN BEYOND THE PRINTED SURFACE

For many centuries, pigment on paper was used as a primary means of communication. From paintings to books and even money, pigment on paper has helped to shape our civilization. In the last decades, we have seen how technological advances in paper and pigment manufacturing have changed the way we define paper. As we become ever closer to a paperless society, artists are using new technologies in some of the most inspired ways. This new arena has not only brought a revolution in poster design but has also altered the way we think about the printed surface. Coupled with a focus on motion design, posters are undergoing another transformation. While this does not mean that paper will disappear, it opens up a new and exciting world for poster artists. In this chapter, we will discuss some of the ways that posters are expanding beyond the printed surface.

(above and facing page) Illustration: Scott Laserow

Interactive Posters

Fundamentally, posters are made to be seen from a distance, draw you in, and present additional content. Yet there is a select group of posters that takes this purpose a step further and lure its audience to participate in the narrative through interaction. Interactive posters use touch, smell, sound, and even taste to make ideas come to life, intensifying the narrative and increasing the potency of the message. Stimulating more than one sense creates greater impact, and in an overcrowded market, emotional engagement with brands is becoming more important and challenging to achieve. By reimagining how a poster is customarily defined, a new generation of artists is creating innovative posters that use the physical world as part of their message.

Flat Life (Figure 7.1) is a poster series by Finn Magee that transforms everyday objects into two-dimensional interactive posters that hang on the wall. Using white space to frame his objects, Finn's wall displays of a lamp that you can plug in and light and a functioning digital alarm clock are visually engaging conversation pieces that serve a practical and useful purpose.

Smell

The olfactory system, which is directly connected to the limbic system,[30] effortlessly evokes memories and triggers emotions without us realizing it. A smell can capture the essence of specific moments, such as the scent of a pine tree on Christmas or roses on Valentine's Day. Therefore, it is a powerful tool when applied to poster design. There are many ways in which designers are

Figure 7.1 | *Flat Time Wood Effect* | **Design:** Finn Magee and Eoghan Hanrahan | *Flat Light* | **Design:** Finn Magee and Bahbak Hashemi Nezhad | *Flat Light:* © Finn Magee and Bahbak Hashemi Nezhad | *Flat Time Wood Effect:* © Finn Magee and Eoghan Hanrahan | **United Kingdom** | 42 x 59.4 cm

Figure 7.2 | *Cinnamon Coke* | © The Aroma Company | AromaCoat—scented encapsulate for large-format printing | **United Kingdom** | Various sizes

using scent, and several agencies now offer, as part of their services for marketing campaigns, scented collateral and sensory branding, known as scent marketing. Some of the uses of scent include posters that release a scent when you touch them and scratch-and-sniff posters. There are also options where no interaction is necessary, such as aroma-infused paper that gently emits its scent over time.

The Aroma Company created a unique billboard campaign for Coca-Cola's limited-edition Cinnamon Coke (Figure 7.2). Displayed in the London Underground, the posters take customers on a sensory brand excursion. The installation includes cinnamon-scented corridors and a vinyl-wrapped escalator with panels that produce a cinnamon scent.

Touch

If a one-year-old's tiny fingers can scroll through a touchscreen, then it should come as no surprise that new generations expect to interact with everything around them seamlessly. From the classic tear-off flyers stapled to telephone poles to advanced papers that react to heat, adding a tactile element to your poster can turn a spectator into a participant. Using Braille and other kinds of embossing can also be more inclusive for people with visual disabilities, allowing the blind to detect and understand a design.

Figure 7.3 | *Free 30+ Sunscreen* | © Cooch Creative | **Australia** | 101 x 152 cm

As the *Free 30+ Sunscreen* poster shows (Figure 7.3), the tactile content of your poster is not limited to the texture of your paper. This interactive design, created by Cooch Creative for the Sun Smart Cancer Council Western Australia, provides passengers with free sunscreen while they wait for their bus en route to the beach. A cut-out area of the image simulating a part of the skin marked for cancer removal surgery holds the sunscreen dispenser, reminding the audience of the dangers they face while providing the solution at the same time.

Taste

Smell and taste are intertwined; both are part of our limbic system and can trigger strong emotional reactions.[31] Approximately 10,000 taste buds cover our tongues.[32] These receptors process five different tastes: sweet, bitter, sour, salty, and umami. Anyone who has been to a food market on a Sunday afternoon has observed taste marketing in action, as multiple brands offer samples to customers. When it comes to printed surfaces, incorporating taste is now achievable with the advancement of edible inks and paper. Many companies offer this type of printing, and if you are feeling crafty, you can even make your own at home. London-based illustrator Rob Flowers created a series of yummy posters (Figure 7.4) for an exhibition at London's V&A Museum of Childhood in partnership with food-design studio Bompas & Parr. The purpose of the show was to encourage children to experiment with food. The participants were asked to describe their food fantasies, which were then turned into ludic designs and printed using edible paper and flavored inks.

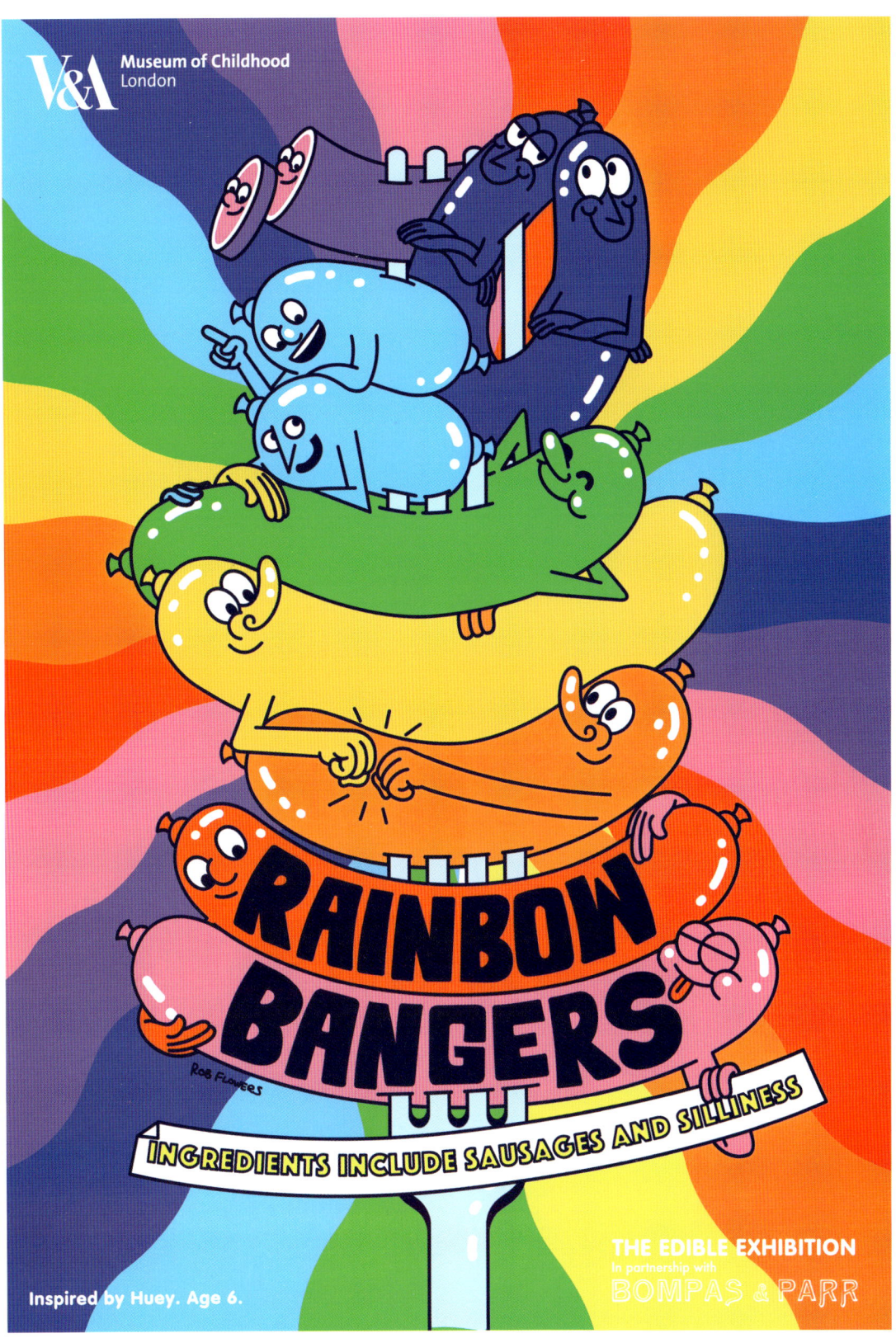

Figure 7.4 | *Rainbow Bangers* | **Illustration**: Rob Flowers | © Bompas & Parr | **United Kingdom** | 42 x 59.4 cm

MAKING POSTERS FROM CONCEPT TO DESIGN

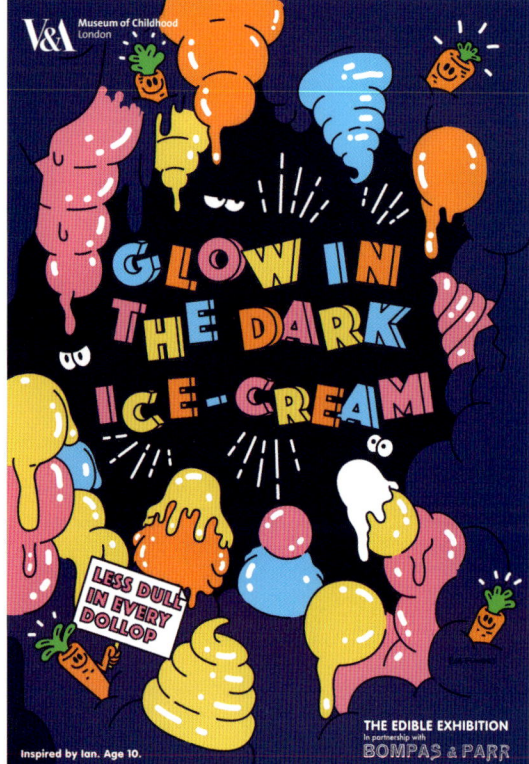

Figure 7.4 | *Eat Your Greens, Parsnip Tornado, Glow In The Dark Ice-cream, Music Juice* | **Illustration:** Rob Flowers | © Bompas & Parr | **United Kingdom** | 420 x 594 mm

CHAPTER SEVEN BEYOND THE PRINTED SURFACE

Sound

As designers, we worry about how our work looks, not how it sounds. A sound is one of the most influential connections to our subconscious reactions. We usually think of sound as something we perceive through our ears, but actually, a sound is a vibration going through matter in the form of soundwaves that our ears register and process. Because of this, we are unable to block sound. We can close our eyes and not see, but we cannot close our ears. Even with earplugs, we can still sense the vibrations produced by sound. Therefore, experiencing a poster with sound is vibrational. Many companies use sound as part of their marketing strategies, from jingles to specific sounds, like a ringtone or the iconic chime that Apple computers emit at startup.

Advancement in printing and ink technology is bridging the gap between traditional printed posters and emerging technologies. Grey London, a leader in this area of blurring the lines of what a poster was and what it is becoming, chose conceptual illustrator Billie Jean for their sonic poster as part of *The Sound of Taste* (Figure 7.5) campaign. Jean combined touch and smell to promote Schwartz Flavor Shots infused with herb and spice blends. To simulate the effects that herbs and spices have on the senses, Grey London produced a poster using innovative touch-sensitive inks that turn the surface area of the paper into an interactive interface. Jean took sixteen herbs and spices and assigned them each a suitable color, filling the composition with colorful, flowing, biomorphic shapes, and related them to a musical tone. Then ink technologist Maria Menicou printed the poster using touch-sensitive inks. Interacting with these inks can be accomplished by downloading a free mobile app that uses Bluetooth to sync a handheld device to microchips embedded into the paper of the poster. The app enables you to play piano chords as you interact with each shape, creating a synthetic, synesthetic sensation. Synesthesia is a neurological condition where one sense stimulates another, like smelling sound. Research shows that approximately four percent of the population is naturally synesthetic, while other people have been shown to experience synesthesia while using psychedelic drugs.[33]

Figure 7.5 | *The Sound of Taste* | **Client:** McCormick | © Grey London | **United Kingdom** | 59.4 x 84.1 cm

Moving Posters

Video projections and guerrilla campaigns have paved the way for contemporary designs that provide a creative and interactive environment for their audience. Motion posters involve the senses, like interactive posters with the added dimension of movement and sound. As posters evolve into visuals that move, they must still maintain their core purpose—to communicate the desired message that is quickly decoded through a powerful visual. Integrating technology into the printed poster is a game-changer; it takes the poster from a purely passive event to something that engages your sense of sound and even touch through interaction. The digital poster is tailor-made for new audiences who have grown accustomed to a flow of digital information. More and more, we see high-resolution display screens integrated into the landscape influencing our daily decisions. They appear in train stations, at bus stops, in airports, on subway platforms, in taxicabs, at gasoline pumps, even in houses of worship. Utilizing new and unexpected locations for these digital screens allows new settings to offer a personalized experience directly to a targeted audience. Poster artists should exercise caution when using digital technology and not allow it to seduce them; instead, they must use it to their advantage and make it work for them so the technology does not impede the concept.

Jung v Matt's poster *It Happens When Nobody Is Watching* (Figure 7.6) demonstrates how new technology can create a smart, educational, one-of-a-kind poster. Jung v Matt, in collaboration with Wall AG, produced a domestic violence poster with eye-tracking capabilities. Since most domestic violence happens behind closed doors while "nobody is watching," Jung v Matt, along with Amnesty International, sought to bring the secrecy out into the open. As Jung v Matt explains, "We mounted a monitor and an 'eye tracking' camera on a poster. This camera registered when people were looking at the poster, and the poster reacted accordingly. As long as nobody was looking directly at the poster, it displayed a typical scene of domestic violence: a man beating his wife. But as soon as somebody looked directly at the poster, it changed into a photo of the same couple pretending to be happy. Since the whole process was programmed with a brief time delay, passers-by were able to catch a glimpse of the violence before the scene changed." Jung v Matt used technology that supports the concept; the eye tracking camera, although hidden, plays an important role, making you an active player with regard to the poster and ultimately the cause.

Figure 7.6 | *It Happens When Nobody Is Watching* | © Jung v Matt JvM | **Germany** | Various sizes

Animated Posters

Animation dates to the 1650s, when Dutch astronomer, mathematician, and physicist Christiaan Huygens developed the *laterna magica* (magic lantern)[34] that projected images from a series of slides onto small glass panes. But perhaps the most famous contributor to animation is Walt Disney, who in 1923 founded the Walt Disney Company, first known as the Disney Brothers Cartoon Studio.[35] The traditional style used by animators like Ub Iwerks of the Walt Disney Studios was frame-by-frame animation, where each movement was painstakingly illustrated, then recorded one cel at a time. This frame-by-frame technique is also used by stop-motion model animators like master Ray Harryhausen, who made subtle changes to poseable figures and recorded them by advancing the camera one single frame. Stop-motion is an art form that creates wonderfully surreal worlds with the sophistication and charm of traditional animation but in three dimensions.[MPR]

Photorealistic three-dimensional animation generated using computers was initially introduced in an impactful way to the public in 1991, with TriStar Pictures' release of *Terminator 2: Judgment Day*. This film was the first to use computer-generated imagery (CGI) to create realistic human movements for one of the main characters. But it was not until the 1995

release of *Toy Story*, produced by Pixar Animation Studios and released by Walt Disney Pictures, that we witnessed the world's first fully computer-animated feature film. *Toy Story* pushed the technological boundaries of computer animation, with digitally modeled actors that performed in a realistic world, moving smoothly without any of the quirks and wobbles of traditional animation. CGI opens the door for the artist who is not a draftsperson or illustrator. With relatively easy access to animation software, designers and artists are now integrating computer technology into their work. Many are collaborating with animators and motion graphic artists from around the world to create a provocative new form of poster design.

Artists interested in adding motion to their posters do not need to be trained animators. There are many software solutions available to artists and designers interested in creating motion graphics like animated gifs, short promotional videos, moving typography, and title sequences. Getting started is as easy as accessing Adobe® Photoshop®, which includes an animation tool. Try building a motion graphic using Exercise 7.1, "A Step-by-Step Guide to Creating an Animation in Adobe Photoshop," at the end of this chapter. This exercise illustrates a simple method for moving an object. However, motion graphics is more than just pushing a shape around in space; it looks at the behavior of the object and how its movement, size, or color can strengthen the narrative and intensify the journey. A solid shape slowly bobbing while moving through a composition will have a calming effect. If that same solid shape is scurrying about and blinking, it will appear to be energetic and excited. If the individual visuals within a composition are the actors on a stage and you are the director, how would you direct your actors to perform? This new role of stage director widens the boundaries of storytelling beyond the flat, static surface. The artists exploring this new horizon are creating some of the most diverse and innovative solutions using emerging technology combined with traditional motion techniques.

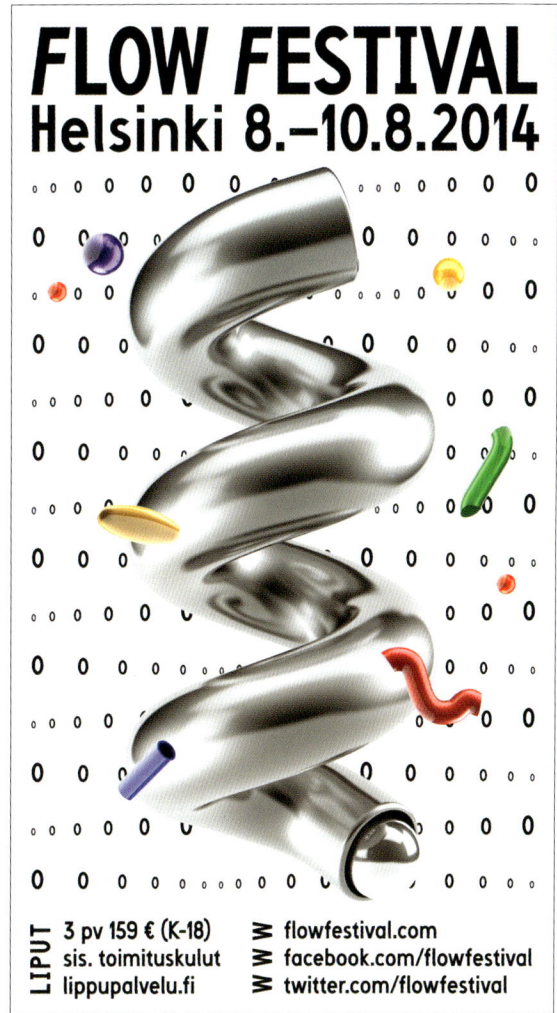

Figure 7.7 | *Flow Festival 2014* | **Design**: Tsto | **Illustration**: Tsto and Kristian Linden | **Animation**: Anima Boutique | © Tsto, Kristian Linden, and Anima Boutique | **Finland** | 38 x 67 cm

On a printed poster, both the type and image must appear at the same time. However, with an animated poster, the designer may choose to present the content by introducing typography first, followed by the visual, or allowing a visual to appear first, trailed by the typography, or a combination of simultaneously moving typography and image. Witness how Tsto handles the flow of visual fixtures in their poster *Flow Festival 2014* (Figure 7.7) by scanning the QR code. Applying both a centralized object and moving typography, Tsto's poster creates the illusion of depth, freeing the silver rotating, three-dimensional tube to float in endless space. The shiny object is then pushed out of the frame, where you witness a series of micro-explosions divulging the artists performing at the festival. In many ways, moving posters employ some of the same best practices used to present type and image on a computer screen or handheld device—keep it simple and easy to read, use contrasts of color and value, and consider your audience. These parameters present new challenges for the poster designer, as size variation and movement are now part of the equation. Elizabeth Reznick, an educator, poster designer, and curator, points out that "ready access to broadband and mobile communications and to digital production technologies has expanded the poster's role well beyond the limitations of the printed surface."[36] As a new generation of global designers begins to study and incorporate animation into their poster design process, we begin to see how this new medium affects narrative by turning the lens onto the human experience as it invites participation with a new kind of storytelling.

Music and Sound

From simple speakers in an auditorium to complex sound systems, music and sound effects have been used in the performing arts for a long time. Before sound systems, live orchestras would add music to the performance, and live sound effects were created using bells, whistles, and ingenious manipulation of common objects. As sound and recording technology has progressed, so has our ability to develop and control multi-layered audible textures, music, and sound effects, as we see in movies and television shows today.

Research shows that music has a powerful effect on our brains, affecting our emotions and even our sensory perception.[38] Music and sound effects can manipulate our emotions and intensify an event. Music has always been present in our lives, from ancient rituals to dancing at nightclubs to the tone and rhythm of our speech. While certain tonalities have calming effects, others are more grating. A semitone is the smallest distance between two different notes, and it is considered the most dissonant when sounded harmonically. Semitones can make your heart start to pound and your palms start to sweat, letting you know that something is about to happen. Rarely have two alternating patterns of semitones (identified as E and F)[39] become more well-known or more memorable than the famous

How to Choose Software

Naturally, you want to use the best software available, but what is the best? Choosing the right software is as important as any other choice you make during the design process, and there are many excellent two-dimensional and three-dimensional options on the market. Although these options may have different user interfaces (UI), the basic idea behind them is very similar. They can animate and edit images, typography, and video by keyframing a timeline. By adding keyframes to a timeline within a finite amount of time, this software creates what is called a tween, which allows for a smooth transitional motion between frames. Most poster designers are familiar with Adobe® Photoshop®. Adobe also offers an animation tool called After Effects®. After Effects is similar to Photoshop in many ways; the first thing you will recognize is the user interface. Like Photoshop, After Effects functions using layers, shapes, and paths and offers you the ability to create, edit, and animate objects and typography. Those familiar with Photoshop will find After Effects a relatively smooth transition.

Choosing the right software tool is subjective. There are many good products on the market, and most offer free trial periods. Take advantage of the offers and then decide which one feels the most comfortable and suits your needs.[MPR] You will find that you settle on a favorite software tool, and that is where you should choose to build your skills. Morr Meroz, the founder of Bloop Animation, makes the excellent point, "It's important to remember that good skills will get you far, regardless of the software you use. Tools are just tools."[37] There are many informative online courses and YouTube videos that teach how to use these new and emerging technologies.[MPR]

Try something fun with the 2002 IKEA *Unböring* campaign's sixty-second commercial spot. Mute your smartphone and scan the QR code below to watch this award-winning spot in its entirety. Then turn your sound back on, re-watch the commercial, and get ready for an emotional roller-coaster ride. Once the sound is added to the mood lighting and the storyline, there is a sense of uneasiness. Now, as you witness the lamp cold and alone in the rain, set to sad music, you begin to feel empathy. When the sound effect of rain is introduced alongside the musical score, watching the old lamp's view of the new light fixture is heartbreaking. If timing is everything, then this spot reels you back in from gloom and despair at the perfect moment, defusing the sadness with humor. This IKEA spot is a combination of well-chosen lighting, sound effects, and music and a simple story brilliantly executed.

IKEA *Unböring* **campaign** | Crispin Porter + Bogusky Advertising Agency | Produced by Morton/Jankel/Zander | Directed by Spike Jonze | Post-production and editing by Spot Welders | Sound design by MIT Out Sound | Sweden IKEA commercial

"dun, dun" from Universal Pictures' feature film *Jaws*. Those two menacing notes are so visceral, they become more terrifying than the shark, making the anticipation worse than the image itself. Sounds can play with our psyche, toy with our emotions, and—as in the case of *Jaws*—evoke dread.

Adding soundscapes to posters elevates the art of storytelling by creating more immersive conditions. Images are powerful, and when appropriately choreographed with soundscapes, the two elements work in unison, both taking a central role in the narrative and affording a more visceral experience for your audience. If a plane takes off silently into a clear, blue sky, we get only half the message. When you add the sound of a roaring engine, you achieve a more primal reaction. If we hear the plane's engine struggle and stall, there is tension and expectation . . . is the plane going to crash? With a simple change in sound, the same image can tell different stories.

When you are enhancing the narrative with sound, there are three types to consider: human voice, sound effects, and music. Since you are creating a poster and not a movie or video short, it is unlikely a voice-over (VO) will be necessary, unless you are accommodating visually impaired people who might appreciate the graphic and the movement but have difficulty reading the typography. VOs should be short and direct; they should not lengthen the process or undermine the poster's core purpose of quickly attracting notice.

The simplest and most effective sound you can add to a poster is a sound effect. This can be anything from a loud crack or explosion to a more subtle sound like birds chirping, a rainfall, a gust of wind, or waves breaking at the beach. The latter, going almost unnoticed by the viewer, becomes a part of the peripheral, making for a more vibrant and captivating adventure. Sound effects will make a striking addition to an animated poster as long as they are short and in rhythm with the visual. Because sound effects can have a significant impact on emotions, choose them wisely, or you can ruin an otherwise strong animation. You can purchase music loops and banks of sound effects from many online sources, or you can record and mix your own. There are many useful tools for mixing sound and music, ranging from simple solutions like GarageBand™ to much more sophisticated technologies offering complete digital mixing boards. Consider collaborating with a sound designer; it can be a valuable experience and strengthen your musical ear.

Choosing the right music can be challenging. When you are selecting music for a moving poster, it is essential that your selection enhance and support the concept, much the same way a color or typeface choice does. Rhythm and musical instruments have different qualities. Drums connect us with the earth, nature, and primitive ceremonies. Harps are ethereal, violins are dramatic, trumpets are sharp and bright, marimbas are joyful and friendly, and electronic instruments can take us to outer space. Always keep in mind the short period you have to capture a viewer. Your musical choice should be simple and seamlessly looped, so the encounter does not become disrupted.

Animation is the foundation for all posters that move. Whether it is an augmented reality (AR) poster that comes to life on your smartphone or tablet, or an interactive kiosk touchscreen display, it will contain some form of motion. Although both printed and moving posters require an understanding of the same principles of concept, composition, image making, and execution, there is a greater need for preparation during the ideation stage of the design process for a moving poster. When developing the narrative, you must plan out how your poster will move. Consider the total time of your poster's animation, what transitions to use (i.e., crossfade, moving objects in frame, dissolve, jump-cut, push, quick-cut, slide, wipe, or zoom), when in the timecode the transitions will take place, and whether the animation will need to be looped.

The best way to plan and organize the flow of an animation is by creating a storyboard (Figure 7.8). A storyboard is similar to a comic—it is a consecutive sequence of panels arranged in a linear order depicting changes and transitions in a narrative. Music and sound effects are timed events and should be considered while you are creating your storyboard. After all, you would not want a sound effect to be out of sync with the action on the screen. The movement should complement and enhance the narrative, together making for a more immersive reality. Although movement adds a wide range of possibilities, it may also impose some restraints. For example, if you have moving typography, the font choice and weight may be less legible than on the printed version of the poster. Other limitations may be color or scale. Animated posters need to have a simple storyline that can be decoded quickly without losing the attention of the viewer.

There are many approaches that artists and designers can take to create a successful animated poster. They can start with something as simple as two alternating images, colors, or patterns and progress to more advanced options, including moving objects, moving typography, divided movements, turning, pushing, camera movements, build, hide and reveal, and live footage. When creating a poster that moves, carefully consider every choice you make, as it must support your concept, or it will become nothing more than window dressing. Award-winning graphic designer and animator Erich Brechbühl says, "A poster is a poster, but the animation acts like a fifth color or a special type of printing."[40] Many poster designers are collaborating with animators and motion artists who have a greater understanding of motion and how to use the software needed to help push this new medium forward.

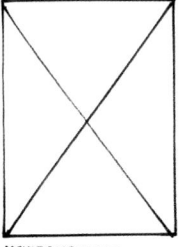  

Figure 7.8 | Storyboard for *Taxi Driver* AR poster | Yibing Wang | © Yibing Wang | **USA**
Scan the QR code to see how this storyboard becomes the foundation for the final animation. To experience the finished artwork, go to the chapter gallery.

White space, contrast, strong composition, and movement describe the poster *Herbstzeitlose* (Figure 7.9), created by collaborators Götz Gramlich, a designer, and Marc Weidenhüller, an animator. The subtle motion adds a level of emotion as the quiet movement of letterforms slowly wilts to reveal the event information that was, until now, intentionally placed upside down, backward, and at strange angles, making it nearly impossible to read. Gramlich and Weidenhüller add depth and dimension to their poster by casting soft and soothing shadows upon the white background. *Herbstzeitlose*'s letterforms are timed to be slow and intentional, but just quick enough to stay a beat ahead of our ability to read the content of each letter. Weidenhüller eases his letterforms into position, giving them the natural movement that a light material would possess. Animating typography can be tricky and should be attempted only with forethought and knowledge. Although a solution may be visually enticing, if you lose legibility, your poster serves no purpose. However, when handled correctly by experts like Gramlich and Weidenhüller, the results can be stunning.

Figure 7.9 | *Herbstzeitlose* | **Design:** Götz Gramlich | **Animation:** Marc Weidenhüller | © gggrafik.de | Germany | 59.4 x 84 cm

Augmented Reality Posters

Imagine directly downloading an app to your smartphone or tablet that allows you to watch the printed poster come to life in its surroundings. This immersive technology is called augmented reality (AR). AR is a type of technology that overlays both two- and three-dimensional computer-generated visuals onto a real-world blended environment that alters the limitations of our perceived space. The term "augmented reality" was first used by Boeing researchers Tom Caudell and David Mizell and was implemented by NASA in 1992.[41] But, believe it or not, the idea of AR has been around since 1968, when Dr. Ivan Sutherland, an American computer scientist and Internet pioneer widely regarded as the father of computer graphics, completed the first AR headset, called The Sword of Damocles.[42] However, AR did not become a part of the popular culture until 2016, when Niantic™ and Nintendo™ launched the mass phenomenon *Pokémon Go*™, which captured the imagination of gamers worldwide. Since then, AR has been popularized in many other smartphone apps from gaming to education, measuring, and planning.

With the use of handheld devices, AR can transform the way you tell your story. By stretching the limits of space, AR posters can reach beyond the visual and may have components that are auditory or even haptic (relating to the sense of touch). Consider these perceptual overlays before the execution stage of the design process. Ask yourself: What will the poster communicate when it stands on its own? How will I motivate the viewer to participate in my AR? How will my virtual fixtures be introduced, and how will they affect the narrative? How will AR enhance my poster and enrich the overall experience? What outcomes am I hoping for?

Although there is a growing appetite for AR, these poster types must do more than merely superimpose virtual fixtures onto the real world. They must strengthen and support the narrative to provoke a reaction. AR has the potential to change the way we interact with our world and should be handled responsibly. Currently, many designers and artists who are using this new technology do so for entertainment purposes; however, eventually, we will need to be conscious that too many visuals will cause overload, rendering them ineffective and largely ignored.

Erich Brechbühl's poster *Open Club Day* (Figure 7.10) demonstrates how AR can enrich a concept. Designed for a daytime open house event for five nightclubs in Luzern (Lucerne), Switzerland, the poster includes a neon sign that is off until evening when the clubs open and the streets come alive. He places the neon typography over the five club names and their locations to complete his composition. On its own, Brechbühl's poster is well designed, informative, attention grabbing, and very successful. The real magic begins with AR, which allows Brechbühl's poster to transition from day to night, becoming dark for a moment before flickering and glowing for your amazement.

Figure 7.11 shows six of the twenty different iterations Brechbühl investigated before settling on one dynamic and informative poster that you cannot help interacting with time and time again.

CHAPTER SEVEN BEYOND THE PRINTED SURFACE

A | **Figure 7.10** | *Open Club Day* | **Design/Animation:** Erich Brechbühl | © Erich Brechbühl | Switzerland | 90.5 x 128 cm

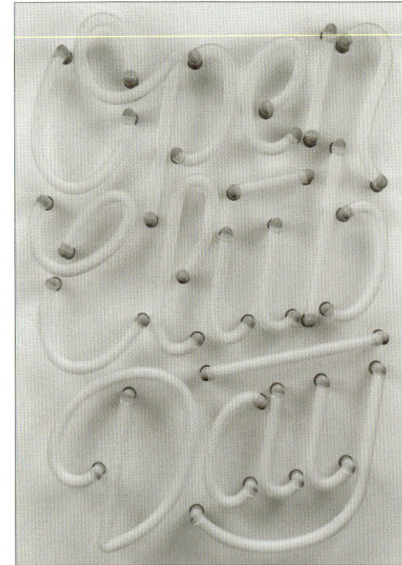

Figure 7.11 | *Open Club Day* | **Design/Animation**: Erich Brechbühl | © Erich Brechbühl | **Switzerland** | 90.5 x 128 cm

Interactive Digital Posters

We live in an age where touchscreens have become integrated into our lives. Most of us interact with touchscreens daily when we use our smartphones. This technology was created to enhance our basic human experience. As large-scale, vertical, digital touchscreens are now more readily available and seen in more places, it is only natural for the poster to take advantage of them due to their broad appeal and accessibility. Interactive digital posters employ layers of interaction revealing additional data, expanding the audience's perspective, and turning them from viewers into users. Interactive digital posters are similar to a kiosk, as they are self-contained, allowing the user to interact with the screen and consisting only of relevant material.

To successfully create an interactive digital poster, you need to consider how the user will interact with your visuals. You must offer them a simple but engaging format while they interact and discover new insights. The interactive digital artist makes decisions on how the poster will transform once the user interacts with it and how the user will acquire the expanded content. This process is the framework that supports the layers of content revealed as the interaction progresses. An artist interested in these new technologies must understand how user interaction can influence a concept and explore all the possibilities to determine the most successful solution. Therefore, the designer must be selective when deciding what to include, remembering that although this is multimedia, it is still a poster with a single focus.

Designing everything from printed posters to moving posters and interactive digital posters, Li Xu is a sort of modern-day poster alchemist. He mixes elixirs of print, animation, AR, and interactive potions into one artistic expression. Xu's poster *Free to Choose Love* (Figure 7.12) is one part art and one part science, blending design and technology for a visually rich presentation. Xu's printed poster uses a sharp contrast of color and energetic line to create perceived movement. Using the printed artwork as his foundation, Xu adds actual movement by alternating images, giving the illusion of keys on a keyboard being pressed. This rhythmic motion seduces you, the audience, into interacting with his poster and becoming free to choose love.

The Future of the Poster
By Erich Brechbühl

Technological development does not stop at an old medium like the poster. In my poster design, I incorporate these new possibilities more and more. First, it started with simple moving posters, which could then be quickly projected into the real world using AR. Eventually, AR turned into virtual reality (VR). I realized that AR posters are a difficult medium to place on the streets because they require you to download an app to activate the motion, which works against the function of a poster—to communicate quickly and directly. VR posters were problematic, as nobody (except for maybe a few geeks) puts on VR goggles to look at a poster, so I changed my focus to interactive posters.

You must acknowledge the relevance of the moving poster. In Switzerland, screens are now being set up on the streets showing moving posters in a loop. And it is only a matter of time before they can react and interact with the viewers. This opens up new possibilities for drawing attention. But even these posters have to be designed with care; otherwise, they remain mere razzle-dazzle.

 **Figure 7.12** | *Free to Choose Love* | **Design/Animation/Development**: Li Xu | © Li Xu | **Client**: Art A&B Studio | **Taiwan** | 70 x 100 cm

As a poster designer and festival organizer, I am always confronted with the history of posters. For several decades now, the poster has been regularly scrutinized and even declared dead several times, and yet it remains persistent. A poster is unique: a printed sheet of paper that hangs on any street corner or in any shop window. No other medium is as democratic. This is the reason why I am skeptical about technical developments, although I remain very interested in the new possibilities offered to us by new technologies. But, of course, these technologies also generate new dependencies. Moving posters cannot simply be hung on every street corner or in every shop window; they require the proper equipment. This is something one must always be aware of before devoting oneself to new technology and denouncing the old one.

Exercise 7.1: A Step-by-Step Guide to Creating an Animation in Adobe Photoshop

(Imagery can be built on a computer or made using traditional media, scanned, and placed into Photoshop.)

Built into Photoshop is a timeline palette that lets you choose between frame animation and a video timeline. Open Adobe Photoshop and create a new document with an artboard size of 350 x 500 px at 72 dpi.

1. Create a new layer and place a filled circle toward the top center of the composition (Figure 7.13).
2. Duplicate your layer and move your object down in the composition. Repeat this process until you have created eight layers total (Figure 7.14).
3. Select all eight layers and duplicate (Figure 7.15). These duplicate layers will be the reverse half of the animation and will create a loop.
4. Reverse the order of the eight new layers (Figure 7.16).
5. Open your timeline palette from the Window menu and select "Create Frame Animation" in the center of the palette.

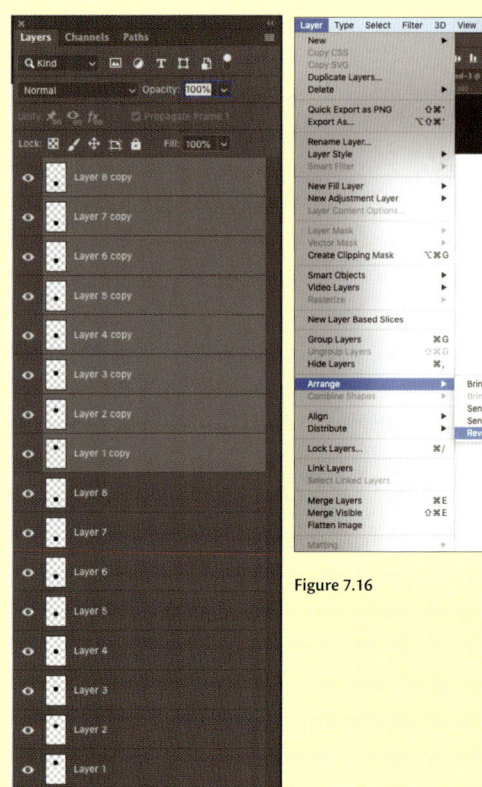

Figure 7.16

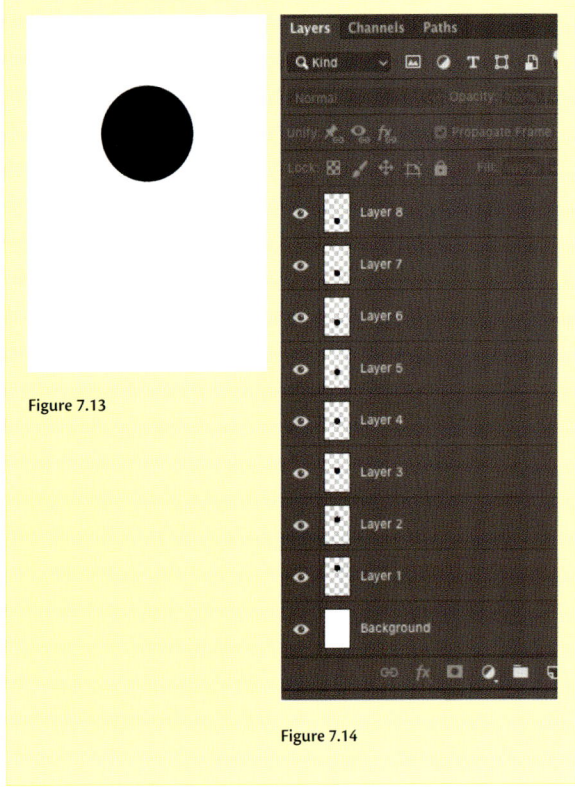

Figure 7.13

Figure 7.14

Figure 7.15

6. In the drop-down menu to the right of the timeline palette, select "Make Frames from Layers" (Figure 7.17).
7. Under each frame, select how long it should appear before switching to the next frame. For this exercise, choose "No Delay."
8. At the bottom of the timeline palette, select how many times you would like the animation to loop. For this exercise, choose "Forever" (Figure 7.18).
9. Preview your animation by pressing the play icon on the timeline palette.
10. Save your file as a gif.

To download a working psd file of this animation, go to www.making-posters.com/psdanimation.

EXERCISES

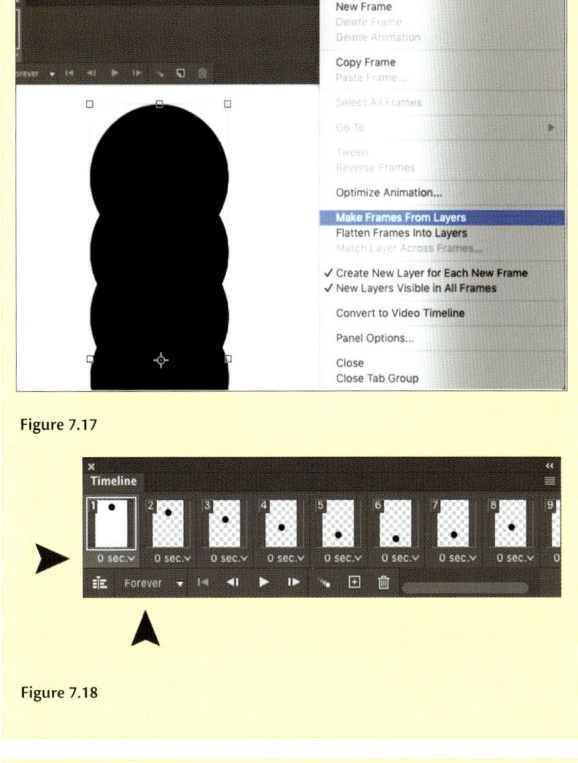

Figure 7.17

Figure 7.18

Exercise 7.2: Behavior

Using the skills that you have learned from Exercise 7.1, build two three-second animations. Create a black circle and place it in the center of a 300 x 400 px composition. Now animate the dot to communicate happiness and joy. Using the same dot from the first animation, create a second animation that communicates sadness and melancholy. Consider scale change, along with movement, distortion, and speed.

CASE STUDY

Blood Oil by Scott Laserow

Creating an interactive digital poster for the first time was an exciting experience. Interactive digital posters are a relatively new medium, and only a handful of poster artists have experimented with this new technology. There is something energizing about working in a niche where the rules have yet to be written. There are, of course, user experience (UX) rules, and I indeed considered them while I was thinking about user interaction. However, UX rules are in place for a different experience, certainly one with many more layers and screens of information than I believe a poster of any kind should have. My mantra, "This is still a poster," played in my head over and over again throughout the entire process.

The goal for the palm oil poster project was to create a printed, animated, and digital interactive poster. Just as with any other poster project that I have worked on, I started to research my topic thoroughly. After learning that there are eight endangered species on the island of Sumatra due to the production of palm oil, I had found my cause. Focusing on just the four critically endangered species allowed me to simplify and not overwhelm the audience with content. My concept was simple. Since palm oil production in Indonesia, and particularly in the vast Indonesian island of Sumatra, comes at a cost to four critically endangered species, the Sumatran elephant, orangutan, rhinoceros, and tiger, I wanted to present their destruction in a horrific pool of bloody palm oil. The visual would be palm oil pouring out of a consumer oil bottle and turning into a pool of blood, where the four critically endangered species would be drowned, metaphorically speaking. The challenge would be creating a poster that could stand on its own and also move and interact. My first thought was, "How would the user interact with the visuals?" This seemed like the next logical step before I began the design process.

Starting with a rough comp, I began to think about what information to include and how to present it to the end user. My early attempts were too detailed, too deep, with too many layers of information to still be considered a poster—it looked more like an information kiosk. It became clear that I needed to simplify, or no one would be enticed to interact. My solution was to float skeletal remains of the four animals in the bloody oil, then place a target over the top of each with which a user could interact. Each tap on the target would reveal simple facts about the destruction of these animals and trigger the sound they make in the wild. The additional sensory layers would make for a more personal connection.

Blood Oil | Design/Illustration/Animation/Development: Scott Laserow | © Scott Laserow | USA | 2056 x 3455 px

Initially, I began to design the printed version of the poster, which was more familiar and more comfortable, but quickly found that there was a need for a back-and-forth between the printed and interactive posters. Primarily, what worked in print did not necessarily translate into digital interaction. Eventually, through a little trial and error, I was able to find balance. The next part of the process was integrating simple navigation, allowing the user to restart the animation or learn how to interact with the poster. Once the design of both the printed and interactive posters was complete, it was time to start the animation process with a simple storyboard. During the animation development, I explored the transition between the end-user interaction and the display of information. It needed to be straightforward but not jolting or abrupt. In the end, a simple scale and fade with a masked type reveal did the trick. Although the animation was relatively simple, it still made use of ease in and ease out to soften the transition. Upon completion of all the interactive components, the final poster was built using HTML5 and JavaScript.

Blood Oil | **Design/Illustration/Animation/Development**: Scott Laserow | © Scott Laserow | **USA** | 2056 x 3455 px

GALLERY

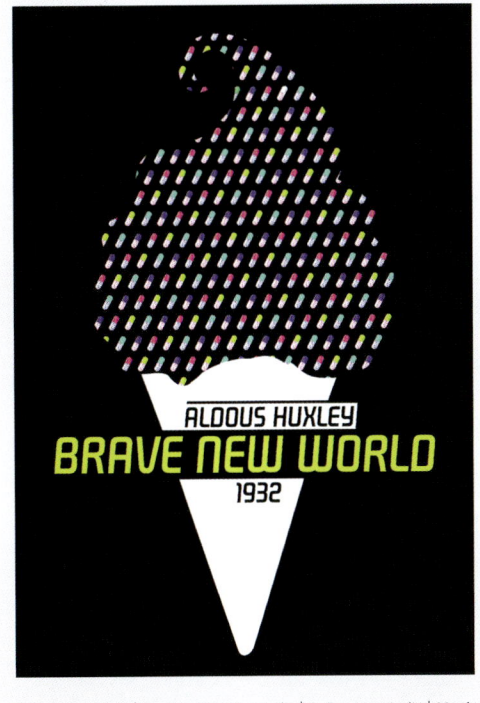

Morainslie's glow-in-the-dark posters paint a retro-futuristic vision of Aldous Huxley's *Brave New World*.

Below: Propague Brazil created their child-abuse awareness posters using a classic folded paper technique—the perfect medium to connect all of us to our childhood—making their posters personal and meaningful.

Brave New World | **Design:** Gus Morainslie | © Gus Morainslie | **Mexico** | 50 x 70 cm

215

Boy-Campaign Against Violence and Sexual Abuse. Stay On Our Side. Report It. | Propague Brazil | **Creative Director:** Rogerio Alves | **Designer:** luiz Dias | **Photography:** Philippe Arruda | © Creative Director: Rogerio Alves | Designer: Luiz Dias | Photographer: Philippe Arruda | **Client:** Government of the State of Santa Catarina | **Brazil** | 40 x 60 cm

MAKING POSTERS FROM CONCEPT TO DESIGN

216

Where Art Happens | **Creative Director**: Anthony P. Rhodes | **Copywriter**: Steven Heller | **Art Direction and Design**: Mirko Ilić | © Mirko Ilić | **Client**: School of Visual Arts, NYC | **USA** | 76 x 117 cm

Created exclusively for NYC subways, Ilić's SVA poster series uses light and shape to create the illusion of speed and motion. As the train comes through the tunnel, its light hits the poster, making the zig-zag grow and creating arrows that point you to the logo, located in the center of the sign. A close look allows the viewer to see the logo and tagline, while a distant view, from either the train or the platform across the tracks, reveals the blue letters spelling the name of the school.

Opposite: Attacking the page with vibrant color and shape, Grilli Type creates an exciting composition that only gets better as the symphony of visuals builds to completion in their animation event poster for Weltformat.

Weltformat | © Grilli Type | **Client**: Weltformat Festival Luzern | **Switzerland** | 90.5 x 128 cm

MAKING POSTERS FROM CONCEPT TO DESIGN

218

Mulheria | **Design/Animation**: Vítor Ventola Bravin | © Vítor Ventola Bravin | **Client**: Sesc Sorocaba | **Brazil** | 500 x 3181 px

When animating, timing is everything; like any poster, you have only seconds to grab someone's attention. Because of the novelty of posters that move, designers, artists, and animators have an advantage. This benefit of unfamiliarity should not be relied on; make sure the movement and timing of your poster support the narrative.

Clockwise: Timing and movement can take different forms, from the quick cuts in Bravin's poster *Mulheria* to the subtle movements in Warner's poster *Rigoletto*. Brechbühl's poster *A Few Messages to Space* has speed and velocity that suck you into the black hole of the spinning vortex.

Rigoletto | **Art Direction/Design**: Daniel Warner | © Daniel Warner | **USA** | 1080 x 1920 px

A Few Messages to Space | **Design/Animation:** Erich Brechbühl | **Client**: Theater Aeternam | © Erich Brechbühl [Mixer] | **Switzerland** | 90.5 x 128 cm

CHAPTER SEVEN BEYOND THE PRINTED SURFACE

A *Pepita* | **Design/Animation**: Josh Schaub | © Josh Schaub | **Switzerland** | 21 × 33 cm

Clockwise: Schaub's poster *Pepita* uses circular shapes and typography as thin veneers of information that animate in a flattened three-dimensional space. Warner's poster *Russia (vote)* mixes quick and jolting cuts that grab your attention with graceful and elegant moves to tell his story. The timing and motion in Brechbühl's poster *Welcome to Lucerne* give the audience a sense of the hustle and bustle of the city.

Russia (vote) | **Art Direction/Design**: Daniel Warner | © Daniel Warner | **USA** | 1080 x 1920 px

A *Welcome to Lucerne* | **Design**: Erich Brechbühl | **Client**: JUSO Luzern | © Erich Brechbühl [Mixer] | **Switzerland** | 90.5 x 128 cm

A *Be Water* | **Design/Animation**: Erich Brechbühl | **Client**: Independent Art Spaces, Beijing | © Erich Brechbühl [Mixer] **Switzerland** | 59.4 x 84.1 cm

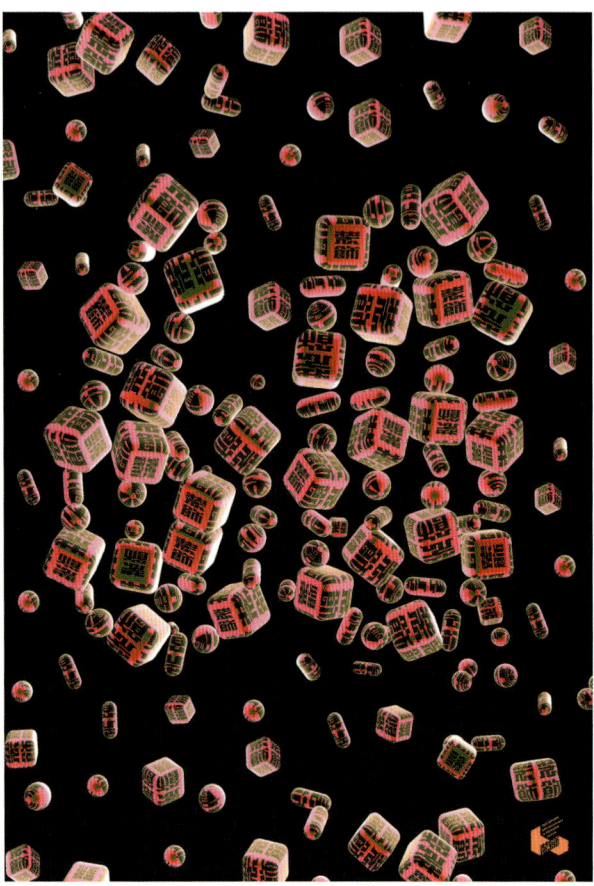

A *60th Anniversary of Zhuangshi* | **Design/Animation**: Li Xu | © Li Xu | **Taiwan** | 70 x 100 cm

Typography, like any other visual, requires timing and movement, but its movement cannot impede legibility. This does not mean that all typographic solutions need to follow any particular set of rules. As long as the typography communicates, experimentation is encouraged.

Clockwise: *Be Water*'s gelatinous amoeba-like creatures move about the page while still exposing enough of the typography so the viewer can read the content. The dramatic *Central Swiss Film Award 2019* poster's pure light and shadow harken back to when spotlights filled the sky at a film premiere.

Central Swiss Film Award 2019 | **Design/Animation**: Erich Brechbühl | **Client**: Albert Koechlin Stiftung | © Erich Brechbühl [Mixer] | **Switzerland** | 90.5 x 128 cm

CHAPTER SEVEN BEYOND THE PRINTED SURFACE

Schoen and Lehmann's poster *15 Jahre Radio 3FACH* glistens, glitters, and shines as it commemorates fifteen years of groundbreaking youth radio in Lucerne, Switzerland.

221

15 Jahre Radio 3FACH | © Raphael Schoen/Kaj Lehmann | **Client:** Radio 3FACH | **Switzerland** | 90.5 x 128 cm

MAKING POSTERS FROM CONCEPT TO DESIGN

Bold black and white, contrast, and scale dominate the spread. All these posters are rich and delightful on their own. However, through AR, these visuals animate and turn from fascinating to wondrous.

A *Le Rex* | © Studio WØT 2019 | **Client:** Neubad | **Sweden** | 29.7 x 42 cm

A *Totally Drunk* | © Studio WØT 2019 | **Sweden** | 29.7 x 42 cm

A *The Great Harry Hillman* | **Design/Illustration**: Benjamin Hermann | © Benjamin Hermann | **Client**: Kulturzentrum Neubad, Luzern | **Switzerland** | 90.5 x 128 cm

A *Life Universe & Everything* | **Design/Animation**: Josh Schaub | © Josh Schaub | **Switzerland** | 90.5 x 128 cm

A *KTV's Music Video Show* | © Amadeus Waltenspuhl | **Client**: Neubad Lucerne | **Switzerland** | 90.5 x 128 cm

Ⓐ *Wo Ist Die Liebe Hin, Für Musik Gegen Musik, You Are at Home Baby* | **Concept**: LWZ & Michael Wittmann | **Design/Illustration/Animation:** LWZ | **Copywriter**: Michael Wittmann | **Chief Marketing Officer FM4**: David Dittrich | © LWZ | **Client:** Radio FM4 | Austria | 59.4 x 84.1 cm

CHAPTER SEVEN BEYOND THE PRINTED SURFACE

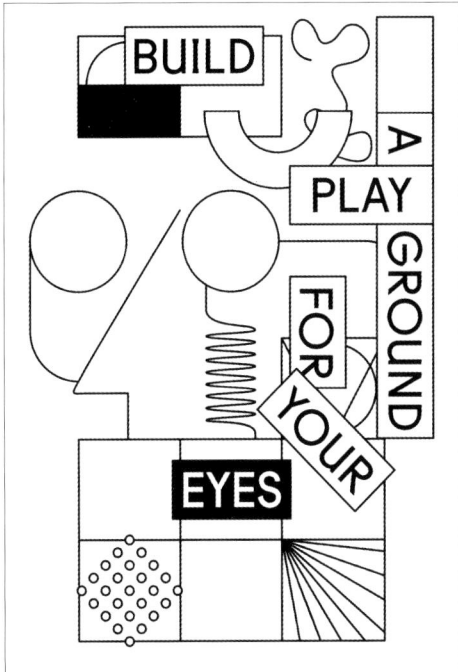
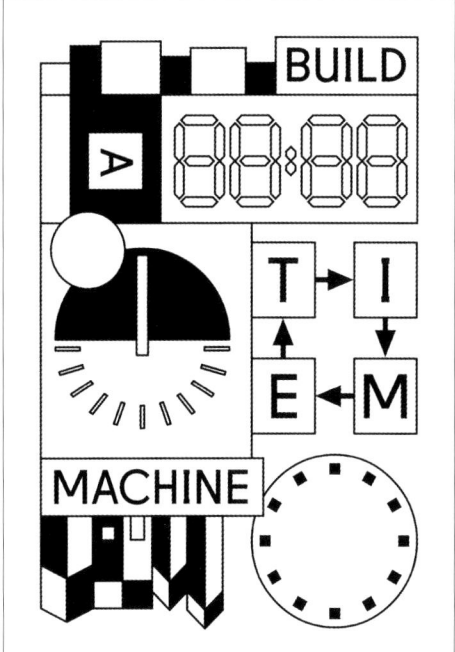

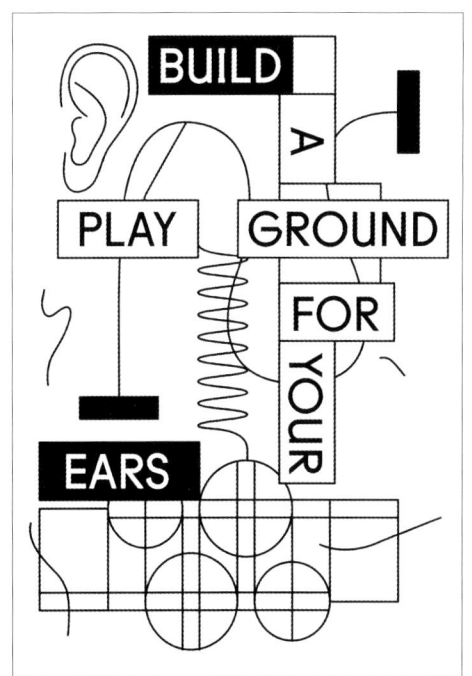

Whether your poster series is animated or not, the same rules of connecting posters across a series apply. In addition, animated poster series should have consistency of movement without repetition. Both series featuring LWZ and all of their talented collaborators demonstrate how to hold together an animated poster series with great success.

A *Build a Playground for Your Eyes, Build a Time Machine, Complete the Half Sentences of Your City, Build a Playground for Your Ears* | **Concept**: LWZ & Michael Wittmann | **Design/Illustration/Animation**: LWZ & Sebastian Pataki | © LWZ & Sebastian Pataki | **Client:** Museum of Applied Arts Vienna, Wirtschaftsagentur Wien, Institute of Design Research Vienna | **Austria** | 59.4 x 84.1 cm

When you bring together good planning, appropriate movement, and timing and blend them with strong transitions and sound, the outcome can be impressive.

Wang's storyboard from Figure 7.8 yielded a great result. Wang's sensitivity to timing, sound effects, and live footage are on display as he incorporates his visual interpretation and an iconic live scene from Martin Scorsese's classic film *Taxi Driver* into a rich sensory event that is unforgettable.

A *Taxi Driver* | **Design/Illustration/Animation**: Yibing Wang | © Yibing Wang | **Film Clip:** Martin Scorsese's *Taxi Driver* (5/8) Movie Clip—You Talkin' to Me? (1976) HD | https://www.youtube.com/watch?v=-QWL-FwX4t4 | **USA** | 43.2 x 55.9 cm

CHAPTER SEVEN BEYOND THE PRINTED SURFACE

A | *International Dessert Festival* | **Design/Illustration/Animation**: Jameela Wahlgren 2019 | © Jameela Wahlgren | **USA** | 61 x 88.9 cm

A | *Mexico City Film Festival* | **Design/Illustration/Animation**: Christian Gaston | © Christian Gaston | **USA** | 61 x 109.2 cm

Clockwise: Wahlgren, Gaston, and Klick all incorporate sound into the movement of their posters by selecting suitable sound effects or music, adding a layer of content that produces a lush and vibrant experience.

A | *Hej! Hej! International Dessert Fest in Malmo, Sweden* | **Design/Illustration/Animation**: Marissa Klick | © Marissa Klick | **USA** | 61 x 91.4 cm

Glossary

Abstraction A non-literal depiction in art.

Aesthetics A branch of philosophy that studies the subjective and sensorial values relating to beauty, art, and taste.

Alignment A straight-line arrangement, parallel to something.

Asymmetry Absence of symmetry.

Audience A crowd of listeners or spectators.

Background The area or ground behind something.

Balance A state with even distribution of weight on either side of an axis.

Baseline An invisible line serving as a base for typography.

Benoît Mandelbrot Responsible for the present interest in fractal geometry; showed how fractals occur in mathematics and elsewhere in nature.

Borders The margins around the printed matter.

Brainstorming Method for developing many ideas spontaneously.

Bricolage Using found objects and assembling them in an organized fashion to create a visual.

Color Also described in terms of hue; the appearance of objects and light sources.

Cognitive antecedent A stimulus that leads an organism to perform a learned behavior.

Cognitive system The mental structure consisting of interrelated beliefs, ideas, and items of knowledge that an individual holds about anything concrete or abstract.

Collage An artistic corpus made of different materials (such as paper, fabric, or plastic) attached to a surface.

Columns Vertical rows of items on a page.

Complementary colors Colors that appear opposite each other on the color wheel. When combined, they cancel each other out, producing gray. However, when used side by side, they cause visual vibration.

Composition The arrangement of objects on a page.

Connotative images Images that offer broader perspectives and help your story by building more profound connections. They are usually made up of many visuals that work together to form one strong message.

Content Typography and imagery that make up a composition.

Context An image's dependence on other visuals, objects, or typography to deliver a message.

Contrast The state of being noticeably different from something else.

Crescendo A gradual increase; specifically, an escalation in the volume of a musical composition.

Critique A detailed analytical discussion of a piece of artwork.

Cropping To cut out.

Crossfade To make a picture appear or a sound become audible gradually as another disappears or becomes silent.

Demographics The statistical characteristics of human populations commonly used to identify markets.

Denotative images Straightforward representations of an object or thing.

Dénouement The last part of a literary work.

Design brief The document that specifies what a project has to accomplish, by what means, and within what timeframe.

Design thinking Problem-solving strategy wherein the collected information is visually depicted to create new methods to solve problems or strengthen weaknesses.

Display type Type fonts that are larger than text fonts and give a distinctive disposition to a printed or displayed publication.

Droste effect The effect of a picture repeatedly appearing within itself forever.

Endorphins Chemicals produced by your body found primarily in the brain that induce pharmacological effects, such as pain relief.

Execution The act of doing or performing an idea or task.

Figure 1. A visual representation of a human form. 2. The foreground of a composition.

Flow To go steadily in a direction with smooth continuity.

Font A set of letters within a type family.

Foreground The closest part of a scene or representation relative to the spectator.

Frame The structure surrounding something, such as a picture or window, and holding it in place.

Framework The basic structure underlying a system, concept, or text.

Freeze frame A motion-picture frame repeated to convey the illusion of a static picture.

GarageBand™ Software supplied with a Mac that gives any user basic capabilities for editing and mixing sound.

Golden ratio See Leonardo Fibonacci.

Grid A structure of evenly spaced horizontal and perpendicular lines.

Grouping Set of objects incorporated in a group.

Gutter The white space between the adjoining inside margins of two facing pages or between adjacent columns of type.

Halo effect A perception distortion that affects the way people interpret information about someone.

Haptic Relating to the sense of touch or conveying the feeling of physical touch.

Harmony A pleasing arrangement of parts.

Hierarchy The arrangement of objects in a composition from most important to least relevant.

Homage An expression of respect toward someone or something, usually in art.

HTML5 The latest version of HTML, allowing for animated movement.

Hue A shade or percentage of a color.

Icon A symbol or graphic representation of an object or form.

Iconography A group of images or symbols associated with a particular subject.

Image A visual representation of something: the likeness of an object on a photographic material or a picture produced on an electronic display.

Immersive technology Any technology that creates an alternate universe by immersing a user in a three-dimensional world.

Interactive Involving the actions or input of a third party.

JavaScript The scripting language used to create interaction and movement on web pages.

Jump-cut An abrupt transition from one shot or scene to another.

Keyframing Points on a timeline that signify a change in the behavior of an object.

Layout Organization of predetermined material placed on a page.

Leading See line spacing.

Leonardo Fibonacci An Italian mathematician who identified the golden ratio, the common proportions of everything in nature, from atoms to the most massive celestial bodies.

Letter spacing The insertion of space between a word's letters.

Light and shadow The contrast that makes vision possible.

Line spacing The space between lines of set typography.

Lock up A typographic design where words and/or characters are fitted together like a puzzle, literally locking up the typography, usually into a specific shape.

Ludic Playful.

Macrocosm An extensive system considered as a single unity.

Matryoshka dolls Also known as Russian nesting dolls; a set of wooden toys of decreasing size placed one inside another.

Meta-emotions Conscious emotions about both one's own feelings and the feelings of others.

Metaphor A figure of speech where a word or phrase indicating one type of object or idea is used in place of another to express a likeness or equivalence between them.

Microcosm A small community resembling a larger unity.

Mind-mapping Using a diagram to organize information that allows for surprising and unexpected connections.

Minimal The least possible; very small or slight.

Mixed media Using or encompassing several media.

Mnemonic A device intended to assist with remembrance; of or relating to memory.

Mock-up 1. A structural model built to scale, mainly for study, testing, or display. 2. A working sample.

Mood boards Samples of color, texture, imagery, typography, photography, materials, and stylistic approach found during the research phase of the design process and collected as a source of inspiration.

Monochromatic Having or consisting of one color.

Motion design A discipline that applies graphic design knowledge to filmmaking and video production through the use of animation and visual effects.

Motion graphics Pieces of digital footage or animation that convey the illusion of motion or rotation; tend to be combined with audio for multimedia projects.

Narrative art The narration of a story through imagery.

Navigation system An electronic system that aids in navigation.

Nostalgia A wistful or excessively sentimental yearning for things past.

Pattern The repetition of a visual over and over again, creating a natural rhythm.

Perceptual overlays Abstract perceptual cues introduced into a user's perceptual reality as constructs overlaid onto the data reflected from the remote site.

Positive and negative space Positive space refers to a picture's main focus, while negative space refers to the background.

Poster A bill or placard, often in a public place, designed to communicate something visually.

Primary colors A group of three colors—red, yellow, and blue—from which all other colors are created.

Proportion Relationship between things, or to the whole, in size, amount, or importance.

Psychographics Market research or statistics classifying population groups according to standardized or newborn psychological variables.

Qualitative data Exploration of material without being inhibited by predetermined findings.

Quantifiable data The capacity to determine or measure the quantity of something numerical or quantifiable.

Quick-cut An animation style involving instant transitions.

Quick sketch Generally applied to graphic art; a fast-paced exercise to produce as many ideas as possible without reviewing them.

Ray Harryhausen American-born British artist, designer, visual effects creator, writer, and producer who created Dynamation, a form of stop-motion model animation.

Reminiscence Recollection of a long-forgotten experience or fact.

Retro Relating to the styles and fashions of the past.

Rising action A series of relevant incidents that create suspense, interest, and tension in a narrative.

Rule of odds A guideline that states that images are more visually attractive when there is an odd number of subjects in their arrangement.

Rule of thirds A system that divides a layout into three equally spaced horizontal lines and three vertical lines, then places the focal point on one of the lines or, ideally, on one of the four points where the lines intersect.

Rhythm Constant and recurrent alternation of strong and weak accents within visuals, sound, and speech.

Roughs Loose, informal presentations of artwork.

Rubin vase Also known as the figure/ground vase or the Rubin face; a famous bi-stable or two-dimensional form developed around 1915 by the Danish psychologist Edgar Rubin.

Rule (line) A one-dimensional path that can also define the edges of a shape.

Sans serif A letterform without serifs.

Saturation Degree of intensity from the achromatic light-source color of the same brightness.

Scale A measure based on contrasts between two or more things.

Script A set of letters of fluid strokes that resemble handwriting.

Secondary colors Colors that result from mixing two primary colors in equal quantities.

Semiotics The theory of signs and symbols that deals with their function and interpretation.

Serif Short lines stemming from the upper and lower ends of the strokes of a letter.

Serotonin A chemical found in the brain, blood serum, and gastric mucous membrane of mammals, the lack of which is thought to be associated with depression.

Shape The visible form that something has, whether spatial or contour structure.

Soundscape The mixture of musical and nonmusical sounds.

Split-complementary color scheme Use of a color and two colors adjacent to its complement.

Stop-motion animation Animation captured one frame at a time where objects are manipulated between frames.

Storyboard Similar to a comic; a consecutive sequence of panels arranged in a linear order depicting changes and transitions in a narrative.

Style A distinctive, personal manner of expression or approach.

Symbol A visible sign that stands for something intangible due to an association, convention, or resemblance.

Symmetry The quality of being the same on both sides or having balanced proportions.

Synesthesia A subjective perceptual phenomenon related to the crossing over of visual or auditory stimuli.

Tagline A phrase related to an individual, group, or product.

Tandem narrative Two or more stories, usually related, running in parallel.

Temperature (color) The spectral properties of a light source.

Tint A variation of a color produced by adding white.

Thumbnail sketches Often made as a preliminary study; represent the main features of an object or scene.

Tracking See letter spacing.

Transparency The quality or capacity of being see-through.

Triadic color scheme A color scheme using three colors situated 120 degrees apart on the color wheel, creating a harmonious and vibrant look even with pale and unsaturated hues.

Type alignment One of four basic arrangements of a line or block of copy: flush left/rag right, flush right/rag left, justified, or centered.

Typestyle Different format of a typeface, e.g., bold, italic, strikethrough, etc.

Typeface A set of characters of the same design that may consist of different fonts.

Typographic design The art and process of designing typefaces.

Typography The visual art of the written word.

Ub Iwerks American animator and innovator who worked at Walt Disney Studios.

Uppercase A typeface consisting of capitals, fractions, symbols, and accents.

Upper Paleolithic Age of man The third and last subdivision of the Old Stone Age, characterized by the emergence of regional stone tool industries.

Variation The difference between similar things.

Vintage Dating from the past.

Virtual fixtures Augmented sensory information to convey the impression of a real environment.

Visual salience (saliency) A perceptual quality that makes some items stand out from others and immediately grab attention.

Visual voice The distinctive way to define your aesthetic.

Visual weight The visual force that appears in an image due to the contrast of light among the visual elements that structure it.

Word bank A set of words made available to support writing.

Word spacing The size of the space between words, designed to aid readability or create aesthetic effects.

Zoom To increase suddenly so that the object's apparent distance from the observer changes.

Bibliography

For more information on qualitative and quantitative research, visit www.making-posters.com/resources.

1 Guffey, E. E. (2015). *Posters: A Global History*. London: Reaktion Books, 7.

2 Resnick, E. (2019). *Graphic Advocacy: International Posters for the Digital Age*. Available online: http://www.graphicadvocacyposters.org (accessed September 15, 2019).

3 Hurston, Z. N. (1942). *Dust Tracks on a Road*. Philadelphia, PA: J. B. Lippincott & Co.

4 Grant, A. (2016). *The Surprising Habits of Original Thinkers* (TED conference, April 10). Available online: https://youtu.be/fxbCHn6gE3U (accessed April 26, 2016).

5 Reason, P. (2004). Critical design ethnography as action research. *Anthropology & Education Quarterly*, 35(2), 269–276.

6 Davis, W. (2010). *Replications: Archaeology, Art History, Psychoanalysis*. University Park, PA: Penn State Press, 4.

7 Cherry, K. (2019). Gestalt laws of perceptual organization. *VeryWell Mind* (updated September 2, 2019). Available online: http://psychology.about.com/od/sensationandperception/ss/gestaltlaws.htm (accessed September 15, 2019).

8 Mambrol, N. (2016, March 21). Claude Levi Strauss' concept of bricolage. *Literary Theory and Criticism Notes*. Available online: https://literariness.org/2016/03/21/claude-levi-strauss-concept-of-bricolage (accessed September 15, 2019).

9 Burke, E. (2001). *On the Sublime and the Beautiful*, Vol. XXIV, Part 2. New York: PF Collier & Son, 1909–14.

10 Jess (2008, September 10). Black, red and white: Colour symbolism throughout cultures. *Nexus Zine*. Available online: https://nexuszine.wordpress.com/2008/09/10/black-red-and-white-colour-symbolism-throughout-cultures-by-jess (accessed September 2, 2019).

11 Papastergiadis, N. (2013). The color of the cosmos: John Berger on art and the mystery of creativity. *Canadian Review of Comparative Literature/Revue Canadienne de Littérature Comparée*, 40(4): 353.

12 Miller, R. (2017, June 7). Tune in to your breath in meditation to find inner peace. *Yoga Journal*. Available online: https://www.yogajournal.com/meditation/tune-breath-meditation-find-inner-peace (accessed September 15, 2019).

13 Rapp, C. (2011). Aristotle's rhetoric. *Stanford Encyclopedia of Philosophy*. Available online: https://stanford.library.sydney.edu.au/archives/win2011/entries/aristotle-rhetoric/ (accessed November 13, 2019).

14 Frascara, J. (2000). *Diseno Grafico Para La Gente*. Buenos Aires, Argentina: Ediciones Infinito.

15 Sanchez-Lozano, C. (2013). Storyweavers. *HapticMind*. Presented November 29, 2013 at Creative-Science 2013 as part of the 3rd Immersive Education Summit, Kings College London, 2.

16 Esqueda, R. (2000). El juego del diseño: Un acercamiento a sus reglas de interpretación creativa. Universidad Autónoma Metropolitana, Unidad Xochimilco.

17 Buchanan, R. (2001). Design and the new rhetoric: Productive arts in the philosophy of culture. *Philosophy & Rhetoric*, 34(3), 183–206.

18 Fazio, J. R. (2010, June 3). How to care for arborvitae, the tree of life. *Arbor Day Foundation*. Available online: https://arbordayblog.org/treecare/how-to-care-for-arborvitae (accessed September 2, 2019).

19 Hichem, N. (n.d.). Art and emotion, in J. Fieser and B. Dowden (eds), *Internet Encyclopedia of Philosophy, Art and Emotion*. Available online: https://www.iep.utm.edu/art-emot (accessed September 15, 2019).

20 Nelson, D. L., U. S. Reed and J. R. Walling (1976). Pictorial superiority effect. *Journal of Experimental Psychology: Human Learning & Memory* 2(5): 523–528.

21 Page, D. (2017, November 6). The science behind why we can't look away from tragedy. *NBC News*. Available online: https://www.nbcnews.com/better/health/science-behind-why-we-can-t-look-away-disasters-ncna804966 (accessed September 2, 2019).

22 Freud, S. and J. E. Strachey (1964). *The Standard Edition of the Complete Psychological Works of Sigmund Freud*. New York, NY: W.W. Norton, 217–256.

23 Catharsis. *Encyclopedia Britannica Online* (2004). Available online: https://www.britannica.com/art/catharsis-criticism (accessed August 10, 2019).

24 Harp seal hunt in the northwest Atlantic ecoregion (2012, March 8). *WWF Canada*. Available online: https://sealsandsealing.net/wp-content/uploads/2017/02/WWF-Seal-Hunt-Position-Statement-Final-March-8-2012.pdf (accessed September 15, 2019).

25 Yim, J. (2016). Therapeutic benefits of laughter in mental health: a theoretical review. *The Tohoku Journal of Experimental Medicine*, 239(3), 243–249.

26 Hernández, J. (2013). El maíz trasgénico en México en 15 píldoras. Available online: https://www.academia.edu/20231865/El_maiz_transgenico_en_Mexico_en_15_pildoras_ver_Oaxaca (accessed July 12, 2019).

27 Once upon a time (1989). *Oxford English Dictionary*. Available online: https://www.lexico.com/en/definition/once_upon_a_time (accessed November 5, 2019).

28 Lucas, G. (n.d.). Lucas Museum of Narrative Art. Available online: https://lucasmuseum.org (accessed September 15, 2019).

29 MacLean, P. D. (1990). *The Triune Brain in Evolution: Role in Paleocerebral Functions*. Berlin, Germany: Springer Science & Business Media.

30 Taste and smell (2012, April 1). *BrainFacts.org*. Available online: http://www.brainfacts.org/Thinking-Sensing-and-Behaving/Taste/2012/Taste-and-Smell (accessed September 15, 2019).

31 Classen, C., D. Howes and A. Synnott (2002). *Aroma: The Cultural History of Smell*. Abingdon-on-Thames, UK: Routledge.

32 Klein, S. (2017, December 6). 8 things you probably didn't know about your tongue. *Huffington Post*. Available online: https://www.huffpost.com/entry/tongue-facts-health-info_n_5952850 (accessed September 14, 2019).

33 Choi, C. Q. (2011, November 22). Why it pays to taste words and hear colors. *Live Science*. Available online: https://www.livescience.com/17156-synesthesia-taste-words-benefits.html (accessed November 5, 2019).

34 Lefèvre, W. (2007). *Inside the Camera Obscura—Optics and Art under the Spell of the Projected Image*. Berlin, Germany: Max Planck Institute for the History of Science, 145.

35 About the Walt Disney Company. (n.d.). Available online: https://www.thewaltdisneycompany.com/about (accessed September 1, 2019).

36 How posters survive and thrive in a digital age (2013, July 15). *Phaidon*. Available online: https://ca.phaidon.com/agenda/design/articles/2013/july/15/how-posters-survive-and-thrive-in-a-digital-age (accessed September 12, 2019).

37 Animation software: Which one should you use? *Bloop Animation*. Available online: https://www.bloopanimation.com/animation-software/ (accessed November 13, 2019).

38 Hallam, S. (2010). The power of music: Its impact on the intellectual, social and personal development of children and young people. *International Journal of Music Education*, 28(3), 269–289.

39 Poyntz, S. (2002). *Visual Storytelling and the Grammar of Filmmaking, Part II, Study Guide 02*. Vancouver, BC: Open Learning Agency.

40 Colombi, G. (2016, November 4). Moving posters: A new poster movement. *Decographic*. Available online: https://blog.decographic.net/moving-posters-a-new-poster-movement (accessed September 1, 2019).

41 Caudell, T. P. and D. W. Mizell (1992). Augmented reality: An application of heads-up display technology to manual manufacturing processes, in *Proceedings of the Twenty-Fifth Hawaii International Conference on System Sciences*, Vol. 2. IEEE: 659–669.

42 Sutherland, I. E. (1968). A head-mounted three-dimensional display, in *Proceedings of the AF/PS Fall Joint Computer Conference*. Washington, D.C.: Thompson Books, 757–764.

INDEX

Page references in *italics* denote illustrations.

A

Access (poster), *162*
ACUD BERLIN (WET in BERLIN) (poster), *102*, 103
Adams, Bryan, 152, *153*
Adobe Photoshop, 202, 210
Aesop, 136
aesthetics, 68
Afshar, Mohammad, 70, *72*, 185
After Effects, 202
Ahmed, Umer, 63, *64*, 129
AIDA formula (Attention, Interest, Desire, and Action), 14
Alcatraz, mind-map for, *32*
Aldriglandet (Neverland) (poster), *184*
allusion, 142–43
Almonte Díaz, José Gerardo, *114*, *121*
Alphabet Insectorum (poster series), 66, *66*
Alzheimer (poster), *157*
Amaranta (poster), *121*
American Dream (poster), *122*
Aminelahi, Onish, 87
Anatomy of a Murder (poster), 24, *25*
Andy Lund in NYC (poster), *92*
animated posters, 200–202
animation, 204
Años de Jazz (poster), *44*
Antony and Cleopatra (poster), 103, *103*
Arena, Luis, 18
Aristotle, 137, 138, 149
Aroma Company, 195
arousal, 152, 158, 160
Art Deco, 17, 21
Art Nouveau, 14
art of persuasion. *See* persuasion
Art of Rhetoric (Aristotle), 138
asymmetry, 62, 64
attention, 101. *See also* grabbing attention
audience, 29–30
augmented reality posters, 206, 208–9
Aux Night and Jaz Ruine (poster), *97*

B

Bad Breath (poster), 24, *25*
Bagley, Caroline, 188, *188*
Baldaia, Mariana, 70, *71*
Bankov, Peter, *91*, *97*, *114*, *116*
Bareis, Felix, *110*, 111
Basel School of Design, 21
Bass, Saul, 18, 24, *25*
Batory, Michal, *43*, 156, *157*
Batten, Barton, Durstine & Osborn (BBDO), 32
Bauhaus, 17

Belle & Sebastian (poster), *90*
Belle Époque, 14
Berg, John, 6
Bernhard, Lucian, 15
Be Water (poster), 220, *220*
Beware (poster), 171, *171*
Beyond Peace (poster), 107, *107*
Big Brother (poster), *95*
A Bite of China (poster), 164, *165*
Bitter Campari (poster), 26, *26*
Bitter Campari Alcoholic Beverage (poster), 26, *26*
Blomqvist, Anders, 168
Blood Oil (case study), 213–14
Blood Oil (poster), *214*
blue, 59
Boguslawski, Tomasz, 68, *69*, 83, *93*
Bolshevik Revolution, 17
Boofe Koor, The Honoring of the Iranian Writer Sadegh Hedayat (poster), *123*
Bouloutian, Matthew, *130*, *181*, 189
brainstorming, 32
Brandt, Erik, 144, *144*
Brave New World (poster), *215*
Breathe (poster), *85*
Brechbühl, Erich, 204, 206, *207*, *208*, *209*, 218, *218*, *219*, *219*, 220, *220*
BRECHT (poster), *157*
Bring in 'Da Noise, Bring in 'Da Funk (poster), 176, *176*
Bring Waste Papers—Help Your School (poster), *161*
brown, 59
Buchanan, Richard, 143
Build a Playground for Your Ears (poster), *225*
Build a Playground for Your Eyes (poster), *225*
Build a Time Machine (poster), *225*
Bundi, Stephan, *134*, *135*, 169, *170*, 180, *180*
Bureaucracy Kills Good Work (poster), *188*
Burke, Edmund, 103
Buzan, Tony, 32

C

Cabañas, Benito, *41*, *87*, *122*
Camper for Kids (poster series), 146, *147*
Canadian Conference of the Arts (poster), 74, *75*
Cappiello, Leonetto, 16, 26, *26*, 117
Cappiello style, 16
Caroff, Joseph, *174*, *175*
Carson, David, 21
Casa de las Américas, 19
case studies
 Blood Oil (Laserow), 213–14
 Converse/Marimekko (Lewis), 117, *118*, 119
 Dead Leaf (Scott), 77–79

 Somos de Maíz (Delgado), 154, *155*
 Splendent Sun (Mac Cormack), 35, *36*, *37*
 Storytelling (Scorsone and Drueding), 177–78
Cassandre, A. M., 17
catharsis, 149
Caudell, Tom, 206
Cavazza, Giulia, *150*, 151
Central Swiss Film Award 2019 (poster), 220, *220*
Cerrella, Coco, 111, *111*, 156
Cézanne, Paul, 108
Chan, Eva May, 162, *163*
channel, 138–39
Chantry, Art, 86, 173, *173*
Chaplin 120 (poster), 160, *161*
Chavez, Cesar, 20
Chekhov Lizardbrain (poster), 189, *189*
Chéret, Jules, *14*
Chicano Poster movement, 20
Chung, Hoon-Dong, 46, 68, 70, *70*
Chwast, Seymour, 24, *25*, 126, *127*
Cinnamon Coke (poster), *195*
Climate Is Changing (poster), 152, *152*
CO_2 (poster), *87*
color, 59
 burst of, 108
 contrasting temperature, 105
 power of three, 107
 triadic color palettes, 107
 using, to demand attention, 103, 105
 using complementary, 105, 107
Colrat, Pascal, *88*, *94*, *95*, 182, *182*
Como no me iba a enamorar . . . mi Fridita (poster), 59, *60*
complementary colors, 105, 107
Complete the Half Sentences of Your City (poster), *225*
composition and hierarchy, 60–61
computer-generated imagery (CGI), 200–201
concept, 23
 defining resources, 30–31
 ideation techniques for, 31–34
 knowing audience, 29–30
 knowing facts, 27
 knowing message, 27–29
 knowing project, 24, 26
 training your eye, 26
conceptualization. *See* ideation techniques
Constructivism, 16
Consumption of This Product Is a Danger to the Planet (poster), 29, *29*
context, 68
Continui (poster), *64*
contrast, power of, 103
Convergence (poster), *108*

233

Converse/Marimekko (case study), 117, *118*, 119
Converse/Marimekko (poster), *119*
Cooch Creative, 196
Costumbre Mexicana (poster), *91*
Cradle of Tortured Peace (poster), *185*
Creativity Has No Bounds (poster), *63*, 64
Crime and Punishment (poster), *120*, 121
Cuban Institute of Cinematographic Art and Industry (ICAIC), 19
Cuban Revolution, 19
Cubism, 16
Curls (poster), 140, *141*

D

Dadaism, 16, 43
The Damp House (poster), 70, 72
Darwin, Charles, 32
David, Michelangelo, 151
David Bowie 1947–2016 (poster), *123*
Da Vinci, Leonardo, 32
Day-Lewis, Daniel, 10
Day of the Dead Anatomical Study (poster), 160, *161*
Dead Leaf (case study), 77, *78*, *79*
Decade Kung Fu Exhibition (poster), *134*
The Decemberists (poster), *45*, *91*
Deconstructivism, 21
Dehar, Zahia, 152, *153*
Delgado, Natalia, *74*, 154, *155*
Der Gott des Gemetzels (The God of Slaughter) (poster), *134*
Desertification of a Tree (poster), *162*
Design by Day, 113, *113*
Design Dogs and Depositions (poster), *158*
design process, 51
    aesthetics, 68
    color, 59
    composition and hierarchy, 60–61
    context, 68
    creating poster series, 67
    evaluating your design, 76
    figure/ground, 58
    focal point, 64
    image making, 52, 54, 80
    line, 54–55
    making mistakes, 74–75
    methods and materials, 70, 72
    rule of odds, 64
    rule of thirds, 62
    symmetry and asymmetry, 62, 64
    type as image, 57–58, 80
    using a grid, 61–62
    white space, 66
De Stijl, 17
Deutscher Werkbund, 15, 16
Diario de un Loco (poster), 114
Digital Medicine (poster), *46*

digital posters, interactive, 208–9
direction, 113
Disney, Walt, 32
Disney Brothers Cartoon Studio, 200
disruption, 114
DMZ International Documentary Film Festival (9th) (poster), 112, *112*
Documentary (poster), 185, *185*
Dogfish Punkin' Ale (poster), 124, *125*
Don't Cry over Spilt Milk (poster), *92*
Doyle, Stephen, *47*, 190, *191*
Doyle Dane Bernbach (DDB), 6
Dracula Is Grotesk (poster), 57, *57*
Drewinski, Lex, 40, *47*, 103, *103*, 122
Drueding, Alice, 144, *144*, 159, *159*, 171, *171*, 177–78, *178*
Duchamp, Marcel, 6
DUMBLAND and After Coronaria-PCI (poster), *98*
Dylan (poster), 6, 7, *24*, 25

E

Easy Horse Rider (poster), *82*
Eat Your Greens (poster), *198*
Ed Sheeran (poster), *45*
8 May 1945—Victory in Europe Day (poster), *47*
Einstein, Albert, 32
Emigrate or Die (poster), *181*
emotional connection, 148–49
Enceladus (poster), 172, *173*
Era of Disinformation (poster), *133*
Esqueda, Román, 140
Ethos (poster), 94, *95*
euphemism, 148
expressionism, 19
eye gaze and pointing, 114
Eyolf (Something in Me Is Gnawing at Me) (poster), 182, *182*

F

facts, 27
fear and shock, 149, 151
Feng, Sha, 94, *95*, *134*, 135, *164*, *165*
Ferrer, Isidro, 146, *146*, *147*
Festival des Films du Monde (poster), *127*
Festival Outre-Mer Veille (poster), *88*
A Few Messages to Space (poster), 218, *218*
Fibonacci, Leonardo, 112
Fiddler on the Roof (poster), *179*
15 Jahre Radio 3FACH (poster), *221*
figure/ground, 58, 89
First World War, 17
Fistula (poster), 177, *178*
5 Years Elmer Sosa & 6 Years Elmer Sosa (poster), *84*
Flagg, James Montgomery, 137, *138*
Flat Life (poster), 194, *194*
Fleming, Sir Alexander, 74

Flow Festival 2014 (poster), 201, *202*
Flowers, Rob, 196, *197*, *198*
focal point, 64, 89
For Sale by Owner (poster), *11*
1492–1992 (poster), *122*
Frankenstein (poster), *88*
Frankenstein Is Franklin Gothic (poster), 57, *57*
Free 30+ Sunscreen (poster), 196, *196*
Freedom of Movement (poster), *157*
Freeman, Sean, 90, *91*, 94, *135*, 181, *181*
Free to Choose Love (poster), 209, *209*
French Revolution, 14
French Revolutionary emblem, illustration of, *14*
Freud, Sigmund, 149
Friedman, Dan, 21
Fu, Yongkang, 58, *58*
Fuentes, Mario, 84, 94, *95*, *96*, *108*
Fukuda, Shigeo, 24, *25*
Futurism, 16

G

Gardi Hutter (poster), 180, *180*
Garla, Ricardo, 143, *143*
Gaston, Christian, 227, *227*
Gautier, Theophile, 50
Gestalt psychology movement, 60
Get Your Hands Dirty (poster), *128*
Glaser, Milton, 6, 7, *24*, 25, 41, 126, *127*
Glasgow School of Arts, 15
glossary, 228–31
Glow in The Dark Ice Cream (poster), *198*
Golden Age, 14
Golden Age of Poland, 19
Golden Week (poster), *187*
Gombrowicz, Witold, 160
Gómez, Santiago, *47*
Gosha, Evdokimov, 52, *52–53*
Go Up, Man (poster), *128*
GQ Magazine (poster), *127*
grabbing attention, 101
    burst of color, 108
    contrasting temperature, 105
    disruption, 114
    eye gaze and pointing, 114
    movement, 113
    power of contrast, 103
    rhythm and pattern, 112
    scale, 111
    triadic color palettes, 107
    using color to, 103, 105
    using complementary colors, 105, 107
Gramlich, Götz, 204
Grant, Adam, 34
graphic design, 8, 9, 10
The Great Harry Hillman (poster), *223*
green, 59
Green Fairy (poster), *186*

Greener, More Beautiful (poster), 28, *29*
Greiman, April, *21*
Grey London, 199, *199*
grid, 92
    rule of thirds, 62
    using a, 61–62
Griffin, Rick, *20*
Gropius, Walter, 17
grunge, 21
Guevara Rangel, Miguel Angel, 12, *39*

H

Hama, Larry, 9
Hamilton (poster), 88
Harnoko, Irwan, *83*
Harris, Natalie, *97*
Hart, Todd, 57, *57*–58
Hasta la Visa Baby (poster), *134*
Heads of State, 44, *45*
Hej! Hej! International Dessert Fest in Malmo, Sweden (poster), *227*
Hemmat, Elham, *98*, *99*, 156, *157*, *183*
Herbstzeitlose (poster), 204, *205*
Hermann, Benjamin, *223*
hierarchy, composition and, 60–61
Hilfiger, Tommy, 59
Hill, Adam, *45*, *92*, 186, *186*
Hohlwein, Ludwig, 15
Holohan, Kelly, *123*, 158, *158*
Homage to Sonia Delaunay (poster), *41*
Homer, 137
Hommage Fukuda (poster), *41*
Honshu Japan study, 54, *54*
Horkay, István, *98*
Houdini (poster), *127*
humor, 151–52, 158
HUNGER (poster), 151, *151*
Hurricane Katrina (poster), *98*
Hurston, Zora Neale, 24
Hut Hut (poster), *82*
Huygens, Christiaan, 200
hyperbole, 144, 163

I

ideation techniques, 31–34
    brainstorming, 32
    making lists, 32–33
    mind-mapping, 32
    mood boards, 33
    quick sketches, 33–34
    reflection, 34
    reviewing past work, 33
IKEA *Unböring* campaign, 203
Ilić, Mirko, 48–49
Illiteracy (poster), 111, *111*
image making, 52, 54, 80, 94
The Immigrant Experience (poster), *81*

Immigration Wall (poster), *156*
Interact 5 (poster), *96*
interactive digital posters, 208–9
interactive posters, 194
International Dessert Festival (poster), *227*
irony, 143–44, 163
Israel Palestine 2003 (poster), 149, *149*
It Happens When Nobody Is Watching (poster), 200, *200*
I've Been Compromised (poster), *183*
I Want You for the U.S. Army (poster), 137, *138*

J

Japan Summer Workshop (poster), *134*
Jaws (film), 203
Jazz Is Like a Picasso (poster), 145, *146*
Jazz Ltd. (poster), 55, *56*
Jenko, Radovan, 128, *129*
Jiménez, David, *129*, *134*, 162, *163*
Jim Henson Exhibition (poster), *188*
Jordan, Esteban, *106*, 107
Jugendstil (*Jugend*-style), 15
Jung v Matt, 200
Jung von Matt/Alster, 142, *142*

K

Kafka, Franz, *39*
Kahlo, Frida, 59
Kaja, Ryszard, *92*, *132*, 133, 179, *179*
Karasova, Maria, 28, *28*
Kath, Gitte, 184, *184*
Katla Vodka (poster), *186*
Kekishev, Marko, *83*
Kepler 186f (poster), *172*, 173
Killer Type (poster), *57*
Kind of Art (poster), *47*
Kiss of the Spider Woman (poster), *87*
Klein, David, 18
Klick, Marissa, 227, *227*
Klutsis, Gustav, 16
Koloman, Moser, 15
Krebs, Soonduk, *98*
Krol Roger (poster), *93*
KTV's Music Video Show (poster), *223*
Kunce, Piotr, *97*, *128*, *129*, *161*
Kunz, Willi, 21
Kyoto Travel Poster, *9*

L

Lacey, James, 140, *140*
Ladies and Gentleman, I Represent the New Symbol of Peace (poster), *90*
La metamorfosis (poster), *39*
Laserow, Scott, *75*, 213–14
Lasseter, John, 192
The Last of the Mohicans (poster), *10*

Lautrec Today (poster), *123*
law of closure, 58
Leete, Alfred, 137
Lehmann, Kaj, *221*
Lemel, Yossi, 68, *70*, *133*, 149, *149*, 158, *158*
Le Rex (poster), *222*
Levi-Strauss, Claude, 70
Lewis, Andrew, *108*, *117*, *118*, 119, *119*, 126, *127*
Liberté (poster), *40*
Libre Libra 2018 (poster), *62*
Lichtenstein, Roy, 19
Life Universe & Everything (poster), *223*
Lindeman, Nicky, *88*
line, design element, 54–55
Lissitzky, El, 16
list making, 32–33, 38
Litfaß, Ernst, 14
Litfaßsäule, 14
lithographic poster, birth of, 14
Living Space (poster), 58, *58*
The Ljubljana Vodnik Guide Found Vodnik (poster), *129*
López Rocha, Manuel, *161*
A Lot of Steak (poster), 27, *27*
Love & Peace (poster), *88*
Lucybell—Peces Tour 20 Years (poster), *125*

M

Macbeth (posters), 68, *70*
Mac Cormack, Dermot, 35, *36*, *96*, *134*, 135
Mac DeMarco (poster), *135*
Macdonald, Frances, 15
Macdonald, Margaret, 15
Mackintosh, Charles Rennie, *15*
MacNair, Herbert, 15
The Madman & the Nun (poster), 68, *69*
Mad Men (poster), 126, *127*
McElroy, Patricia, 35, *36*, *96*, *134*
Magaloo (poster), *75*
Magee, Finn, 194
Mais GMO (poster), *42*
Make It Possible (poster), 105, *105*
making lists, 32–33, 38
making mistakes, 74–75
Man and Nature (poster), *108*
Mandelbrot, Benoît, 112
Marcolla, Tomaso, *42*
Marco Tóxico, *44*, *124*, *125*, 126, *127*
Marinetti, Filippo Tommaso, 16
Maryland Institute College of Art (MICA), 108
Matchsticks Forest (poster), *42*
Matter, Herbert, 24, *25*
Mayer, John, 149
Mazhar Haddad, Wesam, *42*, 159, *159*, *162*, *163*, *185*
Mazzenga, Francesco, 72, *73*
Medeia (poster), *108*

Memory Capsules (poster), 96
Memphis Style, 21
Méndez, Leopoldo, 18
Menicou, Maria, 199
Mercedes Salgado, Maria, *62*
Merinos Arrieta, Daniela, *91*
Mermaid Tears (poster), *159*
message, 27–29, 138
metaphor, 139–40, 156, 160
metonymy, 140, 156, 164
Mexico City Film Festival (poster), *227*
México Dulce y Querido (poster series), 30, *30, 31*
Meyer, Hannes, 17
Meza Romero, Obed, 29, *29*
M for Mantis (poster), 66, *66*
"M" Fritz Lang (poster), *89*
MICA SMART Recruitment Poster (poster), 108, *109*
Michalowska, Karolina, 124, *125*
Mies van der Rohe, Ludwig, 17
mind-mapping, 32, 38
Minini, Marcos, 64, *65, 68, 70*
mistakes, making, 74–75
Mizell, David, 206
Mondrian, Piet, 17
mood boards, 33, 38
Montreal Black Film Festival (13th) (poster), *106,* 107
Morainslie, Gustavo, 27, *27,* 124, *125,* 163, 215
Morris, Phoebe, 89
Moscony, Craig, 66, *66*
Moto (poster), *122*
movement, 113
moving posters, 200
Mucha, Alphonse Maria, 14
Mulheria (poster), *218*
Murga, Julieta, 30, *30, 31*
Museo Nacional de Arte (poster), *132*
music, sound and, 202–4
Music Is Oxygen (poster), *121*
Music Juice (poster), *198*
MŮSÎQÂT (poster), 70, *71*
Muthesius, Hermann, 16

N

narratives
    across a poster series, 175–76
    art, 168
    multiple, 175
NASA Jet Propulsion Laboratory, *172,* 173
The National (poster), *94*
NEST (poster), *61*
Newman, Jon, 92, *128*
Newton, Isaac, 32
New Wave, 21
New York School, 18
Nicholson, Gary, *64*
Nicolaus, Christian, *110,* 111

Niessen, Richard, *128*
The Nightmare of Edgar Allan Poe (poster), *122*
Niklaus Troxler Design, 20
Ninkovic, Nina, 181, *181*
Nitsche, Erik, 19
Nixon, Richard, 9
No + Acoso Sexual 2016 (poster), *157*
No H2O (poster), *159*
No Size Limits (poster), 142, *142*
Nostalgia, 171, 173
Nothing Punny campaign, 164
Now Hiring! (poster), *163*

O

Oberholzer, Sabina, 107, *107*
O'Higgins, Pablo, 18
Oldenburg, Claes, 19
Olivotti, Sergio, 94, *95,* 158, *158,* 188, *188*
1 Trick Pony, 82
On the Sublime and Beautiful (Burke), 103
Open Artist Studios (poster), *87*
Open Club Day (poster), 206, *207,* 208
Open Relationship (poster), *83*
orange, 59
Orosz, István, *108,* 180, *180*
Orquesta Típica Agustín Guerrero (poster), *67*
Osborn, Alex, 32
Over 1,000,000 Sold (poster), 144, *144*

P

Paddick, Damien, *133*
Pan's Labyrinth (poster), *97*
Parachute (poster), *91*
Pardekhane (poster), *183*
Pareidolia (poster), 133, *133*
Parsnip Tornado (poster), *198*
The Path (poster), *46*
People for the Ethical Treatment of Animals (PETA), 152, *153*
Pepita (poster), 219, *219*
Perez Ñiko, Antonio, 19
Periférica (poster), 114, *115*
persuasion, 136, 137–39
    allusion, 142–43
    arousal, 152
    building an emotional connection, 148–49
    channel, 138–39
    euphemism, 148
    fear and shock, 149, 151
    humor, 151–52
    hyperbole, 144
    irony, 143–44
    message, 138
    metaphor, 139–40
    metonymy, 140
    prosopopoeia, 146

    receiver, 139
    rhetorical figure, 139
    sadness and despair, 151
    simile, 146
    source, 138
    synecdoche, 140, 142
Pesic, Ana, 120, 121
Peter and the Wolf (poster), *89*
The Pianist (poster), 181, *181*
Picasso, Pablo, 146
Pierre de Ronsard (poster), *129*
Pig Iron Theatre Company, 189
pink, 59
Piotr Kunce Workshop in Mumbai (poster), *97*
placement, 113
Plakatstil, 15
Plastic Soldier Seamline (poster), *158*
Plastic Waste/Real Threat (poster), 28, *28*
Platonov Mais (poster), *95*
Plunkert, David, 108, *109,* 124, *125,* 161
pointing and eye gaze, 114
Pokémon Go™, 206
Polish Film Festival (5th), Australia (poster), *125*
Pontresina Engadin (poster), *25*
Pop Art, 19, 21
poster(s)
    animated, 200–202
    augmented reality (AR), 206, 208–9
    creating series, 67
    future of, 209
    interactive, 194
    interactive digital, 208–9
    moving, 200
    music and sound, 202–4
    pictorial communication, 13
    smell, 194–95
    sound, 199
    taste, 196
    touch, 195–96
Poster for Tomorrow, 10
Poster Passion (poster), *158*
Poster Poster, 10
Posters with Letter #A (poster series), *52–53*
Postmodernism, 20
power of contrast, 103
presentation. *See* poster(s)
printed surface, 193
Profanity (poster), *55*
Propague Brazil, 215
prosopopoeia, 146
Prstojević, Luka, *46*
Psychedelia, 20
psychology, color, 59
punk, 20
pure gray, 59
purple, 59

Q

quick sketches, 33–34
quick sketching, 38

R

Rainbow Bangers (poster), 196, *197*
Reason, Peter, 51
receiver, 139
red, 59
Reese, Ralph, 9
reflection, 34
Reid, James, 20
Rejected Poster (poster), 144, *144*
reminiscence, 171, 173
Requiem pour les Artistes (poster), 43
research, 24, 38
    defining resources, 30–31
    knowing audience, 29–30
    knowing facts, 27
    knowing message, 27–29
    training your eye, 26
Resnick, Elizabeth, 81, *81*
resources, defining, 30–31
Revell, Giles, *85*
Revolution of 1917, 16
Reyes, Rodolfo, *89*, 186
rhetorical figure, 139
rhythm and pattern, 112
Rieben, John, 55, *56*
Rigoletto (poster), 218, *218*
Rivera, Diego, 59
Rock'n Ink (poster), 186
Rodchenko, Alexander, 16
Rodriguez, Robert, 26, *26*, 186, *186*
Rok Gombrowicza (poster), *160*
Romero Vargas, Moisés, *40*, 105, *105*
Rompo, Max, 67, *67*
Room 17B (poster), *161*
Rosenquist, James, 19
Rubin, Edgar, 58
rule of odds, 64
rule of thirds, 62
Russia (vote) (poster), 219, *219*
Russian Constructivist movement, 16
Rusted Tears (poster), *159*
Rutz, Luis, *102*, 103

S

sadness, 151, 159
Saeedi, Mehdi, 31, *31*, 90, 123
Safety Against Violence (poster), 169, *169*
Salati, Michele, *124*
Samurai (poster), *82*
Sanderson, Brandon, 166
scale, 111
Schaub, Josh, 219, *219*, 223
Scher, Paula, 176, *176*
Schmidt, Joost, 17
Schoen, Raphael, *221*
Scorsese, Martin, 226
Scorsone, Joe, 144, *144*, 159, *159*, 171, *171*, 177–78, *178*
Scott, Christopher, *40*, 77, 78, 79, 159, *159*, 169, *169*
Second World War, 18
Serve Marketing Inc., 164
sex, 152, *153*
Sex Pistols, 20
Shakespeare, William, 64
shape, 55
Shaxpeare/Shakespeare/Shagsbere (poster), 64, *65*
Shendrick, Natasha, 180, *180*
The Shining (poster), 183, *183*
shock and fear, 149, 151
Shoot Out Rock (poster), *82*
Shut Up and Dance (poster), 130, *131*
simile, 146
Simpson, Steve, *45*, 161, 187
60th Anniversary of Zhuangshi (poster), *220*
sketching, quick, 33–34, 38
SKIN (poster), 173, *173*
The Sleepers—Forest of Hands (poster), *45*
smell, 194–95
software, 202
Sommese, Kristin, *83*
Sommese, Lanny, 55, *55*, *83*, *88*
Somos de Maíz (case study), 154, *155*
Sosa, Elmer, *42*, *84*, 148, *148*
Sottsass, Ettore, *21*
sound, 199, 202–4
Sound of Taste (poster), 199, *199*
source, 138
Splendent Sun (poster), 35, *36*, *37*
Sposato, Mark, 183, *183*
Staniszewski, Jacx, *96*, 151, *151*, 183, *183*
Stay on Our Side. Report It (poster), *215*
Steben, Eve, *90*, *91*, *94*, *135*, 181, *181*
Stenberg, Georgii, 16
Stenberg, Vladimir, 16
storytelling, 167–68
    case study, 177–78
    creating your visuals, 168–69
    multiple narratives, 175
    narratives across a poster series, 175–76
    nostalgia and reminiscence, 171, 173
    structuring your story, 171
    telling your story with type, 173
Storytelling (case study), 177–78
STRIKE! (poster), 110, 111
Studiolo of Plans, Building Sets Storage (poster), *128*
Style Moderne, 17

Suelo de Vino (poster), 72, *73*
Sumatra, 212, *214*
The Sunshine Way from Balkh to Konya (poster), 31, *31*
Sun Smart Cancer Council Western Australia, 196
Surrealism, 16
Sutherland, Ivan, 206
SVA NYC poster series, *216*
SVA Subway Posters (posters), 190, *191*
Swiss Punk Typography, 21
Swiss Style, 19
Sycamore Trees (poster), *89*
symmetry, 62, 64, 85
synecdoche, 140, 142, 164
Szabó, Kristóf, *185*

T

Tagli, Renato, 107, *107*
Take Your Umbrella Knight (poster), *99*
Talavera Paz, Sophia, 59, *60*
Tales from the Vienna Woods (poster), *180*
Taller de Gráfica, Mexico, 18
taste, 196
Tatlin, Vladimir, 16
Taxi Driver (film), 226
Taxi Driver (poster), *204*, 226
Teatr Pinezka (poster), *92*
Tello, Claudia, 156, *157*
10 Najlepszych Horrorów (poster), *129*
Terminator 2: Judgment Day (film), 200
Terror (poster), 169, *170*
This House (poster), *96*
This Is England (poster), *181*
Tjung, Handoko, 152, *152*
Typical Story (poster), 114, *116*
Toronto Jewish Film Festival (20th) poster, 140, *141*
Totally Drunk (poster), 223
touch, 195–96
Toy Story (film), 201
training your eye, 26
triadic color palettes, 107
Túlsúly (poster), *185*
Tyler School of Art, Temple University, 8, 9
type as image, 57–58, 80
typography, 57, 90, 92, 111, 131, 173

U

Un Desierto para la Danza 13 (poster), 104, *105*
United Farm Workers (UFW), 20
University of Bath, 51
University of Ulster, 77
Unspooling (poster), 113, *113*
Unzueta Arce, Ana Luisa, 114, *115*
Ups! (poster), 148, *148*
Upside Down (poster), *123*
Use Your Head (poster), 177, *178*

V

V&A Museum of Childhood, 196, *197*, *198*
Valenzuela, Ivette, *104*, 105, 156, *157*
van de Velde, Henry, 15
van Doesburg, Theo, 17
Van Gogh 100 Years (poster), *41*
Ventola Bravin, Vítor, 218, *218*
The Ventures (poster), 86
Venus (poster), 172, *173*
Victor, Victoria (poster), 140, *140*
Vienna secession, 15
Vilen Künnapu exhibition "Magical Tallinn" (poster), 83
violet, 59
Viramontes, Xavier, 20
Visions of the Future (travel posters), 172, *173*
visuals, creating, 168–69

W

Wahlgren, Jameela, 227, *227*
Waiting for Godot (poster), *40*
walk (poster), 143, *143*
Walt Disney Company, 200
Wang, Yibing, 226

War and Peace (poster), 84
Warhol, Andy, 19
Warner, Daniel, 121, *122*, 126, 218, *218*, 219, *219*
War Peace, Peace War (poster), *133*
War Unmasked (poster), *129*
Was/Saw Dyslexia (poster), *47*
Watergate (poster), 9
Water Is Life (poster), 95
Weidenhüller, Marc, 204
Welcome to Lucerne (poster), 219, *219*
Weltformat (poster), 216, *217*
We're Not All Well-Born in the Maze (poster), *162*
West Side Story (poster), 174, *175*, 180, *180*
Where Art Happens (poster), 216
Whiplash (poster), *42*
white space, 66, 87
White Tiger Melts (poster), *40*
Wilco (poster), *45*
Wildhack, Robert J., 15
Willey, Matt, 85
WITH (poster), *124*
Wo Ist Die Liebe Hin, Fur Musik Gegen Musik, You Are at Home Baby (poster), *224*
The Wolf Man Is Helvetica (poster), 57, 57–58

Woman and Man's Legs (poster), 24, *25*
word bank, 33
World War I, 17
World War II, 18
Wright, Erin, 88, *133*, 160, *160*

X

Xiamen Echoed (poster), 83
Xu, Li, 209, *209*, 220
XVIII Certamen Internacional de Cortos, Ciudad de Soria (poster), *125*

Y

Yañez, Luis, *41*, 123
yellow, 59
Yong, Zhang, *28*, *29*
Your Indifference (poster), 150, *151*
Yugoslav Drama Theatre (series), 48–49

Z

Zagorski, Stanislaw, 74

ACKNOWLEDGMENTS

This book is the result of combined efforts, and therefore we would like to thank all of those who, in one way or another, contributed to its completion. We are very grateful to the incredibly talented professionals and studios who allowed us to reproduce their outstanding work. Special thanks are in order for Erich Brechbühl, Andrew Lewis, Dermot Mac Cormack, Joe Scorsone, and Alice Drueding and Christopher Scott for their images and for writing the essays featured in each chapter. We would also like to give a special thank-you to Elizabeth Resnick for writing our foreword and for recommending us to Bloomsbury Publishing. We are also grateful to Louise Baird-Smith, Senior Commissioning Editor—Design and Photography, Bloomsbury Visual Arts, for offering us this tremendous opportunity. Thanks to Felicity Cummins and the rest of the Bloomsbury Publishing team for helping us along the way. We owe a debt of gratitude to Molly Montanaro for her professionalism and attention to our project.

First, I (Scott Laserow) want to thank my wife Roe for keeping me sane while I wrote this book. Your unwavering support and thoughtful suggestions, and the way you challenged me with your questions, made me a better writer and this a stronger book. I love you, and I am ready to get back to work in supporting your animal advocacy. I would also like to thank my co-author, Natalia Delgado, for bringing all that you did to make this book happen. Our styles and how we approached this project meshed well and kept me balanced. I always looked forward to our weekly Skype calls and your outlook and honest criticisms, which made me a more focused writer. Your enthusiasm for everything poster was infectious and made for a rewarding experience—I thank you. Thank you, my dear friends Joe Scorsone and Alice Drueding, for your help and guidance over the years. Joe, I'll never forget you telling me back in 2004, "Hey Scott, you should start designing posters." You were my most influential teacher and my mentor. To my mom and dad, thank you for believing in me when nobody else did. Without your love and encouragement, I would not be where I am today. And to my sister Leslie Weinfeld for stepping in and taking on the lion's share of caregiving for our parents while I was in the process of writing this book.

I am forever grateful for the backing of my school, Tyler School of Art and Architecture, Temple University, Philadelphia, PA, USA. My sincere gratitude to Dean Susan Cahan and Vice Provost Kevin Delaney for allowing me to refocus my study leave to write this book. Finally, to Professors Dermot Mac Cormack and Kelly Holohan and the rest of the Graphic and Interactive Design program, I appreciate your patience and encouragement during a demanding year and a half.

I (Natalia Delgado) would like to begin by thanking my co-author Scott Laserow, who kindly invited me along for one of the most amazing journeys of my life and was the best working partner anyone could dream of.

I would like to thank my teachers for their guidance and support and my students for being my inspiration and motivation for this project. Your questions and insights were the foundation for the contents of this book.

To my parents, I thank you for instilling in me a love for reading and writing, allowing me to discover a wonderful world that fueled my imagination. To my dad, thank you for sharing your passion for literature and the classics and always pushing me to do better. To my mom, thank you for being my role model, critic, shoulder to cry on, and neverending support. You inspire me every day, always.

I would also like to thank all my friends and colleagues who supported me in this endeavor: Moriana Delgado for your assistance with edits and research; Roman Esqueda for your help with the rhetorical analysis and figures; Paulina Arroyo for your enthusiasm and encouragement.

Finally, we would like to acknowledge all the great poster designers who have inspired us along the way, especially those who are no longer with us.